'*Postcolonial Theories* is among the most
ductions to this important field now avai
pay due attention to the variety of new dir
taking.' – **Robert Spencer**, *University of Manchester*

'[Provides] students with a clear sense of the evolution and complexity of the
field.' – **Shailja Sharma**, *DePaul University*

Postcolonial Theories is a lively introduction to postcolonial theories,
contexts and literatures which presents both the theory and practice to
students in approachable and attractive ways. Jenni Ramone includes
discussion of a wide range of influential theorists such as Frantz Fanon,
Homi Bhabha, Rey Chow, Edward Saïd, Ngugi wa Thiong'o, Paul Gilroy
and Trinh T. Minh-ha. She also demonstrates postcolonial ideas through
compelling readings of a wide range of exciting literary texts, including:

- Nawal El Saadawi's *God Dies by the Nile*
- Aravind Adiga's *The White Tiger*
- Shyam Selvadurai's *Funny Boy*
- Jamaica Kincaid's *My Brother*.

Covering a diverse array of geographical locations, this is essential reading for anyone with an interest in postcolonial theories and how they have
continued to adapt in the wake of globalization, digital technology and
neo-colonialism.

Jenni Ramone is Senior Lecturer in English at Newman University College,
Birmingham.

Transitions critically explores movements in literary theory. Guiding the
reader through the poetics and politics of interpretative paradigms and
schools of thought, **Transitions** helps direct the student's own acts of critical analysis. As well as transforming the critical developments of the past
by interpreting them from the perspective of the present day, each study
enacts transitional readings of a number of well-known literary texts.

transitions

General Editor: Julian Wolfreys

Published titles
TERRY EAGLETON David Alderson
JULIA KRISTEVA AND LITERARY THEORY Megan Becker-Leckrone
BATAILLE Fred Botting and Scott Wilson
NEW HISTORICISM AND CULTURAL MATERIALISM John Brannigan
HÉLÈNE CIXOUS Abigail Bray
HOMI K. BHABHA Eleanor Byrne
GENDER Claire Colebrook
POSTMODERN NARRATIVE THEORY 2nd edition Mark Currie
FORMALIST CRITICISM AND READER-RESPONSE THEORY Kenneth Womack and
    Todd F. Davis
IDEOLOGY James M. Decker
QUEER THEORY Donald E. Hall
MARXIST LITERARY AND CULTURAL THEORIES Moyra Haslett
ROLAND BARTHES Martin McQuillan
LOUIS ALTHUSSER Warren Montag
RACE Brian Niro
JACQUES LACAN Jean-Michel Rabaté
POSTCOLONIAL THEORIES Jenni Ramone
LITERARY FEMINISMS Ruth Robbins
SUBJECTIVITY Ruth Robbins
DECONSTRUCTION ● DERRIDA Julian Wolfreys
TRANSGRESSION Julian Wolfreys
ORWELL TO THE PRESENT, 1945–1999 John Brannigan
CHAUCER TO SHAKESPEARE, 1337–1580 SunHee Kim Gertz
MODERNISM, 1910–1945 Jane Goldman
POPE TO BURNEY, 1714–1786 Moyra Haslett
PATER TO FORSTER, 1873–1924 Ruth Robbins
BURKE TO BYRON, BARBAULD TO BAILLIE, 1790–1830 Jane Stabler
MILTON TO POPE, 1650–1720 Kay Gilliland Stevenson
DICKENS TO HARDY 1837–1884 Julian Wolfreys
SIDNEY TO MILTON, 1580–1660 Marion Wynne Davies

Forthcoming titles
NATIONAL IDENTITY John Brannigan
SPACE Christina Britzolakis

Transitions
Series Standing Order
ISBN 978- 0- 333- 73634- 0
(*outside North America only*)

You can receive future titles in this series as they are published. To place a standing order please contact your bookseller or, in the case of difficulty, write to us at the address below with your name and address, the title of the series and the ISBN quoted above.

Customer Services Department, Macmillan Distribution Ltd, Houndmills, Basingstoke, Hampshire RG21 6XS, England

transitions

Postcolonial Theories

Jenni Ramone

First published 2011 by
PALGRAVE MACMILLAN

Palgrave Macmillan in the UK is an imprint of Macmillan Publishers Limited,
registered in England, company number 785998, of Houndmills, Basingstoke,
Hampshire RG21 6XS.

Palgrave Macmillan in the US is a division of St Martin's Press LLC,
175 Fifth Avenue, New York, NY 10010.

Palgrave Macmillan is the global academic imprint of the above companies
and has companies and representatives throughout the world.

Palgrave® and Macmillan® are registered trademarks in the United States,
the United Kingdom, Europe and other countries.

ISBN 978-0-230-24302-6 hardback

ISBN 978-0-230-24303-3   ISBN 978-0-230-34407-5 (eBook)
DOI 10.1007/978-0-230-34407-5

A catalogue record for this book is available from the British Library.

A catalog record for this book is available from the Library of Congress.

10   9   8   7   6   5   4   3   2   1
20   19   18   17   16   15   14   13   12   11

For Scotty, with love and thanks

Contents

General Editor's Preface   x
Acknowledgements   xii
Timeline of Key Events and Texts   xiii

Introduction: The Colonial Exotic   1
- Case study: the exotic   4
- Colonial representation and literature   6
- Global consumption: Zingolo   10

Part I   The Emergence of Postcolonial Thinking   15

1 Anticolonial Resistance   17
- Barbados, sugar, and the 1816 slave uprising   19
- Anticolonial responses: Toussaint L'Ouverture; Aimé Césaire   21
- The Communist Party and anticolonialism: C. L. R. James   24
- Claudia Jones   26
- Feminism and anticolonialism: Claudia Jones; Una Marson   27
- Algerian resistance   29
- Literary responses: Chinua Achebe; George Lamming;
  Édouard Glissant; Aimé Césaire   31
- In theory: Frantz Fanon; Albert Memmi   37
- Aboriginal responses   40
- Affective communities   42

2 The Postcolonial Moment   46
- The post(-)colonial   49
- 'A borrowed place on borrowed time': Hong Kong   51
- Queer Hong Kong   55
- The Partition of India   58
- Partition in literature   61
- Partition memories   66
- Partition histories   70

Part II   Postcolonial Theories   77

3   Otherness   79
    ● Defining the other   80
    ● Orientalism and othering   82
    ● The nation and the novel   86
    ● Saïd's other   89
    ● Trinh T. Minh-ha's dissatisfaction with the 'other'   90
    ● Trinh and film   94
    ● Rey Chow, language and the other   100

4   The Postcolonial Migrant   102
    ● The Sapir–Whorf hypothesis   102
    ● Fanon on language   103
    ● Fanon's migrations   107
    ● Fanon and psychopathology   109
    ● Bhabha and hybridity   112
    ● Questions of cultural theory   116
    ● Gilroy's conviviality   118
    ● Gilroy and music   124

5   Native and Nation   127
    ● Ngugi and English in Africa   127
    ● Indigenous concerns: a different kind of nativism?   131
    ● Mudrooroo   135
    ● Textuality and orality   136
    ● The native informant   139
    ● Spivak's concept of the subaltern   146
    ● *God Dies by the Nile*   148
    ● *The White Tiger*   150

Part III   Reading Postcolonial Literature   155

Introduction to Part III   157
6   The Text in the Colony   159
    ● Joseph Conrad, *Heart of Darkness*   159
    ● Chinua Achebe, *Things Fall Apart*   163
    ● Tsitsi Dangarembga, *Nervous Conditions*   166

7 The Postcolonial Counter-Text   169
   ● William Shakespeare's *The Tempest* and Aimé Césaire's
     A Tempest   169
   ● Charlotte Brontë's *Jane Eyre* and Jean Rhys's
     Wide Sargasso Sea   172
   ● Charles Dickens's *Great Expectations* and
     Peter Carey's *Jack Maggs*   175

8 The Diaspora Text   180
   ● Shyam Selvadurai, *Funny Boy*   180
   ● Salman Rushdie, *The Satanic Verses*   183
   ● Jamaica Kincaid, *My Brother*   187

Part IV   **Postcolonial Futures**   191

9 Afterword: Postcolonial Futures   193
   ● Postcolonial ecocriticism   194
   ● Global and local voices   196
   ● Digital postcolonialism   199
   ● Postcolonial queer   201
   ● Postcolonial prize books and bestsellers   203

Annotated Bibliography   207
Bibliography   211
Index   221

General Editor's Preface

> Transitions: *transition-em*, n. of action. 1. A passing or passage from one condition, action or (rarely) place, to another. 2. Passage in thought, speech, or writing, from one subject to another. 3. a. The passing from one note to another b. The passing from one key to another, modulation. 4. The passage from an earlier to a later stage of development or formation [...] change from an earlier style to a later; a style of intermediate or mixed character [...] the historical passage of language from one well-defined stage to another.

The aim of *Transitions* is to explore passages and movements in critical thought, and in the development of literary and cultural interpretation. This series also seeks to examine the possibilities for reading, analysis and other critical engagements which the very idea of transition makes possible. The writers in this series unfold the movements and modulations of critical thinking over the last generation, from the first emergences of what is now recognized as literary theory. They examine as well how the transitional nature of theoretical and critical thinking is still very much in operation, guaranteed by the hybridity and heterogeneity of the field of literary studies. The authors in the series share the common understanding that, now more than ever, critical thought is both in a state of transition and can best be defined by developing for the student reader an understanding of this protean quality.

This series desires, then, to enable the reader to transform her/his own reading and writing transactions by comprehending past developments. Each book in the series offers a guide to the poetics and politics of interpretative paradigms, schools and bodies of thought, while transforming these, if not into tools or methodologies, then into conduits for directing and channelling thought. As well as transforming the critical past by interpreting it from the perspective of the present day, each study enacts transitional readings of a number of well-known literary texts, all of which are themselves conceivable as having been transitional texts at the moments of their first appearance. The readings offered in these books seek, through close critical reading and theoretical engagement, to demonstrate certain possibilities in critical thinking to the student reader.

It is hoped that the student will find this series liberating because rigid methodologies are not being put into place. As all the dictionary definitions of the idea of transition above suggest, what is important is the action, the passage: of thought, of analysis, of critical response. Rather than seeking to help you locate yourself in relation to any particular school or discipline, this series aims to put you into action, as readers and writers, travellers between positions, where the movement between poles comes to be seen as of more importance than the locations themselves.

Julian Wolfreys

Acknowledgements

I am very grateful to Julian Wolfreys for his support on this project.

I would also like to express my sincere thanks to colleagues and friends who read draft chapters of this book and provided helpful feedback: Helen Cousins, Louise McDonald, Esther Eidinow, Matthew Day, Noelle Plack, Louise Hickman, Anna Hartnell, Dave Gunning and Clare Barker. Thanks, too, to Nicholas Wong and Tammy Ho for sharing their knowledge of Hong Kong literature.

I am also very grateful to my friends and family for their patience and understanding while I was busy completing this book.

Timeline of Key Events and Texts

This is a selective list presenting some key historical events and important publications, plotting items covered within this book in a chronological format.

1271   Marco Polo travels in China, Sri Lanka, Southern India and the Persian Gulf (–1295)

1492   Christopher Columbus makes first voyage to America, arriving in Cuba, then Hispaniola

1498   Vasco da Gama of Portugal first sails to India

1524   Vasco da Gama made Viceroy of India

1611   First recorded performance of Shakespeare's *The Tempest*

1625   Dutch East India Company founds Cape Colony in South Africa; Barbados first populated by white settlers

1704   Antoine Galland's first European edition of *The Arabian Nights (The Thousand and One Nights)*

1716   Mary Wortley Montagu's Turkish Embassy Letters, written 1716–18, published posthumously 1762

1770   Cook sails to Australia

1775   American War of Independence (United States Independence 1783)

1784   Bengal jointly governed by East India Company and British Crown

1788   Penal colonies first established in Australia

1789   French Revolution begins

1791   Toussaint L'Ouverture's rebellion (–1802)

1798   Napoleon's invasion of Egypt

1807   Slave Trade Act (coming into effect 1 January 1808) banned slave trade in British Empire

1814   Jane Austen, *Mansfield Park*

1815   Barbados House of Assembly rejects Slave Registry Bill

1816   April 14–17 Barbados slave uprising (Bussa's rebellion)

1819   Singapore: settlement and trade port set up under British control

1821   San Domingo gains independence from Spain

1829   Sati Abolition Law passed by Bentick in India
1831   Jamaican Slave Uprising (Christmas Uprising)
1834   Abolition of slavery in British colonies (with four-year implementation period)
1835   Macaulay's Minute on Indian Education
1837   Accession of Queen Victoria
1838   Myall Creek massacre, Australia
1839   Manifest Destiny proposed in America
1840   Masters and Servants Act, in force until 1937;
        New Zealand claimed part of British Empire in The Treaty of Waitaingi following colonial settlement there by individuals and missionary groups.
1842   British territorial acquisition of Hong Kong following the Opium Wars
1857   Sepoy Mutiny (Indian Rebellion)
1867   Canada established as dominion in British North America Act
1877   Britain claims ownership of the Transvaal
1879   British–Zulu War
1880   First Boer War/Transvaal War (–1881)
1884   Berlin Conference divides Africa into colonies of Europe in the 'Scramble for Africa'
1885   H. Rider Haggard, *King Solomon's Mines*;
        Richard Burton's translation of *The Arabian Nights* (–1888)
1890   British colonial control of Rhodesia
1899   Boer War/Second Anglo–Boer War (–1902);
        Joseph Conrad, *Heart of Darkness*
1900   Nigeria becomes a British protectorate
1903   W.E.B. Du Bois, *The Souls of Black Folk*
1906   Zulu uprising (Bambata Rebellion)
1912   South African Native National Congress formed (later the African National Congress)
1913   Rabindranath Tagore wins Nobel Prize for Literature
1914   First World War (–1918);
        Egypt becomes a British protectorate
1916   Easter Rising, Ireland
1917   October Revolution in Russia, leading to establishment of the Soviet Union
1918   Declaration of Irish Republic
1919   Amritsar Massacre, India

1920	Britain gains control over Iraq, Palestine and Transjordan and France gains control of Syria and Lebanon, in League of Nations mandates following First World War; Government of Ireland Act partitioned Ireland
1921	Non-Cooperation Movement, India
1922	Constitution of the Irish Free State Act
1924	E.M. Forster, *A Passage to India*
1931	British Commonwealth of Nations established in Statute of Westminster
1936	Spanish Civil War (–1939)
1937	Eire established as Republic
1938	C.L.R. James, *The Black Jacobins*
1939	Second World War (–1945); Joyce Cary, *Mister Johnson*; George Antonius, *The Arab Awakening*
1944	Jamaica gains self-government
1946	Aimé Césaire elected mayor of Fort de France; BBC Caribbean Voices radio programme begins
1947	Midnight 13 August: Partition of India; Midnight 14 August: Indian Independence
1948	Independence: Burma and Ceylon (Sri Lanka); Apartheid made law in South Africa; Assassination of Mahatma Gandhi
1949	Mao Tse-tung establishes People's Republic of China; Pioneer Press established by Una Marson
1950	The Korean War (–1953)
1952	Mau Mau Resistance in Kenya; Frantz Fanon, *Black Skin, White Masks*
1954	Algerian War of Independence (–1962)
1955	Final withdrawal of British troops from Egypt
1956	Official Language Act in Sri Lanka; Independence: Sudan
1957	Independence: Ghana, Malaya
1958	Chinua Achebe, *Things Fall Apart*
1959	Fidel Castro governs Cuba; Mardi Gras celebrations first organised by Claudia Jones in London
1960	Independence: Nigeria; Aboriginals first recognized as Australian citizens; George Lamming, *The Pleasures of Exile*

1961   Frantz Fanon, *The Wretched of the Earth*
1962   Independence: Algeria, Jamaica, Trinidad and Tobago, Uganda
1963   Independence: Kenya
1965   Rhodesian Unilateral Declaration of Independence from Britain
1966   Independence: Barbados;
        Jean Rhys, *Wide Sargasso Sea*
1968   Assassination of Martin Luther King;
        Paris May Uprising;
        Prague Spring Uprising
1969   Aimé Césaire, *A Tempest*
1971   East Pakistan becomes Bangladesh in Partition of Pakistan
1972   Ngugi wa Thiong'o, *Homecoming*
1975   State of Emergency declared in India after Indira Gandhi's election
        fraud;
        Chinua Achebe's lecture, 'An Image of Africa: Racism in Conrad's
        Heart of Darkness'
1977   Syed Hussein Alatas, *The Myth of the Lazy Native*
1978   Dominican Republic gained independent government from Haiti;
        Edward Saïd, *Orientalism*
1980   Rhodesia renamed Zimbabwe at independence
1982   Falklands War;
        First publication of the Subaltern Studies Group
1983   Attack on Sri Lankan army 23 July recorded as the beginning of
        the civil war (–2009)
1984   Communalist violence follows assassination of Indira Gandhi
1986   Wole Soyinka wins Nobel Prize for Literature
1987   Gilles Deleuze and Felix Guattari, *A Thousand Plateaus*
1988   Salman Rushdie, *The Satanic Verses*;
        Tsitsi Dangarembga, *Nervous Conditions*
1989   Tian'anmen Square massacre;
        Ashcroft, Griffiths and Tiffin, *The Empire Writes Back*;
        Salman Rushdie fatwa imposed by Ayatollah Khomeini 14 February
1990   Freedom of Nelson Mandela;
        Homi Bhabha, *Nation and Narration*
1991   South African apartheid laws repealed;
        Benedict Anderson, *Imagined Communities*
1992   Riots follow demolition of Babri Masjid mosque, Ayodhya
1993   Renaming of Ayers Rock to Uluru
        Paul Gilroy, *The Black Atlantic*;
        Edward Saïd, *Culture and Imperialism*

1994   Homi Bhabha, *The Location of Culture*;
        Fatima Mernissi, *Dreams of Trespass: Tales of a Harem Girlhood*;
        Shyam Selvadurai, *Funny Boy*
1997   Midnight 30 June: end of British colonial control of Hong Kong;
        Peter Carey, *Jack Maggs*;
        Jamaica Kincaid, *My Brother*
1999   Gayatri Chakravorty Spivak, *A Critique of Postcolonial Reason*
2000   Sardar Sarovar dam project underway
2001   Attack on World Trade Centre, New York, 11 September;
        Afghanistan War begins;
        China begins sustained programme of mining and business in
        Africa
2002   Zimbabwe's Robert Mugabe pledges rapid land reform
2003   Iraq War begins
2004   France bans conspicuous religious symbols in schools;
        Paul Gilroy, *After Empire*
2005   Israeli troops and settlers pull out of Gaza Strip but retain border
        control
2007   Israel intensifies blockade of Gaza following council vote where
        Hamas wins seven out of ten councils in Gaza Strip
2008   Barack Obama becomes first black American president;
        Banking Crisis begins, directly affecting mainly America and
        Europe
2009   Beirut World Book Capital City
2010   Talks resume between India and Pakistan over Kashmir, unresolved
        since 1947

Introduction: The Colonial Exotic

Postcolonial literature and theory react to colonial encounters, and the primary function of both is to critique the assumptions and representations on which colonialism is based. This book is intended as an introduction to a range of postcolonial theories, contexts, and literary texts. The timeline of events and introduction serve to introduce the context and some of the questions that postcolonial theories engage with; the remainder of the book is structured into four sections. The first section contains Chapters 1 and 2 and expands on postcolonial contexts and the emergence and development of postcolonial thinking. Chapter 1 brings together a number of key anticolonial thinkers and activists whose work contributed – directly, in many cases – to the process of decolonization. The majority of these figures are from the Caribbean, and respond to a unique context of the history of slavery and plantations involving mass population movement and production on formerly largely uninhabited islands. The second chapter considers the idea of decolonization and of the moment at which a territory is, according to the pretended fixity of the historical timeline, no longer a colonial property. The postcolonial moment in both South Asia and Hong Kong is shown to be an imprecise and ongoing social change, as is explored through representations of the Partition of India and of homosexuality laws in Hong Kong. The second section provides a more sustained presentation of theories in Chapters 3, 4 and 5. These chapters offer introductions to the works of a number of dominant postcolonial theorists, alongside critiques offered by emerging scholars and applications of those theories to a range of contemporary sources including literary texts, advertisements and music, as well as reference to other important literary works and historical events. As will become clear, these three chapters are interdependent and are organized in order to aid negotiation of theorists' work, although they are best considered as interlacing fields of attention in postcolonial studies. The focus of this book is predominantly on the way that postcolonial theories are applicable to the study of literary texts, and with this in mind, Chapters 6, 7 and 8 in the third section bring together literary texts exploring the colony, rewriting of canonical literature, and the diaspora. These three chapters are intended to show the diversity of texts categorized by the chapter titles, while all three short chapters practice some of the theoretical and contextual concerns that have been highlighted in earlier chapters. A focus on the literature in these three chapters instead of the histories or the theories reveals that sometimes the more cutting-edge postcolonial thought happens first of all within literary texts. The final section includes Chapter 9, a survey of the newest debates raised by postcolonial studies, and an annotated bibliography including suggested further reading on areas that could not be addressed in detail in this book due to the limitation of space. The final chapter explores some of the most recent debates in postcolonial studies and areas of future scholarship, including explorations of sexuality, digital and virtual identity, interdisciplinary connections made with ecocriticism, and textual culture including postcolonial prize-books and bestsellers, all of which are negotiated through an awareness of the impact of globalization and neocolonialism.

Postcolonial theories consider international relationships from the earliest to the most recent examples, but the discipline is concerned with a particular period of colonial history, and does not consider all instances of colonization (or, settlement on a geographical territory) in the same way. Britain and the USA are not considered postcolonial locations, even though both places have in the past been colonized, Britain by the Romans and Vikings and the USA by European settlers. Postcolonial theory responds, in the main, to the particularly rampant colonial expansion undertaken in the nineteenth century. This is the period during which South Asia was under British Imperial rule, following a longer history of trade between Britain and South Asia and formerly, Portugal and South Asia. Trade is often the precursor to more aggressive domination of territories. Trade and violence came together in the colonization of the Caribbean: in order to extract profit from the Caribbean, the European colonizers employed slave labour, taking men and women from Africa and enslaving them in plantations. Slavery was in operation mainly in the eighteenth and early nineteenth centuries, although colonial control remained in the Caribbean islands through education and law after slavery ended.

Colonialism made a further claim on Africa at the Berlin Conference of 1885: one of the key historical events in postcolonial history is the rapid division of the African continent into European colonies, often referred to as the Scramble for Africa. Neither cultural or linguistic groups nor natural geographical markers such as rivers or mountain ranges were taken into proper consideration during this process; the emphasis was on speedily dividing up the land between the most powerful European colonizing nations. Previously, major European colonial powers – Germany, France, Britain, Belgium and Portugal – had colonized small areas, generally along the coast. And there had been a long history of trade and colonization of Africa with the Middle East and Europe. The German Chancellor Bismarck had called the 1885 conference in order to establish international trade rules, but once the question of territorial acquisition was opened, it remained open: the European nations continued altering boundaries until 1914. During the first and second world wars, Africa remained colonized; after the Second World War, African nations began to exert political pressure and gradually gained independent status.

The USA, Canada and Australia have a different postcolonial relationship with their former colonial centres. Large numbers of (mainly European) settlers moved permanently to these locations and displaced the indigenous populations. First the USA and then Australia was used by Britain to house its criminals: convicts were transported to Australia until 1868, but postcolonial writers have reconsidered Australia's nineteenth-century representation as a hive of criminality. Many more migrants travelled to Australia during the 1851–1871 Gold Rush. It is also important to remember the definition of criminality that was applied to those transported to Australia: there were many political prisoners including those involved in Chartism, an effort to gain voting rights for working people, the Merthyr Rising, in response to exploitative working and living conditions for ironworkers, and the Tolpuddle Martyrs, agricultural workers who formed a rudimentary type of trade union. Postcolonial theorists are also interested in the representation of indigenous groups in Australia, Canada and the USA, as well as migrants from formerly colonized locations. Postcolonial thinking has its clearest origin in the anticolonial activism and writing that emerged during periods of resistance and negotiation in colonized territories; this is the subject of Chapter 1.

This book intends to demonstrate just how heterogeneous postcolonial studies can be. However, there are a number of key questions that this book intends to ask: one of these questions is over the notion of historicity. History tends to represent a place or an event from one perspective, and to fix it within certain dates: postcolonial thinking questions the historical mode by revealing multiple perspectives and the ongoing impact of events. Another key focus is on the citizen affected by the postcolonial context: this book is repeatedly concerned with the body and identity of the postcolonial subject. In addition, this book endeavours to identify the complexity of interactions between the local and the global, a concern that is particularly pertinent in ongoing, neocolonial trade and globalization.

One of the principles of postcolonial thinking is to resist certainties and instead to ask questions: certainties tend to be based on the dominant view and this inevitably excludes the views of many others affected by postcolonial history. This book responds to the need to be aware of multiple voices and to resist the temptation to find clear and certain answers in style as well as content: case studies and brief enquiries into the discipline are combined in order to convey the extremely diverse range of postcolonial writers, thinkers, and contexts, but also to place the reader in the open, questioning mindset required by postcolonial theories. The first of these case studies is presented in the introduction and serves to introduce the breadth of scholarship in the discipline. This case study is concerned with the idea of the exotic, a preoccupation which has been present since the earliest precolonial travel narratives, and prevails in neocolonial thinking today.

Case study: the exotic

The colonial project which operated in earnest between the early nineteenth and mid-twentieth century attempted to justify occupation and control of distant territories on the assumption of Western European cultural, intellectual and even evolutionary superiority. Rather than admitting that colonization was, in the main, an exercise in the exploitation of distant nations and inhabitants by the European privileged classes, colonial discourse maintained that the colonized were primitive, infantile peoples in desperate need of the enlightenment that the colonizers could provide. This assumption was supported, to an extent, by the limited and flawed knowledge that Europe read about the colonized territories, gathered from the travel diaries and letters written by explorers and adventurers, and also from fictional accounts like adventure novels and stories; frequently, the supposedly factual accounts were as fanciful as the fiction.

In his book *The Ethics of Travel*, Syed Manzurul Islam discusses thirteenth- and fourteenth-century explorer Marco Polo's travelogue as a machine of othering (1996, p. 118). Islam is suggesting, in other words, that a book that claims to objectively record the sights and encounters experienced by the explorer on his voyage to places never before visited by Europeans or recorded in European histories actually performs the function of setting up the 'us' and 'them' or 'self' and 'other' binary that colonialism relies upon. Othering is achieved in claims that the native inhabitants of those unfamiliar places are different from Europeans and therefore flawed – monstrous, primitive, immoral; indeed, Polo's travelogue frequently describes the inhabitants of various locations as brutally wanton, repeating of various peoples: 'they do not regard any form of sexual indulgence as a sin' (Polo, 1958, p. 240). In setting up this relationship, the idea that the European represents the human ideal and that anything that does not conform to that ideal is somehow flawed (and must be corrected) enables the maintenance of later colonial binaries. Describing India, Marco Polo writes:

> The country produces a diversity of beasts different from those of the rest of the world. There are black lions with no other visible colour or marks. There are parrots of many kinds. Some are entirely white – as white as snow – with feet and beaks of scarlet. Others are scarlet and blue – there is no lovelier sight than these in the world [...]. Everything there is different from what is with us and excels both in size and beauty. They have no fruits the same as ours, no beasts, no birds.   (Polo, 1958, p. 261)

On first reading, such a description seems fairly harmless, and appears to be an enthusiastic celebration of an encounter with beautiful and unfamiliar animals. However, on further analysis of the language used, it becomes clear that the enthusiastic explorer is repeatedly drawing attention to the extent of the difference between the two places, Europe and India: those beautiful animals are, above all, 'different'. In fact, 'everything there' is different. While Polo appears to celebrate the beauty of India, at the same time his description is an example of exoticism: disturbing, wild differences are presented to the European reader within the safe boundary of the text. Marco Polo goes further, though: he reports seeing mythical creatures – unicorns and gryphons – and these gryphons, he claims, are vast birds resembling eagles, big enough to lift an elephant to a great height and drop it to the rocky floor, smashing the elephant's body to a pulp to feed on the carcass (1958, p. 274). Furthermore, he describes species of human–animal hybrids, or the *homo monstrum*: men with long tails, and men with 'heads like dogs, and teeth and eyes like dogs' (p. 33), images that evoke ideas of breeding between animals and humans and so invite the European reader to view those foreign places as immoral and barbaric.

This impression is intensified by reports of cannibalism, the practice of killing, cooking and eating anyone who is deemed seriously ill, in order to prevent their dead body from being consumed by worms, which in turn, according to custom, would torment the dead man's soul (Polo, 1958, p. 228). Such stories perpetuated the notion of European superiority and were a precursor of the kind of exoticism and horror that featured in later colonial records of encounters with foreign places.

Colonial representation and literature

H. Rider Haggard's *King Solomon's Mines* is a fictional encounter with the foreign other. The novel is dedicated, by the fictional narrator Allan Quatermain, to 'all the big and little boys who read it'; little boys who will grow up to be imperialists, learning their colonialist attitudes from those big boys who instruct them and encourage them to read such novels. As the story begins, the narrator insists repeatedly on the truth of his tale and his own incidental part in telling it, his reasons eluding any charge of disingenuous motive or ideological purpose: he writes 'Because Sir Henry Curtis and Captain John Good asked me'; 'Because I am laid up here at Durban with the pain in my left leg' and writing breaks the monotony; 'Because I want my boy Harry [...] to have something to amuse him and keep him out of mischief for a week or so'; and, finally, 'Because I am going to tell the strangest story that I remember' (Haggard, 1961, p. 12). The implication is that he has no choice but to write. Accused of exaggeration by Sir Henry, Quatermain is affronted, only to be pacified with a heartfelt apology which again works to convince the reader of the veracity of the tale: 'I see very well you do not wish to deceive us, but the story sounded so strange that I could hardly believe it' (p. 27).

He excuses his 'blunt way of writing', apologising for his inability to supply 'the grand literary flights and flourishes' sometimes found in 'novels', as if this is not a novel at all, but a genuine record of events (p. 10). He, in contrast, claims to write in the only way he can – a 'plain, straightforward manner' which is another claim for truth, because, 'a true story, however strange it may be, does not require to be decked out in fine words' (p. 10). Despite claiming a lack of expertise in language and a humble position in relation to the tale he tells, Quatermain nevertheless feels sufficiently qualified to precede his narration by remarking that Zulus often use 'strange bursts of rhetorical eloquence' – far from appreciating these, though, as a man of 'plain, straightforward', 'blunt' language might, he prescribes such speeches as 'full [...] of vain repetitions' which only serve the purpose of informing the white European that contrary to their expectations the Zulu race is 'by no means devoid of poetic instinct and of intellectual power', as if it might be logical to assume such a thing (p. 54).

The character–narrator is visible beyond the boundaries of the fiction as he provides the dedication and the foreword, which would normally be presented from the author's perspective (Haggard's). When Quatermain voices these paratextual sections, there is an illusion of realism, of reality, even, which has a profound impact. In claiming that the text is a representation of reality, his presentation of Africa is accorded an authority normally restricted to factual accounts (though these, admittedly, are often similarly flawed, as Marco Polo's description of gigantic, elephant-carrying gryphons proves) and so the imperialist position adopted by the text is presented as if it was the logical one. Thus, the novel claims that the wild, exotic landscape is in need of the taming hand of Western civilization: 'however beautiful a view may be, it requires the presence of man to make it complete, but perhaps that is because I have lived so much in the wilderness, and therefore know the value of civilisation' (p. 31). This land in need of a taming hand is also figured as feminine – and even wanton, whorish, naked and reclining:

> These mountains [...] are shaped after the fashion of a woman's breasts, and at times the mists and shadows beneath them take the form of a recumbent woman, veiled mysteriously in sleep [...] and upon the top of each is a vast hillock covered with snow, exactly corresponding to the nipple on the female breast.   (p. 66)

Figured as female, the wild African landscape doubly invites the mastery of European masculinity, in the colonial mindset. The native people are equally subject to the imperialist gaze; they are monstrous like Gagool, a 'frightful vulture-headed old creature' (p. 125), and like the terrible one-eyed King Twala: 'an enormous man with the most entirely repulsive countenance we had ever beheld' (p. 106). The natives are repeatedly subordinated to the European explorers, even to the extent that they are sacrificed for white men; a stampeding elephant is prevented from killing Captain Good, stranded on the ground in its path because of his refusal to wear snag-proof clothing instead of his European long trousers, only with the death of a Zulu guide:

> Khiva, the Zulu boy, saw his master fall, and brave lad as he was, turned and flung his assegai straight into the elephant's face. [...] the brute seized

the poor Zulu, hurled him to the earth, and placing one huge foot on to his body about the middle, twined its trunk round his upper part and *tore him in two.* (p. 50)

Directly opposing the textual representations of colonized natives was the ideal of European culture that was presented, like a gift, to the colonies. The domesticating project involved a literary negotiation: while poetry from India was translated into English, Shakespeare's plays were regularly performed for elite groups of Indians. Jyotsna Singh insists that, colonial domination being 'as much a cultural as a political process', performance of Shakespeare's plays and promotion of Western literary texts in colonial India was 'crucial in producing a discourse of cultural colonialism' (1989, p. 447). The British colonials built theatres in India, the first in Calcutta in 1775, and Shakespeare's plays figured prominently in theatre programmes in the eighteenth and nineteenth century. The reproduction of Shakespeare in this context is part of the process of creating replica home societies in the colonies, which has often been equated with translation, the imperial culture being translated in a foreign landscape. Like translation, which was, in the past, considered a second-rate copy, in the colonial context the replica England in India was never intended to be an exact or equal copy: to create an equivalent culture in the colony would be to admit equality, and to undo the principle of benevolent mastery upon which the colonial project relied. This apparent benevolence is a presumption present in *King Solomon's Mines*; having witnessed a brutal killing the group of adventurers extract a promise from chief Ignosi that 'the killing of men without trial shall no longer take place in the land' (p. 132). This is, of course, a fictional creation, but a similar very public demonstration of civilization over superstition was carried out by the British administration in India when *sati*, the Hindu practice that demanded that widows must sacrifice themselves on their husbands' funeral pyres, was banned. On the surface this appears to promote women's welfare; at the same time, though, it is a wily diplomatic move: an act preventing women's premature and painful death proclaims publicly and internationally the worthiness of the colonial cause, justifying other acts of colonialism: economic exploitation, subordination of other nations, and the accumulation of status.

Audiences for performances of Shakespeare's plays in India comprised colonial dignitaries, governors, and elite groups of Indians, proof, for postcolonial readings which pay attention to literature and ideology, that Shakespeare's plays were 'invaluable in promoting and privileging the culture of the colonizers' (Singh, 1989, p. 449). Anxieties over the literary audience and ideology echo in current debates over postcolonial literature. For John Marx, global literary taste for books with postcolonial themes is to be seen as a positive impact of the decolonizing process, which has expanded the literary canon. He suggests that 'the mainstreaming of post-colonial literature confirms that such writing is equipped to represent the local cultures that imperialism has wrought as well as those it strove to demolish' (2004, p. 95). Others question how many postcolonial narratives actually achieve positive aims, suggesting instead that many simply present the East in accessible packages for Western consumers. Kiran Desai, for example, has been accused of presenting a simplified South Asian culture, the dialect words in her novels being repeated in translation to simply add an exotic flavour rather than to convey an authentic India (Sen, 2006). Desai apologized for her novel *Hullabaloo in the Guava Orchard*, agreeing with reviewers who described it as exoticist, and calling it 'frivolous' (Sharma-Jensen, 2006), thereby rejecting the book just as her second novel, *The Inheritance of Loss*, won the Man Booker Prize in 2006. There are extensive descriptions of food, cookery and eating in *Hullabaloo in the Guava Orchard*, expressing need: Kulfi's 'hunger that had overtaken her in recent months' (Desai, 1998, p. 4); desire: 'Gall nut, cinnabar, mace. Senna, asafoetida, quail eggs, snail eggs, liver of a wild boar, tail of a cat [...] Nasturtium leaves, rhododendron flowers, cicada orchids! [...] What would her dish be without them?' (pp. 200–201); and food as the ultimate solution to all social problems, conveyed by the idea of cooking and eating unruly alcoholic monkeys who are terrorizing the area (p. 181). Descriptions like these, particularly in the light of the exotic spices and flowers described, seem to offer up India for the consumption of Western readers in the manner that Graham Huggan has described in *The Postcolonial Exotic*. India, and Indian literature in English, has become, Huggan argues, very fashionable, literature a consumer item and India a consumable for the West (2001, p. 59). An example he gives is Salman Rushdie and Elizabeth West's anthology, *The Vintage Book of Indian Writing, 1947–1997*. The fact that all texts collected in this anthology are written in English is confirmation for many that, rather than being an accurate record of contemporary Indian literature, the text – and others like it – is produced solely to market India and Indian literature to a Western audience.

However, Desai's novel seems almost too preoccupied with consumption, suggesting that the drunken monkeys, dreams of eating peacocks and tigers, and the spies falling into cooking pots is more than a simple offering up of the exotic for consumption. Every event is determined by food: the relief parcel dropped from a Swedish aeroplane announces Sampath's birth (p. 11) and Sampath's position as sage is dependent upon the treats cooked as offerings and laid at the foot of his tree by devotees, collected at the end of the day to be re-sold (p. 93) – this is surely an explicit engagement with consumerism as a cycle dependent on dishonest profiteering; and more than that: the characters are all in some way edible. As well as Sampath's metamorphosis into a guava (p. 207), his mother is named Kulfi (ice cream); Pinky's romantic interest is the Hungry Hop Boy – he sells food at the cinema and so is named for his job, but it is perhaps his hunger that transforms Pinky's love rival, a girl chosen for him by his parents, into an edible delight, as he renames her 'Miss Pudding and Cake' (p. 193). The extent to which food and eating constructs the book implies that, at some level, the text itself raises questions about the desire to present India for Western consumption.

Global consumption: Zingolo

There are no such qualms in Cadbury's recent advert for Dairy Milk (broadcast in Autumn 2009), newly launched as a fair trade product in the UK and Ireland. The advert celebrates the 101-year trading relationship with Ghana by presenting the country as a kind of African Willy Wonka's chocolate factory, a place of constant, joyful cocoa production. The television advert is known as 'Zingolo', after the song that accompanies it, and begins with a painter talking to his friend while finishing a large sign advertising the Big Plant Cocoa Farm. He is interrupted by a giant face constructed from wood, stone and cocoa beans which emerges from a garage, and starts to spin as the 'Zingolo' theme music begins. The face continues spinning and dancing through the village, and the image cuts rapidly and frequently between the mask's procession and images of people dancing, laughing and smiling, as well as images of cocoa production. These images of production seem calculated to produce a specific impression of the Cadbury's–Ghana partnership: cocoa beans and trees and people picking cocoa are shown on a very small scale, and the cocoa beans are only ever shown in transport on the back of a child's bike. The image of the child carrying cocoa beans was perhaps misjudged, when a glance at the official Ghanaian Cocoa Board website shows that subscribers can read a report on child labour. These images suggest simplicity, small-scale community farming, and certainly not mass production, a running theme throughout the advert. At the end of the sequence, the painter and his friend watch the giant cocoa bean head fly up into the sky and away, as if magically, under its own spectacular powers. In fact, this resembles the exported beans being taken abroad, but without having to disturb the quaintness of the scene with cargo planes or freight shipment containers. The painter and his friend discuss the event in relaxed, happy tones and continue painting the sign – but the sign is in English, unlike the language that they converse in, or the language of the 'Zingolo' song. The English sign demonstrates the villagers' actual disconnection from the process of global cocoa trade, production and export, while the happy, dancing advert had seemed to convey a connection between Ghanaian village lifestyle and the cocoa trade, implying willingness on the part of the population. The sign actually acts as a slogan or an international billboard, creating the impression that Ghana is in full control of its cocoa export, that it is, in fact, actively seeking customers like Cadbury's, and that this has only a positive impact on their community. A few moments after the beans have been transported away, one cocoa bean drops to the ground near the painter. Perhaps this is intended to convey a charming, carefree method of farming and production, again in sharp contrast with the production methods of large corporations and global industry. However, an unintended meaning is inevitably suggested by this image when read from a postcolonial perspective: when the large crop of Ghanaian produce is taken away, leaving just one pitiful bean dropping back to Ghanaian soil, the exploitative nature of global trade is revealed. This is even the case with a system of 'fair' trade, which still relies upon the poverty of the producers, even if they are slightly better off financially than other farmers and producers under more competitive systems. For Yuri Smertin, fair trade may have further hidden dangers due to the closer interference from apparently benevolent international agencies:

> By the start of the 1960s, immediately following the national liberation of most of the African countries, more than 600 missionary, educational, philanthropic and other private and government-sponsored US organisations were at work in Africa.   (1987, p. 80)

This, Smertin suggests, is a form of neocolonial expansion involving the dissemination of values and religious views, as well as control of the media and education. This is directly relevant to Cadbury's, who are donating the proceeds of the 'Zingolo' single to Care, a charity working with cocoa communities in Ghana. However well-intentioned, this is potentially an outlet for cultural intervention reminiscent of colonial missionary work and other social and legal changes implemented with the apparent good of the colonized community in mind.

The global and corporate nature of the cocoa trade is alluded to within the chocolate advert in a number of ways. The 'Zingolo' song is performed by Tinny (or Nii Addo Quaynor), an established Ghanaian musician, and accompanied by a famous Ghanaian dance troupe, High Spirits. The performance area is a village clearing which at one point resembles a computer or arcade game floor which lights up under the dancers' feet. Tinny is dressed differently from the villagers, in typically American sports clothing, and rather than engaging with the crowd, he appears as if from nowhere (or, at least, elsewhere) in a flash of sparkling light, which positions him on a roof high above the crowds. His clothing and his position seem based on American rather than Ghanaian performance norms: performers of traditional Ghanaian dance and music occupy the nucleus of the *vufofe*, a designated performance area, but this is not an elevated position in traditional dance (Burns, 2009, p. 49). Of course, contemporary popular music in Ghana is influenced by other international music and dance and is not restricted to its traditional origins. But at the same time, the implication in the very American-influenced performance is that a Western or an international lifestyle is an aspirational one, and, in turn, that global trade can help local communities to accomplish this desire. The very fact that this song is available to buy internationally – online, what's more – determines that Ghanaian culture (music) is internationally exportable, like its cocoa. At one point a white European style hairdresser's dummy wearing black wigs spins around and this image is interspersed with shots of the cocoa bean head and Ghanaian villagers; the implication is that the Western consumer can perform, can buy, and can become Ghanaian, by consuming the culture and its produce.

The language used to describe these relationships between local producers and global corporations conveys the extent to which globalization resembles colonialism in certain aspects. In fact, it was a Ghanaian thinker who first proposed the term 'neocolonialism', the first president of independent Ghana, Kwame Nkrumah. In 1965, Nkrumah wrote *Neocolonialism: The Last Stage of Imperialism*, which described 'the role that transnational corporations play in draining surplus from Africa, hence fostering the continent's underdevelopment' (Zack-Williams, 2006, pp. 190–1). The term 'neocolonialism' is often used to describe the continuing hegemonic power of imperialism after independence in an exertion of economic, cultural and political pressures. Hegemony, a term first used by Antonio Gramsci to describe the subordination of the Italian working class, is a form of control by surreptitious means rather than by force. It describes a kind of power which allows the dominant to retain control, while encouraging the less powerful (the working class, or in a strictly postcolonial context, the 'natives' living in a formerly colonized place after independence) to accept an unequal system. Hegemony is the force that convinces people that hierarchical structures in society are necessary or inevitable – that certain people hold all the wealth, land and power, while others do the work to maintain the wealth of that country yet will never own an equivalent share of the wealth, land and power. Hegemony is different from imposed control, like slavery, which requires physical force to compel people to work. Edward Saïd has described the way that imperialist ideology and colonialist occupation enforced an overlap between different places and cultures which has grown since, in what has been called by George Ritzer a 'McDonaldization' of the globe, an economic and electronic homogenization. This involves global labour forces: call centres set up to answer British bank customers' calls in India, factories producing goods for American markets in Thailand, for example, and globalization has been accompanied by an unprecedented level of movement (of people, goods, data and technologies) across geographical boundaries.

Nkrumah campaigned for neutrality in trading relationships, fostered a socialist ideology, and is remembered as a key figure in anticolonial politics and a key actor in the decolonization process (Holden, 2008, p. 117). The presentation of Ghana as available for the world to buy is appropriate, considering that Ghana hosted World Tourism Day for 2009, which takes place on 27 September each year (to coincide with the date that the advert was shown on UK television). The theme for 2009 was 'Tourism Celebrating Diversity', and the aim of the event was to 'celebrate and highlight the importance of tourism and Globalization' (Ghana Tourism, 2009). Globalization is becoming an increasingly more positive image in official Ghanaian media, with the Cocoa Board demonstrating its global thinking by producing a display to welcome US President Barack Obama to the country, depicting Obama's face constructed from cocoa beans. The image shows three cocoa workers constructing the image, accompanied by the message of welcome, 'Akwaaba Obama'. Ghana is repeatedly portrayed – from both internal forces like the Cocoa Board and external ones like the Cadbury's advert – as an international player based on cocoa production and global trade. The influence of global corporations is inevitably a neocolonial one, as Nkrumah warned.

Part I

The Emergence of Postcolonial Thinking

1 Anticolonial Resistance

You taught me language; and my profit on't
Is, I know how to curse: the red plague rid you,
For learning me your language!

The Tempest, 1.2.363–5

Shakespeare's Caliban, the disobedient slave in *The Tempest*, eventually understands that he has behaved badly and promises to 'be wise hereafter, And seek for grace' (5.1.294–5). The only native human inhabitant of a tropical island, he was quickly dominated by the exiled European duke Prospero, and forced into slave labour, allowing Prospero to maintain his position of authority, which might have been compromised had he been compelled to do the hunting, cooking and building. The Prospero–Caliban dynamic has resonance in anticolonial thought, especially in the Caribbean because of the island setting and the Caribbean location of colonial plantation slavery. George Lamming has used the Caliban figure at length in his fiction and non-fictional prose, most notably in *The Pleasures of Exile* (1960), a memoir which is at the same time an analysis of West Indian writing and cultural history in a global context. George Lamming was born in Barbados in 1927, and has worked as a university lecturer as well as a writer. Engaging with Caliban, Lamming produces a direct assault on colonialism, revealing the flaws in the assumption that the colonizing mission was a civilizing and necessary one, by questioning the monstrosity of the Caliban figure and the benevolence of European master–teacher, Prospero.

Lamming claims that language fundamentally alters Caliban: 'only the application of the Word to the darkness of Caliban's world could harness the beast which resides within this cannibal. This is the first important achievement of the colonizing process' (1992, p. 109). In the play, Caliban's mother died giving birth to him, so rather than replacing his own language with a new one, the colonizing process is more profound: Caliban is made aware that he must accept his inadequacy because he lacks language before quickly acquiring Prospero's language in order to be complete, but as Lamming explains, Caliban is both colonized and excluded by language. In learning the language of the colonizer, he simultaneously learns that he is unable to ever become whole: the new language separates him from the identity he had once been sure about, and he is left 'exiled from his gods, exiled from his nature, exiled from his own name' (Lamming, 1992, p. 15).

Caliban represents the universal exile: having been torn from their history by leaving, or being taken from, their place of origin, exiles must accept their 'inadequacy', their 'irrelevance of function' (Lamming, 1992, p. 24). The place of exile for the West Indian is frequently England, the 'Headquarters' in Lamming's terms where not only the colonial mother-land but also Shakespeare, the writer who has in some ways determined the exile's position, may pass judgement. Under the colonial education system, the exile was taught that England is the place where 'culture' comes from, and this 'culture' may be summarized by the works of 'Dickens, Jane Austen, Kipling and that sacred gang' (Lamming, 1992, p. 27) – the literary canon. In order for the West Indian writer ever to achieve a sense of adequacy in the face of an overwhelming expectation of failure (which asks, how could a writer from Barbados ever write as well as an English writer, when England is the place where English literature comes from?), the solution is, Lamming suggests, 'to make English his' (1992, p. 31). With this intention comes a shift in attitude which understands both the West Indian writer and the West Indies as a location as valuable and relevant:

> I am not much interested in what the West Indian writer has brought to the English language; for English is no longer the exclusive language of the men who live in England. [...] A more important consideration is what the West Indian novelist has brought to the West Indies.   (Lamming, 1992, p. 36)

Like Caliban who planned to steal Prospero's books which he assumed would strip him of his powers, the West Indian writer is empowered by turning the weapon against the master in an act of anticolonial resistance, or against his former master in an act of postcolonial revision. For Lamming, the colonial condition described by *The Tempest* was somehow sanctioned by the specific product of colonialism: sugar. Something so sweet was produced by the brutal colonial regime: 'it sweetened, hot and black, the irretrievable cup of Prospero's wealth' (1992, p. 151). After the sugar plantations, Barbados and the other sugar-producing islands of the Caribbean remained, for Lamming, a 'sad and dying kingdom of sugar' (1992, p. 17), a very different image to that sweet and hot cup of colonial wealth that belied the process of its production. Part of this changing

process, the slave uprising in Barbados of 1816 was instrumental in decolonization. Beginning with a discussion of this uprising, this chapter gathers
diverse instances from within a long, slow process of anticolonial resistance involving organized uprisings, political movements, and literary and
other textual responses in the struggle for decolonization.

Barbados, sugar, and the 1816 slave uprising

In April 1816, Barbados, the Caribbean plantation reputedly providing
slaves with the best working and living conditions, was the location for
a significant rebellion. It is known as Bussa's rebellion after its leader
and also The Easter Rebellion, in recognition of its date, which had symbolic significance in the Christian calendar and signified its importance
as a symbol of hope for the ongoing emancipation struggle (Cleve Scott,
2007, p. 90). The uprising is not significant because of its length, size or
outcome: it lasted just three days, was no larger than other rebellions elsewhere, and had little impact on the abolition of slavery which ultimately
came into force in 1834. Its significance derives from its aims and intentions: the slaves wanted to end slave ownership and the plantation system
altogether by instituting black leadership in Barbados (Cleve Scott, 2007,
p. 90). Although a common demand of the black working majority elsewhere in the Caribbean, as Karl Watson has explained, the specific demo-
graphic history of Barbados meant that it was quite unexpected by the
white masters in Barbados.

When Barbados was first populated by white settlers between 1625 and
1643 there was a majority white population, which meant that in the white
landowners' psyche, white Barbadians were 'authentic inhabitants, true
insiders, settlers as opposed to transient exploiters' (Watson, 2009, p. 180).
Even after large numbers of slaves were brought to the island, the population comprised a large, socially stratified white population, a larger poor
white population, and a black population with approximately equal numbers of males and females. This differed from other plantation systems
where a vast majority of black, male slaves were governed by white colonial masters with European connections. As well as making Barbados
self-sustaining, meaning that there was no need for a constant influx of
new black slaves, the community was more stable. There was not the sense
of transient labour and temporary habitation which prevailed in other
Caribbean colonies. This may have produced the illusion in the landowners' minds that the social system was a reasonable one, a workable one that

would continue. In fact, the black slaves were enabled by this system, to an extent, with its complacent government and slightly improved working and living conditions which meant the slaves were in a more capable physical and emotional position to revolt.

Planning the rebellion began in November 1815 after the Barbados House of Assembly rejected the Registry Bill. This bill to create a register of slaves was intended to ease the transition from slavery to emancipation. Yet uncertainty about the purpose and the process of its implementation led to its rejection in Barbados. Ambiguous reports led the slaves to believe that the authorities were preventing emancipation by holding up the process, and this was the major cause of the rebellion (Welch, 2003, p. 36). The rebellion was carefully planned. Its timing was significant not only for its religious symbolism but also because at a time of celebration there would be minimal supervision from guards. The state of the sugar crop itself was a significant aspect in the timing and the objectives of the rebellion: the mature sugar crop would provide cover, and its burning in maturity would cause the most serious financial damage to the plantation owners (Cleve Scott, 2007, p. 90).

That the Barbadian plantations produced sugar was not incidental to the rebellion. As Bill Ashcroft has explained, sugar is the most significant key to understanding the colonial process. According to Ashcroft, 'sugar became the focus for changes in notions of race, power, cultural dominance, and the geography of the world' (2001, p. 68). This is because of the way that sugar is used internationally; the 'relentless invention and promotion of its consumption as a staple' led to the reconstitution of Barbados, which had once been a settlement with a varied agricultural output, as 'little more than a sugar factory' (Ashcroft, 2001, p. 69). Such a singular focus renders society unstable because it is explicitly constructed on the production of a fetishized product to be consumed by what was at the time a privileged class in the West. There was extensive burning of the crop across a number of plantations in Barbados on the night of 14 April, before the armed forces reacted and eventually put down the rebellion on 17 April.

Even after their legal emancipation following the abolition of slavery in 1834, slaves had little freedom. Perhaps the most damaging law that followed slavery was the Masters and Servants Act in 1840, which remained in force until 1937. This act meant that former slaves were still controlled by the plantations as it was illegal for them to seek alternative employment. As Karl Watson has described, the shift in power in Barbados was a slow process, as 'white power was slowly whittled away by black perseverance and repeated challenges to the status quo' (2009, p. 181).

Anticolonial responses: Toussaint L'Ouverture; Aimé Césaire

The slave trade cannot be separated from the colonial project in the Caribbean. The only way to colonize the Caribbean, to extract profit from the land, was to work people to death. The Industrial Revolution in Britain operated under similar principles, but slavery exerted new levels of control and direct brutality over the workforce. San Domingo was the location of what C. L. R. James calls 'the only successful slave revolt in history' (1938, p. vii). The revolt of 1791 lasted twelve years and brought down what had been considered by those who wanted to maintain colonialism and slavery 'the finest colony in the world' (James, 1938, p. 109). San Domingo was a vast colony with 599 sugar and 3379 indigo plantations, and half a million slaves, all of whom were from Africa – the white slaves (white *engages*, mostly from Ireland) initially working in the colony could not tolerate the climate. Sugar must have held an important symbolic place in the minds of the slaves, who were repeatedly punished by tortures derived from methods of crop production. In *The Black Jacobins* (1938), C. L. R. James describes sugar cane labour as 'exacting and ceaseless', from daybreak until night, digging ditches in the hard sun-baked earth (p. 4). Because the crop could grow at any time of the year, there would have been no sense of completion or variety in the exhausting job. As well as digging in the fields, other slaves worked up to eighteen hours a day in mills extracting juice and manufacturing raw sugar. In order to maintain this level of labour, slaves endured near starvation, and were forced to wear a tin-plate mask designed to prevent them from eating the sugar cane (James, 1938, p. 6). Slaves were punished for what was considered disobedient behaviour – whipping was common, but this punishment was elaborated cruelly, and slaves underwent practices of torture that made particular use of the sugar. For example, as James describes, slave-masters poured boiling cane sugar over slaves' heads, or 'buried them up to the neck and smeared their heads with sugar that the flies might devour them' (1938, p. 6).

Despite the slaves' living conditions, eventually they were able to organize. They began the San Domingo revolt in 1791 (lasting until 1802), during which slave gangs murdered their masters and burned the plantations to the ground. *The Black Jacobins* is a history of the San Domingo revolt and an analysis of Toussaint L'Ouverture (commonly known simply as Toussaint, having changed his name from Toussaint Bréda), the most prominent figure in the slave revolt, who had worked as a livestock steward and been well educated. He initially maintained order and prevented slaves from killing white slave owners, preferring to organize an army with European-style titles with which to face those who perpetuated slavery (and associated colonialism). In adopting titles like 'general', 'colonel', 'commander', 'brigadier' and 'viceroy', a practice that James calls absurd (1938, p. 73), the leaders of the slave army were claiming an equivalency with the colonial armies that attempted to destroy them. Under a corrupt and unjust colonial system, military titles must have been considered by those who opposed that system as flimsy. To make use of those military titles is not to show subservience towards them, but to demand equal status. Toussaint's use of language was strategic, though James questions its clarity. James analyses a letter written by Toussaint to rally the black slaves, in which he seems to adopt two contradictory positions: he uses both the language of the French Revolution – urging 'Liberty and Equality' – while at the same time positioning himself within the royalist system that the revolution was fighting to overturn, by adopting in his signature the military position of 'General of the Armies of the King' (1938, p. 100). Rather than showing a lack of clarity or direction, Toussaint's linguistic choices position the slave revolt and his army as somewhat separate from both the revolution and the royalist colonial system, but informed by both. This conveys the careful position that his army would need to adopt in order to avoid becoming a low-ranking segment of one side or the other. Eventually, Toussaint's command took the form of a military dictatorship, and though he necessarily changed allegiance at times and resorted to violence when his allies attempted to restore slavery, his government implemented a fairer system and established schools, agricultural prosperity, and a simplified taxation system. His rule was remembered as a success, and San Domingo gained independence from France in 1804, and renamed the area Haiti. France only formally recognized Haiti's independent status on the agreement that they would pay a hefty fee to compensate France for lost territory and resources. Haiti only finished repaying this debt in 1947. As an aside, in 2010 a number of academics and activists, including Noam Chomsky, Naomi Klein and Cornel West, wrote an open letter to the French President Nicolas Sarkozy urging France to repay this money to Haiti, to help rebuild the country following the devastating earthquake in Haiti in January 2010. Toussaint's role was a geographically specific one, concerned with the independence of San Domingo, but it had worldwide impact regarding the possibilities of revolt.

Long after the 1821 revolt, in the middle of the twentieth century, Aimé Césaire fought a political battle to achieve independence for Martinique, staged in political campaigns, public address and literature. Born in the French colony of Martinique in 1913, Césaire studied in France and then followed a political career, being elected to the position of mayor of Fort de France in 1946 and serving as President of the Regional Council of Martinique from 1983 until 1988 before his retirement in 2001. In contrast to his openly revolutionary literary texts, Césaire's *Discourse on Colonialism* (1955) is a more straightforward political statement, an essay that exposes the corruption and brutality of colonialism and promotes liberation. Colonization, Césaire reminds the reader, is not a product of evangelism, or a 'philanthropic enterprise' (1972, p. 10). It is instead a process that works to 'decivilize' and 'brutalize' the colonizer so that they can permit brutality, and within such a system, 'no one colonizes innocently' (1972, pp. 13, 17). With an irresistible turn of phrase, Césaire mimics the colonial attitude that claims to impose colonial rule for the good of the colonized: 'Start the forgetting machine!' (1972, p. 32), he writes, after quietly revealing what the colonial rulers want to hide, that pre-colonial societies, giving as examples Vietnam and Madagascar, were 'refined', had 'poets, artists, administrators', 'sculpture', 'art' and 'music' (1972, p. 32).

To attempt to return to pre-colonial society – pre-colonial society that was 'democratic', 'cooperative' and 'anti-capitalist' – is, for Césaire, impractical, and instead he campaigned for the emergence of a new society that rejects colonization in two ways: by embracing the Communist Party or Marxist objectives, and by celebrating negritude, the term coined by Césaire to describe pride in black culture, language and identity, and to end a feeling of shame in being black. Negritude is an insistence that 'Africa was not some sort of blank page in the history of humanity', but that instead, 'Negro heritage was worthy of respect' (Depestre, 1972, p. 76). This means a rejection of the colonial system, and Césaire effects this in his own writing by purposely renouncing French literary forms, emphasizing the need to create a new language instead (Depestre, 1972, pp. 66–7). Using Communist discourse, Césaire affirms that 'the bourgeoisie, as a class, is condemned to take responsibility for all the barbarism of history', which of course includes racism, slavery and colonialism (1972, p. 49). The only method of overcoming colonialism in the absence of what Césaire cites as an ideal, a 'classless society' in which all citizens would work and benefit equally, is 'revolution' (1972, p. 61). However the Communist Party in the early and mid-twentieth century did not always satisfy Césaire, and it was not always able to comprehend his insistence that black people were 'doubly proletarianized and alienated: in the first place as workers, but also as blacks' (Depestre, 1972, pp. 78–9). Considering Césaire's point that blacks were doubly alienated, due to their working conditions and their race, it seems logical that many anti-imperialist activists were also members of the Communist Party, which primarily sought representation and rights for working people. The next section considers examples of black intellectual activism in the Communist Parties of Great Britain and America.

The Communist Party and anticolonialism: C. L. R. James

Paul Buhle has claimed that cricket '"proved" to the colonizer [...] that "civilizing" had been a successful mission', a problematic concept that anticipates questions about why an anticolonial activist like C. L. R. James should remain so steadfastly loyal towards the game. But Buhle indicates that this is not the only thing that cricket proved: it showed the colonized that 'civilization was by no means the monopoly of the mother country but a larger game that anyone could play' (1988, p. 18). While this analysis opens up a space for general participation in the culture of the imperial mother country and its games, roles, and occupations, it implies that the imperial way is the only way, that assimilation and excellence in the ways of the English empire is the ultimate goal for the colonized subject. This shuts down any opportunity to question the legitimacy of that empire, its history and practices, or to forge new anticolonial and postcolonial systems which might involve new literatures, languages, laws, and sports, including those that had been forcibly abandoned by slaves when they were removed to the Caribbean.

James's relationship with cricket is interesting; in his autobiographical work, *Beyond a Boundary* (1963) he examines cricket as an emblem of Caribbean and international culture and politics. A prominent participant in colonial and English customs and culture, a famous cricket writer in England with celebrity status, James had not followed a conventional path while growing up in colonial Trinidad. James excelled academically, securing a scholarship for his secondary education. His colonial education instilled a love of Englishness: his school headmaster, Mr W. Burslem was an autocrat, but 'beloved':

> How not to look up to the England of Shakespeare and Milton, of Thackeray and Dickens, of Hobbs and Rhodes, in the daily presence of such an Englishman and in the absence of any nationalist agitation?   (2000, p. 29)

However, he was not an ideal student. Instead of conforming to others' academic and professional expectations, James turned away from his studies and focused instead on cricket, which he pursued in practice and theory, playing the game while studying its rules and tactics, history and personalities. James wrote about the dual identity that he found within himself, 'one, the rebel against family and school discipline and order; the other, a Puritan who would have cut off a finger sooner than do anything contrary to the ethics of the game' (2000, p. 28). His experience is reminiscent of colonial and postcolonial duality: his rebellion was not just against authority, it was against a colonial authority, while what he describes as his Puritanism was equally problematic because it meant adherence to a set of rules imposed by the colonial regime.

As a young adult, James was active in developing the intellectual landscape in Trinidad in new ways, but his early choices reflect just how much James was still influenced by his colonial education. He was a founder of the Maverick Club in 1919, an intellectual gathering which published and delivered lectures and wrote essays, and although the club seemed to turn away from colonial control because it was for non-whites only, still, the lectures and essays discussed English literature and drama (Buhle, 1988, p. 26). However, James's subsequent journals, *Trinidad* and *The Beacon*, supported new voices and challenging literary subjects like slum life and prostitution. It was not until he moved to England in 1932 that James gained some critical distance from English literature and culture. He was supported by Learie Constantine, a cricketer originally from Trinidad and later a politician, who introduced James to anti-imperial politics. His time with Constantine may have provided some impetus for James to write *The Black Jacobins*, a work that Paul Buhle has described as a forerunner for international black history, and a text that 'revolutionised historical scholarship simply by discrediting the history of abolition as pure philanthropy' (1988, pp. 41, 59).

James was a committed Marxist, but it was not until he moved to America in 1938 that he was able to devote his time to political activism. During this time, as well as giving lectures on anti-imperial and socialist politics, he wrote *Mariners, Renegades and Castaways*. This study of Herman Melville's *Moby Dick* analyses the social structures on which the novel is based and its resonance for both American society and colonialism. As Bill Schwarz has claimed, in both this text and *Beyond a Boundary*, James is 'explicitly interrogating the precepts of a civilisation' (2006, p. 131). Underlying this interrogation of an organising system is a questioning of the colonial system that underpins the civilization of America, Britain, and the West Indies. Ultimately, Schwarz suggests, of the first importance was his 'determination to understand that blacks historically had been active in the making of modern America, that they were in his own times fully modern subjects, and that in the future they would take a leading role in bringing about freedom for all' (2006, p. 146). Claudia Jones was another important black member of the Communist Party.

Claudia Jones

Founder of the biggest street parade in Europe – the Notting Hill Carnival which takes place in London every August Bank Holiday – Claudia Jones is a lesser-known figure of both Communist and anticolonial activity, although she played an active role in developing the foundations for racial equality legislation in Britain. Claudia Jones was born in Port of Spain, Trinidad, in 1915. She had emigrated to New York in 1924, and was to become a prominent member of the Communist Party of the USA, working as editor for Negro Affairs in the *Daily Worker* and later editing *Negro Affairs Quarterly*. It was after her imprisonment for Communist activism and subsequent migration to the UK in 1955 as an alternative to deportation to Trinidad that she questioned the ability or willingness of the Communist Party to address issues of colonialism and race. A sustained campaign by the party's black members eventually led to the issuing of the Charter of Rights for Coloured Workers in Britain which purported to oppose racism by stating that racial discrimination should be made a penal offence, and demanding equality of employment, wages and working conditions. Yet the charter demanded equality between British and 'coloured' workers, failing to recognize that many black workers were also British, by birth or by citizenship. Jones wrote in a letter to a New York colleague that the Communist Party was dominated by imperialist ideas (Sherwood, 1999, p. 76), a feeling supported by reports that a number of Nigerian students attending Marxism classes claimed that they were not consulted when the party formed its policy and wrote its pamphlet on the Nigerian political situation. Leela Gandhi has discussed the sometimes 'explicitly antagonistic' (1999, p. 24) relationship between Marxism and postcolonialism, the origins of which can be traced to Marx's imperialistic writings on India which assumed a 'fundamental inequality between East and West' (Gandhi, 1999, p. 72) and a regenerative role for the incoming European.

Disengaging somewhat from the Communist Party after she was unable to secure a leading role or to make sufficient impact in fostering party awareness of race, Jones worked with and even founded a number of other organizations, including the Association for the Advancement of Coloured

People, the Inter-Racial Friendship Co-ordinating Council, and the Afro-Asian-Caribbean Conference. She also helped to establish the *West Indian Gazette*, and reflected on her writing in an autobiographical statement, saying: 'all weavers know of tangled skeins. The Bard thought they became "threads to deceive". Sometimes they can be untangled and sometimes they serve as webs. How I believe in the Loom of Language!' (Sherwood, 1999, p. 55). Jones probably had an ambivalent relationship with her 'Loom of Language', or with her life in political journalism, as this image implies; Jones learned to weave while in prison, winning a state prize for her woven place mats (Sherwood, 1999, p. 23). She was in the strange position of receiving state recognition for a skill practised while imprisoned by that state. State recognition for the craft was in sharp contrast with what she felt was the lack of recognition for her political abilities when she was living in exile in Britain.

Feminism and anticolonialism: Claudia Jones; Una Marson

Claudia Jones's anticolonial work straddles both Marxism and feminism. Yet, nowadays, some of the events that she actively promoted, like beauty contests for black women, might be seen as contrary to feminism. Jones's black beauty pageants were the main event of the Caribbean carnivals held in St Pancras town hall, beginning in January 1959, which were the precursors of the Notting Hill Carnival. Jones set up the beauty pageants in direct response to the mainstream (white) beauty contests.

The Miss Great Britain beauty contest began in 1945, originally named the Bathing Beauty Queen competition as it took place for many years in British seaside resorts and holiday camps. Beauty contests thrived during the 1950s and 1960s, and it was not until later in the 1960s that feminists would start to protest against them, one example being Michelle Anderson, a 1969 Miss America contestant who entered the competition in order to pull a feminist banner out of her bra on stage in protest (Craig, 2002, p. 69). Rather than joining in with a popular activity, Jones repositioned beauty as something that black women could be part of. Jones's black beauty competitions were about taking pride in black identity and to an extent, expressing Césaire's concept of negritude, but in a way that connected black women in Britain with their British identity as well as their black identity. Helping women to become visible in Britain, even through what might nowadays be understood as an objectifying practice, was part of a broader political agenda to create racial harmony and equality. Nevertheless, as Maxine Leeds Craig writes, 'black contestants challenged the content of the beauty contest but not its form', symbolising both defiance and convention (2002, p. 70) when they maintained traditional constructions of gender in every way except by asserting the right of black women to be considered beautiful along with white women.

Una Marson fits more straightforwardly into a feminist category. Marson, born in 1905 in rural Jamaica, was the daughter of a Baptist parson. She was a journalist, playwright and poet who travelled to London, Geneva, Haifa and also spent eight years in the United States. Unlike other prominent anticolonial intellectuals from the West Indies, though, Marson only ever lived abroad for short periods. She used her experience gained elsewhere to reconsider Jamaica from an international perspective, 'as part of the larger colonial, Caribbean, and later African, picture', as Alison Donnell has pointed out (2003, p. 116). Marson returned to Jamaica after both of the periods she spent abroad. The first period was spent in Britain and Geneva, where Marson worked as personal secretary to Haile Selassie, Emperor of Ethiopia (Abyssinia) and was the first black woman invited to attend the League of Nations. Later, she worked as a BBC radio journalist and editor in London. Each time she returned to Jamaica her career bloomed, and unlike many other anticolonial activists, such as Claudia Jones, she had a high profile and attained recognition within her lifetime (Donnell, 2003, p. 121).

Marson is best known for her work at the BBC, where she established the Caribbean Voices radio programme and changed for the better the 'fortunes of West Indian writers in the metropolis' (Donnell, 2003, p. 122). Caribbean Voices emerged out of the Caribbean section of the BBC World Service which delivered news and patriotic messages with the intention of boosting the morale of Caribbean troops during the Second World War. Marson, the presenter, started to read out some of the letters and poems written by Caribbean listeners and momentum gathered until Caribbean Voices emerged. The programme consisted of literature readings and also literary critical discussion, adding something very new to the literary landscape at a time when literary education in the Caribbean was all about England. As well as making literature about the Caribbean widely accessible, it presented a positive public image of the West Indian, and it fostered Caribbean writers practically: George Lamming claims in a recent BBC documentary that he wrote *In the Castle of My Skin* funded entirely by money received for his readings on Caribbean Voices; for each poem, the writer was paid a guinea, a sum acknowledged as a very good amount (Grant, 2009). The programme ended in 1958. Alison Donnell notes that

one of Marson's most important contributions to the anticolonial movement was in achieving international recognition for Caribbean writers.
This began with Caribbean Voices, and was strengthened by the Jamaican
publishing house Pioneer Press, which was established by Marson in
1949.

Despite her significant contribution, Marson has often been sidelined.
Donnell suggests that this may be due to her elite education and privileged
middle-class upbringing. Marson certainly lived in a position of privilege in comparison to the majority of Jamaicans, who would never have
been able to afford a large household with four servants where the family budget was 'ample', and where there were often 'elaborate' meals with
visitors: 'parishioners came in for rose-tea parties with Ada Marson', her
mother (Jarrett-Macauley, 1998, pp. 5–6). She attended the elite Hampton
High School, a school for upper-middle-class girls, on a scholarship, but
she 'did not thrive' there (Jarrett-Macauley, 1998, p. 20), experiencing racism, and receiving an education that was 'directed towards ideas of service
rather than intellectual grandeur' (Donnell, 2003, p. 114). Her independence from her family and her first job in social work perhaps allowed her
the distance from her wealthy upbringing to raise questions about social
inequality in Jamaica. She campaigned actively on agricultural and environmental issues, questions of education and housing, industry, leisure
facilities and public representation. Marson's agenda is most interesting
because of her very early conjunction of ideas about race and gender; as
Alison Donnell describes, Marson possessed an awareness of 'the colloca-
tion of African subjects and women within the political matrix of British
colonialism' (2003, p. 129). As a result, the boundary between feminist and
anticolonial agendas in Marson's work is movable. The same might be
said of later feminist postcolonial Arab scholars like Fatima Mernissi and
Fadwa El Guindi, whose work follows Marson's, conjoining feminist and
postcolonial concerns. Both Mernissi and El Guindi have written about
the female body, the harem, and also the role of the veil in colonized contexts, a potent emblem of resistance in the Algerian War of Independence,
1954–62.

Algerian resistance

In Algeria the veil was symbolic for both parties in the colonial encounter,
and was itself a tool used in violent anticolonial resistance. The French
colonial programme had targeted the veil and other aspects of women's

lives. According to Frantz Fanon in his 1969 essay, 'Algeria Unveiled', the French unveiling of women was an attempt to destabilize the Algerian social system. Like the British colonial system in India which pinpointed *sati* (Hindu widow burning) in particular, the French colonial system had assumed a protective position towards Algerian women in an effort to gain their support and disrupt underlying gender relationships. The colonial position assumed that veiled women were oppressed by men; this was not necessarily a view shared by Muslim women, when in some areas female seclusion was considered 'a source of pride' and a privilege of wealthy women (Mernissi, 1987, p. 142). For Assia Djebar, it is important to reveal that colonial ideas and even Western feminism did not necessarily offer 'ready-made recipes that would save us', which is why, she says in an interview, in *Women of Algiers in Their Apartment* it is 'the Algerian woman who comes to the help of the French one' (Zimra, 1992, p. 177). Gender roles were carefully moderated spatially in Muslim societies and to break these rules would be, according to Fatima Mernissi, to disrupt 'Muslim sexual order' (1987, p. 137). The colonizer's desire to unveil Algerian women is constructed in erotic terms by Fanon, who claimed that 'every rejected veil disclosed to the eyes of the colonialists horizons until then forbidden, and revealed to them, piece by piece, the flesh of Algeria laid bare' (1969, p. 167). Colonial acquisition is often described in these erotic terms, where the colonizer plays a dominant masculine role and the colonized land is figured as feminine, as virgin territory to be conquered.

From 1955, Algerian women started to play an active role in anticolonial resistance. Assuming a newly Westernized, unveiled identity, some Algerian women began to carry weapons past colonial checkpoints in suitcases. They were not suspected or subject to security checks like Algerian men were, and so they were able to help the violent anticolonial resistance. Unveiling was not, thus, a success as was assumed by the French, but an act of war against the colonials. In this way, by unveiling and taking an active role in anticolonial resistance, the Muslim woman was committing an act of aggression against the masculine colonial system, but also against the gendered spatial roles that governed her society, because in strict Muslim society 'a woman has no right to use male spaces' such as the street and she commits an act of aggression against him by being where she should not be – and 'if the woman is unveiled the situation is aggravated' (Mernissi, 1987, p. 144).

Once the colonizers became aware that unveiled Algerian women posed a threat to the colonial system, the women had to adopt a new resistance tactic, and they started to wear the veil again, disguising weapons underneath: 'a bomb, or a sack of grenades, bound to her body by a whole system of strings and straps' (Fanon, 1969, p. 184). The female body was continually repositioned in the anticolonial struggle. On the one hand, this could be understood as an example of the ultimate objectification of the female body, that the women were in fact simply male-dominated victims within their own society, used to attack what threatened the traditional system (where women were not permitted in public spaces). However, the veiled bombers also represent a feminist response to the colonizers, because colonization is itself so frequently considered a masculine act of conquest over the virginal colonized territory. The ambiguous position occupied by Algerian women is clear in Djebar's *Women of Algiers in Their Apartment*: the women who carry bombs are revered in feminist terms as 'sisters', as empowered 'fire carriers' who have 'liberated the city'. Yet, their public act makes them vulnerable, an object of the male gaze: 'in the streets they were taking pictures of your unclothed bodies, of your avenging arms in front of the tanks'. This must be borne, though, in reaction against other forms of objectification and abuse carried out by both colonial men, 'rapist soldiers', and Algerians, poets who described the female body 'only in parts, bit by little bit' (1992, p. 44). The veil continues to be a subject that is particularly difficult for the French system to tolerate within its directly secular system. If its postcolonial diaspora Muslim citizens wear what is deemed a conspicuous sign of religion, then this implies that the country is a fractured system and not a 'singular, united entity', as Joan Wallach Scott has discussed in her study of the ongoing politics of the veil (2007, p. 12). The Algerian example conveys direct action, but the literary text can itself respond to colonialism in a similarly active way. This is the focus of the next section.

Literary responses: Chinua Achebe; George Lamming; Édouard Glissant; Aimé Césaire

At the most fundamental level, a literary text can convey its anticolonial standpoint by telling a familiar story from an alternative perspective. This may take the form of translation or rewriting, where a canonical literary text with a colonial subject matter is retold by a writer from a colonized location who might usually be excluded from the traditional literary canon. When it engages with a canonical text, the anticolonial literary text takes a directly combative stance. Aimé Césaire's *A Tempest* is an example of such a rewriting, an anticolonial retelling of Shakespeare's *The Tempest* which revises the position of Caliban, allowing him more awareness of his situation which enables him to demand and take his freedom instead of remaining subject to colonizer Prospero's control.

However, revising a text so directly is not the only way to retell a familiar story. Colonial literature on the subject of explorers, missionaries and adventurers in pre-colonial societies or in previously unexploited pockets of colonized areas was highly regarded and taught in schools and universities. In these stories, good, intellectual, civilized white colonizer figures invariably struggle in their quest to enlighten the savage black natives who are often cannibals, and who certainly always fail to understand what the novel takes for granted: that the colonizer knows what is best for the colonized. It was inevitable that such texts would be utterly unconvincing to African students in colonial university systems, where they were taught on English literature courses. Chinua Achebe was one of these students, who, with his fellow students, protested angrily during seminars on Joyce Cary's *Mister Johnson*, which was presented to the Nigerian students as the 'best novel ever written about Africa' (2003, p. 23). In a recent work, Achebe has written about the impact that this novel had on him as an individual, and as a writer. *Mister Johnson*, Achebe writes, portrays the African subjects in a thoroughly offensive way, describing them as 'demonic', 'naked', 'grinning, shrieking, scowling', 'dislocated, senseless and inhuman' (2003, p. 24). These barbaric images are typical of colonial literature which worked to maintain imperialist ideology by implying that colonized subjects were not fit to govern their own societies because they were infantile and undisciplined. This portrayal is often emphasized in the depiction of highly emotional and unstable characters, which in this way attempts to justify colonial government on the basis of a humanitarian endeavour. In Cary's novel, not just individuals, but society itself is portrayed as infantile and undeveloped: the town is described as 'a dwelling-place at one stage from the rabbit warren or the badger burrow, and not so cleanly kept as the latter' (Cary cited by Achebe, 2003, p. 24). This claim about people's homes implies a cultural inferiority and invites direct comparison with European achievements in construction. Such a portrait of African society clearly indicated to Achebe 'distaste, hatred and mockery' (2003, p. 24), yet this was the text that he was expected to praise and to analyse in detail in university seminars. The novel was to have a fundamental impact, as Achebe describes: *Mister Johnson* 'was to call into question my childhood assumption of the innocence of stories' (2003, p. 33). Achebe's response came in the form of his seminal text *Things Fall Apart* (1958), a novel which rewrites the African colony and the colonizer from the perspective of Okonkwo, a prominent member of an Ibo community which is ravaged by the advent of the colonial regime, yet revealed as complex, in direct opposition to colonial narratives which portrayed the African colonized communities as inferior and lacking.

A further method for resisting colonial thinking is through narrative structure. A number of Caribbean writers have used the English language in non-standard ways, by disrupting narrative structures and using vernacular. George Lamming's *In the Castle of My Skin* switches between narrative and prose script, and includes long episodes in vernacular, or informal Barbadian-accented English. In one such extract, a group of young boys discuss the beating that one of them had received from the school headmaster, and forge a half-hearted revenge plot to punish him for what they feel was not a 'nat'ral beating' (Lamming, 1991, p. 44). Although the boys' conversation is in many ways typical of discussion between children anywhere under a school system involving corporal punishment, it has a more imperative function in an anticolonial novel. One boy's lament that his father would support the teacher's decision and 'tell you the teacher didn't lash you properly an' he'll do it all over again' (p. 45) is on the one hand a complaint that adults sometimes unfairly support each other's decisions. At the same time, when a father upholds a teacher's decision in a colonial school system he implicitly supports the wider system of government that forces him to remain under colonial rule. The colonial community is unsettled, in a condition of temporary labour and habitation, and people worry when Mr Slime, a former teacher, sets up the first savings bank. Old Man and Old Woman, elderly members of the black community, contemplate the impact of Mr Slime's bank and his new position of power. Again, their conversation is conveyed in informal language as they discuss Mr Slime's challenge to the white landowner, Mr Creighton:

> [o]l' as you think Mr Creighton is, he won't have it; he ain't goin' to sit back an' let Mr Slime chase him off the village like a lappy dog. He too great for that, an' if he see the worse comin' to the worse he'll sell it. [...] It ain't the nature o' earthborn to sit back an' give up all like Christ would have do if he wus landlord an' he see trouble comin'.   (p. 79)

The old couple anticipate trouble, but they have been forced to defer their authority to others – in particular, to the white landowner, Mr Creighton – and are unable to see the possibility of a different system of government. While they express what seems obvious to them, that people are not likely to 'sit back' and give up their possessions and their power, they can only see this in terms of who currently holds the possessions. It is inconceivable that Mr Creighton is not the legitimate owner of the island, and that any 'trouble comin'' might be in the form of revolutionary action that could put them in a better position.

Mr Slime's savings bank is a prelude to bigger changes: soon after, the community learns that they are expected to vacate the land, taking their homes with them. The flimsy houses collapse when the villagers try to move them in a last act of obedience before they revolt against changes that push them too far into complete disenfranchisement. Like the conversation between the boys, the old couple's discussion is presented on the page in a style that reads like a play script rather than prose narrative mediated by a narrator. There is interruption from the narrator at certain points, but for long stretches the old people's voices are presented in direct speech and in this way, their words are largely unmediated. This is in itself a powerful statement to make in the literary text, as it provides a vehicle for the old people's ability to speak for themselves. In other words, the conversations in vernacular Barbadian-accented English are a call of protest and a claim for unmediated government and the independence of black citizens in Barbados. This claim comes from the senior characters who, it is clear, should be more in control of their own destiny yet they are restricted by a system which renders them largely impotent and only able to protest by discussing their ideas in their own bed, at night, while the rest of the community is asleep. The young boys whose voices are also represented in unmediated dialogue represent the willingness of the new generation to fight against injustice, and determination to find an effective way to begin that fight. The novel as a whole gives voice to a number of characters and, as Sandra Pouchet Paquet has observed, it is intentionally difficult to establish who has narrative dominance when the depersonalized narrator whose narration is frequently deferred to other voices is employed to 'establish collectivity' (in Lamming, 1991, p. xi).

The urge to represent the collective voice is shared by Martiniquan writer Édouard Glissant, who considers the singular narrative persona as faulty, and instead works to represent a communal voice by dramatising 'a range of voices from the past and present', and even having 'his narrator marginalised by this polyphony of voices' (Dash, 1995, p. 5). Michael Dash observes the political defiance inherent in Glissant's assertion of a 'creolized collective presence' (1995, p. 5). Indeed, it is far easier to dismiss a literary character in a play or a novel as a flawed individual, but when a whole community is united in revolt against colonial control, the literary text presents a much more forceful argument for change. Édouard Glissant was born in Martinique in 1928 and as a young man was politically active, taking part in Aimé Césaire's election campaign in 1945. After studying at the Sorbonne in Paris he wrote a number of plays, novels, collections of essays and poetry, before following an academic career in Martinique and the United States.

Glissant's experimental literary style is representative of a wider agenda in his creative and critical works to challenge textual boundaries and expectations, and with them, conceptual and political boundaries. As Michael Dash writes, 'one of the distinctive features of Glissant's work is the fusion of the imaginative and the theoretical' (1995, p. 1). Although many anticolonial writers produced both theoretical and creative works, Glissant's output was more difficult to categorize; because he was 'neither exclusively poet, novelist, dramatist nor essayist', in his work he 'combined all categories, often simultaneously' (Dash, 1995, p. 1). Indeed, his theoretical work *Poetics of Relation*, which explores notions of belonging in terms of roots and rhizomes (connected networks in a multiple root system, as discussed at length by Deleuze and Guattari), nomads and exiles, is written in very poetic language. Describing the kind of exile experienced by slaves, Glissant writes:

> The asceticism of crossing this way the land-sea that, unknown to you, is the planet Earth, feeling a language vanish, the world of the gods vanish, and the sealed image of even the most everyday object, of even the most familiar animal, vanish. The evanescent taste of what you ate. The hounded scent of ochre earth and savannas.   (1997, p. 7)

The beauty of this image of a remembered home is presented in stark contrast to the description of the conditions of the slave-ships carrying those exiled towards a 'sentence of death' (Glissant, 1997, p. 6). It may seem unusual to describe the slaves' passage in such poetic terms, but in doing so Glissant asserts the emotional and intellectual impact of the voyage on those people, in contrast to colonial representations of the slaves as 'cargo'. In an epic poem, Aimé Césaire recreates the experience of a journey to the Caribbean under different circumstances: his *Return to My Native Land* contemplates his return home to Martinique following a period studying in France.

Return to My Native Land is a long narrative poem. Césaire uses the opposition of speech and silence repeatedly throughout the poem, where speech both symbolizes and explicitly represents power. The colonized town is at the beginning of the poem 'a stranger to its own cry' (Césaire,

1969, p. 38): its only voice is unfamiliar, because it is a colonized voice. The poem's speaker is positioned at something of a distance from the crowd and in this way is detached from the community, and able to ask by what logic the crowd should be 'deaf to its own cry of hunger and misery, revolt and hatred' (p. 39) and thus rendered 'strangely' dumb. To remain dumb is fatal, though, as is demonstrated by the man who commits suicide by 'rolling back his tongue to swallow it' (p. 40). The colonized must speak in a voice that is different from the colonizer's. The speaker openly rejects discipline and reason which belong to the realm of the colonizer in the binary language of colonial prejudice and accepts 'dementia', 'cannibalism' and 'madness', a 'madness that screams' when it is used as a weapon to gain a voice in the only method available, an anger or controlled hysteria that 'unchains itself' (p. 55). The poem is a cry for revolution, a powerful reaction that allows the colonized to take back full control of their voice after 'The End of the World' (p. 60) or the end of Empire. Suddenly, aware of the possibility of revolution, it is the European imperial voice that is constrained, visibly constrained on the page and rendered ridiculous by its repetitive style that indicates desperation – 'niggers-are-all-the-same, I tell you / they-have-every-conceivable-vice, I'm telling you' (p. 64) – and by its punctuation in parenthesis with the words flowing together so that they become meaningless utterances. No longer can the master's pronouncement dictate the way that the colonized individual is understood. Verbs and nouns to do with speech (tell, telling, the old saying) are rendered impotent when they are repeated in empty phrases which deliver racist insults. The formerly colonized subject, in the hope of revolution, can announce 'I speak', and he dictates the terms on which he speaks when he states: 'I may invent my lungs'. This new speech embraces that which has been rejected as madness, the 'bark', the 'laughter' and the 'bad nigger dances' and have become 'the it-is-beautiful-and-good-and-lawful-to-be-a-Negro dance', presented in joined up words forming a new slogan to replace those that were harmful (pp. 90–1).

This cry, this new slogan, that 'it-is-beautiful-and-good-and-lawful-to-be-a-Negro' (p. 91) is the cry of negritude, the term that celebrated and validated the power and the validity of black cultural expression and identity that is not formulated by colonialism or crushed by it. It is the need to reject the 'good nigger' like the speaker's grandfather whose death is celebrated because it must be, because there can be no place for the 'master's good Negro' who lives in misery with 'no power over his own destiny' and believes 'honestly in his unworthiness' (p. 87). This 'good nigger' is eaten up by disease, by 'an atrocious tapeworm' that destroys slavery instead of accepting it, in a reversal of the image at the opening of the poem, the image of the 'scab', 'hail-marked with smallpox' (p. 37), the disease of acceptance that prevented revolution and maintained the system of colonial slavery. Césaire and many other anticolonial thinkers discussed here were active in more than one field, and in addition to political and literary works, they wrote theoretical or academic texts.

In theory: Frantz Fanon; Albert Memmi

Two anticolonial theorists who have maintained a prominent position in academic thinking and the ongoing development of postcolonial studies are Frantz Fanon and Albert Memmi. Frantz Fanon was a psychiatrist, born in Martinique in 1925. He studied in France and worked in Algeria, becoming an activist in the anticolonial movement. Fanon's most influential works include *Black Skin, White Masks* (1952), a psychological analysis of the colonized Caribbean black subject, and *The Wretched of the Earth* (1961), an anticolonial political statement.

Black Skin, White Masks highlights the psychological impact of white colonial culture on black colonized subjects, including schoolboys. Comic books, Fanon argues, can have a devastating and lasting psychological impact on the colonized child, and he discusses comic books emblematic of a range of damaging intersections of black and white cultures under colonial regimes. Adventure stories and comics for boys, Fanon writes, are 'put together by white men for little white men' (1986, p. 146). In other words, they represent imperialist ideologies with the intention of maintaining those ideologies in succeeding generations. Yet, they are read by the colonized black schoolboys as well as by white children, all of whom identify, as the text dictates, with the explorer or adventurer, who is white. When the black child reads repeatedly that the bad or savage enemy of the hero is black or 'Indian', he distances himself from those figures:

> The Antillean does not think of himself as a black man; [...] The Negro lives in Africa. Subjectively, intellectually, the Antillean conducts himself like a white man. But he is a Negro. That he will learn once he goes to Europe. (Fanon, 1986, p. 148)

Many people from the Caribbean studied or worked in Europe during the colonial period, as they had British or French national status and had been taught to regard the colonial motherland as their home. To succeed in European society, though, in the face of unexpected prejudice, there was a need to break with the Caribbean. For Fanon, this is undertaken through language choice, language being fundamental to identity, and the adoption of a language involving the assumption of its culture (1986, p. 17).

The ruptured state of the colonized subject more often than not manifests in violence among the black colonized community (1967, p. 40). This 'fraternal blood-bath' is a method of avoiding the real obstacle: the colonial system. The violently implemented colonial system eventually elicits an equally violent response in the colonized subject, which, once organized, can be harnessed in anticolonial protest. In India, Mahatma Gandhi's policy of non-violent protest was an attempt to avoid fraternal violence, but in *The Wretched of the Earth*, Fanon's anticolonial manifesto, he states that decolonization is always violent, necessarily a 'programme of complete disorder' because it 'sets out to change the order of the world' (1967, p. 27). By placing the cause of anticolonial violence firmly within the colonial system as a whole, *The Wretched of the Earth* seeks to justify the aggressive nature of decolonization in response to a system built on violence.

Just as Fanon has proposed in *The Wretched of the Earth* that decolonization is an inevitably violent process, Albert Memmi has claimed that revolt is the only way out of the colonial situation, suggesting that the condition is absolute and requires an absolute solution, and not a compromise (2003, p. 171). However, Memmi's position is an ambivalent one that seems to offer hope for an equal society of 'complete liberation' (2003, p. 195), even while the positive outcome can only be achieved by violent means – self-destructive means – as his choice of language clearly conveys when he suggests that 'to live, the colonized needs to do away with colonization. To become a man, he must do away with the colonized being that he has become', just as 'the European must annihilate the colonizer within himself' (2003, p. 195). Albert Memmi is a Tunisian novelist, academic and theorist, born in 1920, who studied at Algiers and the Sorbonne, and taught in Tunis and Paris. Though he lived in French colonized Tunisia, as a Jew his position was somewhat ambiguous. In colonial North Africa, Algerian Jews adopted the French style and language, and fought alongside the colonial army. Resembling the colonizer was, for Memmi, a necessity in order to escape the colonized condition which he describes vividly in *The Colonizer and the Colonized* (1957), his influential first academic text.

Many of Memmi's ideas in *The Colonizer and the Colonized* have been influential in the development of postcolonial studies as a whole. The study is separated into two main sections, and in the second part, the presentation of the colonized subject's psyche, Memmi proposes that the most serious effect of colonialism for the colonized subject is their exclusion from their history and community. Memmi claims that the colonized cannot feel like a true citizen because identity is constructed through a series of negations opposing colonizer with colonized. Under the colonial education system, the pupil is taught a history that is not their own and the compulsion to learn the colonizer's language means that the colonized individual is forced to operate in two separate 'psychical and cultural realms' (2003, p. 151). The colonized young man is emasculated under a colonial regime because his lack of prospects make him reliant on his family, and the result of these limitations mean that the colonized society as a whole is rendered operative only in a 'passive present', being exempt from both its history and future (2003, p. 145).

Memmi's position is that assimilation is not desired by the colonizer, because to eliminate distinctions between colonizer and colonized would eliminate the colonial relationship and this would mean that there was no one to exploit (2003, pp. 193–4). This anticipates ideas presented in recent postcolonial translation theory, that the colonial project aimed to reproduce the motherland in necessarily inferior 'translations' in the colonies. Memmi explicitly states that the colonialist 'never planned to transform the colony into the image of his homeland, nor to remake the colonized in his own image' (2003, p. 113) because to do so would be to admit an equivalency. Although Memmi's text seems on the surface to present the colonial situation as a too rigid binary opposition between colonizer and colonized, in fact his work is focused on the colonial system, and the system, he claims, has an equal impact on both figures: it 'manufactures both colonialists and the colonized' (2003, p. 100).

More recently, Memmi has contributed to postcolonial diaspora studies in *Decolonization and the Decolonized* (2006 [2004, French]). Of particular note is his reconsideration of the myth of return, the concept that has been frequently applied to both literary characters and to ethnographic studies of diaspora communities to account in part for examples of incomplete integration into the new location. The myth of return is the idea that life as a migrant is temporary and that, at the right time, usually determined by financial and career success, the migrant will return home a wealthier and happier individual, able to support their family. For Memmi, this notion is a false one, for the migrant knows that 'the myth is over', that in fact, a return 'home' would be a 'catastrophic upheaval' because it is inevitable that, having remained a migrant for some time, it will soon be impossible to decide 'which is here and which is there' (2006, pp. 106, 109).

The position of migrant is reversed in relationships between indigenous groups and white settler populations. The colonial situation has been explored somewhat separately in relation to aboriginal contexts, where large migrant settler populations displaced the native inhabitants.

Aboriginal responses

Though Aboriginal children were placed in English school systems in late-nineteenth and early-twentieth-century Australia, the colonization of Australia was not at first a 'civilising' mission, as was claimed in South Asia and Africa. Instead, the process seemed intent on erasing the Aboriginals altogether, sometimes by force but initially by making them invisible. Australia, first claimed as British territory following Captain Cook's arrival in 1770, was designated *terra nullius*, land belonging to no one, which thus rendered the Aboriginals 'no one', invisible because their habitation of the land looked different from the kind of ownership marked on the European landscape. Soon afterwards, colonial settlers began using expanses of land in Australia as a penal colony for British prisoners, a practice that continued until the mid-nineteenth century. During this time, articles appeared in British periodicals and newspapers on the subject of Australian penal colonies, but these articles focused on the experiences of the colonial governors and the convicts, debating the merits of transportation as a method of punishment and assessing the resulting society of white settlers comprising convicts and former convicts who, having served their sentence, had the right to independent work and land ownership in Australia. In 1901, Charles Slaughter wrote that this lack of representation of Aboriginal peoples had been just as prevalent in the laws and practices of Australian government as it was in British journalism. Slaughter claimed that 'much has been said concerning what is subversive of the rights of the colonial population, but what is subversive of the rights of the Aboriginal, does not appear to have received equal consideration' (1901, p. 412).

Ignored and thus rendered invisible, Aboriginals resisted colonization by means of violence. Very early in the period of British colonization of Australia, Pemulwuy, an Aboriginal considered as leader of the Botany Bay tribe, 'mounted a sustained resistance to the colonial invasion, including an attack on Parramatta, until in 1802 he was shot down' (Macintyre, 2004, p. 38). Pemulwuy had attempted to resist a colonial project that resembled the concept of Manifest Destiny in America, the notion that it was God's will that the Native American be slaughtered to make way for the so-called progressive white American. Australian Aboriginals were slaughtered and forcibly driven into remote and inhospitable regions. In particular, the Myall Creek massacre in 1838 was an exceptional case which has been described by Bronwyn Batten as 'one of the most widely known accounts of a massacre targeting Aboriginal people in Australian history' (2009, p. 83), not least because of the hanging of the seven white men who perpetrated the massacre of 28 people, including women, elderly people and children, all of whom had previously been living with the white colonials peaceably. The colonials burned the bodies of those they had killed, so the only remaining evidence was the remains of a child's skull, another act of eradication of the Aboriginals. At the first trial the men were not found guilty of committing any crime amid widespread support for the massacre in the press which, as Batten has described, claimed that the Aboriginals were living contrary to God's will because they were farming the land incorrectly and thus their murder was an act of legitimate protection of the white man's property (2009, p. 83). The men were only eventually found guilty of the murder of an Aboriginal child rather than mass murder, and the sentence of hanging was, according to Batten, only imposed because a change in attitude and increased humanitarian support for Aboriginals in England exerted pressure on the courts in Australia (2009, p. 84).

The Australian writer Mudrooroo has analysed the impact of colonization on Aboriginal literature. Both the literature and culture were, he suggests, observed through British eyes and inaccurately translated. Aboriginal literature was traditionally oral narrative, memorized and retold, usually in verse form. Prose was used, Mudrooroo suggests, where there was less need to remember the narrative precisely: religious tales would be rendered in verse in order to maintain the content rigidly, while stories and histories could be told with more variation as these were considered less important. When translated, though, Mudrooroo claims that 'methods of Aboriginal storytelling are edited out and the content forced into forms akin to the fairy tale, an oral tradition in itself which has been forced into a nineteenth century written format' (1995, p. 229). Mudrooroo had for many years occupied a position as an acclaimed Aboriginal writer and activist. However, his stated Aboriginal heritage has been disputed in recent years following his sister's research into their family history in 1996, and his own extensive genealogical research which revealed uncertainty in his parentage, meaning that his Aboriginal status could not be proved or disproved, as Adam Shoemaker has discussed in some detail (2003, pp. 1–6). For Gerhard Fischer, Mudrooroo's role as Head of Aboriginal Studies at Murdoch University until 1996 and his acceptance of a prize for Aboriginal writing should not necessarily be revoked, though they inevitably raise questions (2000, p. 98). Fischer disputes the notion that Mudrooroo's work is suddenly 'less Aboriginal' or of less literary value because it has been claimed that he may have Irish and Black American heritage instead of Australian Aboriginal parents. To claim that he has no right or authority to represent Aboriginals implies that identity in post-colonial societies can be rigidly fixed and corralled, which only seems to uphold colonial dualities. This unusual position leads on to the final type of anticolonial resistance addressed in this chapter: activists from within the colonial settler community.

Affective communities

Acts of brutality and the impact of colonization on colonial areas raised questions about the imperial project for some colonial settlers. A number of individuals who might be expected to benefit from colonialism began to convey anticolonial messages and to work towards ending colonization. Leela Gandhi's recent work *Affective Communities* (2006) presents the stories of a number of these figures with the intention of showing that anti-imperialism was not confined to those non-Western individuals and groups who were colonized. Gandhi suggests that anticolonialism is primarily understood as having taken two forms: oppositionality and infiltration (2006, p. 1). Oppositionality includes the defensive preserva-tion of native traditions and culture, including things as fundamental as language and religion, as well as specific cultural symbolism, or indeed the reinstatement of those traditions where they have been lost altogether. An example of this is the drumming and stick-fighting performed as part of Trinidadian carnival at the turn of the twentieth century in an effort to recapture traditional African celebratory ceremony (but suppressed by the British administration, who were scared of the rebellious potential implied by the power of the performance). In very recent years, such oppo-sitionality has taken new forms: Creole is taught in Caribbean schools as an alternative to English and as a legitimate language rather than a subor-dinate one, as part of a project to research and reinstate native traditions, languages, memories, and knowledge of histories and culture. Infiltration is an alternative to this method, which was again a prominent Caribbean response. Children were given an 'English' education which included English literature and history. This might be expected, and perhaps the colonial administrators could – to an extent – legitimately argue that these were valuable things to learn for West Indian children and students. But certain aspects of this English education showed up its absurdity: the Caribbean schools taught English geography, and even botany, as Delia Jarrett-Macauley describes in her biography of Una Marson, so children would have learned the characteristics of English primroses and oak trees instead of the plants that grew around them. The same is true of French colonies in the Caribbean. Despite this, Caribbean children thrived in French and English schools and many, C. L. R. James being a key example, attended French and English universities, thoroughly infiltrating those cultures – except that their infiltration could never be entirely complete. This is where Homi Bhabha's term 'hybridity' and the term 'interpellation', used by Bill Ashcroft and others, have been used to describe the sense of uncertainty experienced by those who seem to have more than one 'home', culture, or place, because of the effects of colonization and migration.

Leela Gandhi adds a further dimension to the subject of anticolonial resistance when she takes a step back from the colonized subject to examine those colonials who worked to end colonialism. Her work is, she suggests, something of a departure from postcolonial studies because of its analysis of internal critiques of empire, by those who might be considered 'treasonous' because of their interpretation of empire, calling it harmful to the colonized location and subjects and self-interested in its motivations (2006, p. 2). In order to analyse the impact of those anticolonial individuals, Gandhi examines a number of figures in detail. C. F. (or Charlie) Andrews is an interesting figure because of his explicit desire to experience and represent India with a degree of detachment not usually found among colonials.

Andrews was an Anglican priest working in India, thoroughly dissatisfied with British rule. Perhaps his most important contribution to anticolonial thinking was his book, *The True India* (1939), which, as Leela Gandhi explains, was written as a corrective response to a number of sensationalist books on India, particularly targeting Katherine Mayo's *Mother India* (1927). Mayo's book is a heavily subjective description of Indian morality, which presents animal sacrifice, child marriage and even child sexual abuse as the norm, as her language choices convey: 'Often', Mayo writes, 'a particularly lovely child' is left in the care of Hindu temple women where, 'by the age of five, when she is considered most desirable, she becomes the priests' own prostitute' (2000 [1927], p. 103). Such a book would have served a number of colonial purposes: by describing Indian society as primitive, superstitious and uncivilized, the assumption that colonization can provide enlightenment is upheld. At the same time, India is presented as an unruly, childlike society that requires the firm parental hand of the colonial administration. It is true to say that for many, Mayo's sensationalist text did not merit a serious response, but it did exert a certain amount of influence over popular thinking about India. One example is a letter published in *The Saturday Review* in February 1935 advising all Members of Parliament to read Mayo's book in order that they maintain colonial control, although British reviews of the book were often scathing, like Edward Thompson's analysis in *The Bookman* in September 1927. Thompson accuses Mayo of being 'unjustifiably complacent' about British and American civilization, which she presents as exemplary despite the condition of the black individual in the American South who 'has civic rights he dare not claim, for the dominant community will not permit it' (1927, p. 322). Responses to Mayo's book from within India and from South Asians living elsewhere were unsurprisingly aggressive. Leela Gandhi notes in particular two anti-American responses, which describe American society as equivalently morally flawed, Kanhaya Lal Gauba's *Uncle Sham: Being the Strange Tale of a Civilisation Run Amock* (1929) and Dinshah Gadiali's *American Sex Problems* (1929) as well as the well-known immediate response by an anonymous writer, *Sister India* (1927) which reflects Mayo's analysis back at her, accusing her of writing the book in an act of sexual frustration. These responses are not unexpected and can be read today as combative discourse, but at the same time an equally sensational response means that no legitimate, direct rebuttal of Mayo's book was published until Andrews wrote *The True India*.

Leela Gandhi suggests that Andrews' complex position – not quite on either the Western or the Indian side, but not quite *not* on one side or the other – was because of his desire for 'friendship' with Indian people (2006, p. 16). Gandhi goes on to explore this as an example of Derridean 'improvisational politics' (2006, p. 19), a position necessarily operating outside politics, yet achieving political, or perhaps, diplomatic goals, at the individual level. Apart from his book, Andrews' anticolonial efforts were largely played out in personal and professional relationships with individuals, including Mahatma Gandhi and Rabindranath Tagore. Since his death in 1940, Andrews has been recognized as a significant figure.

In contrast to C. F. Andrews, Leela Gandhi presents the more public and prolific figure of Edward Carpenter, who she summarizes as 'late nineteenth-century socialist, animal rights activist, prison reformer, and homosexual' who also wrote poetry and supported the journal *Justice*, produced by the Social Democratic Foundation. Carpenter's efforts for equality of recognition politically and socially were distributed across a number of areas; Gandhi suggests that in addition to his anti-imperialist sympathies, Carpenter campaigned for the rights of 'criminals, prostitutes, workers, women, and animals' (2006, p. 36) as well as to legitimize homosexuality, which was his over-arching project, founded in his belief that homosexuality possesses 'a capacity for radical kinship' (2006, p. 36). Clearly, many of those categories are not mutually exclusive, but perhaps it was Carpenter's methods which led them to be considered by his critics as separate interests, even as 'evasive' politics (Gandhi, 2006, p. 37) which prevented him from addressing homosexuality with sufficient focus. Carpenter's contribution could instead be understood as a progressive view which recognized the need to combat all forms of injustice, with imperialism as a dominant aspect of late-nineteenth-century politics.

Decolonization followed the onslaught from multiple methods of anti-colonial resistance, some of which have been addressed here. The process was a long, varied and complex one. Peter Childs and Patrick Williams question the commonplace assumption that the term 'postcolonial' refers to the period coming immediately after the end of colonialism, because the required 'sense of an ending' is difficult to maintain meaningfully (1997, p. 1). This is logical, given that the event of colonization varies so much from place to place, that independence has been achieved in different places at different times, and that there have been successive versions of colonialism in some locations. If it is difficult to pinpoint the postcolonial, then what meaning can be attached to the concept of a 'postcolonial moment'?

The next chapter will explore the idea of the postcolonial moment to consider whether it is in fact possible to identify such a thing, by analysing two very significant and very precisely timed end-of-Empire moments: the Partition of India which formally took place 24 hours before South Asian Independence from British colonial rule (partition taking place at midnight on 13 August 1947), and the end of the British colonial leasehold control of Hong Kong, which took place, again at midnight, on 30 June 1997. These two events invite an exploration of the notion of the postcolonial, and posit the idea that the postcolonial moment might not be conceivable in terms of historical phases.

2 The Postcolonial Moment

Decolonization never takes place unnoticed, for it influences individuals and modifies them fundamentally.

Frantz Fanon, *The Wretched of the Earth*

The impact of decolonization on the individual that Fanon describes should be understood as a response to a prolonged period of change. There is usually a specific date associated with the moment when a colonial regime formally ends, but this date, though often commemorated and highly symbolic, is always just part of a longer, gradual process of change and adjustment. For Hong Kong, British colonial administrative control ended at midnight on 30 June 1997, meaning that Hong Kong was no longer a British colony from 1 July 1997. This date marked the end of a 99-year lease which Britain had held over the majority of the land area, the New Territories. The date had been fixed in place when a leasehold arrangement was imposed on China by imperial decree in 1898, following the territorial acquisition of Hong Kong in 1842 at the culmination of the Opium Wars. In India, the end of colonial rule occurred 50 years earlier, at midnight on 14 August 1947 – 15 August being the date of independence. The planning process for this handover took place over a shorter time and was characterized most dramatically by the accompanying act of Partition: the vast Indian subcontinent, formerly a large number of principalities which under British colonialism had been re-mapped as one country (India) was given a new map, separating the land into two countries, India and Pakistan. Partition is officially recorded as taking place exactly 24 hours before independence in a highly contested final act of British government. In fact, Partition had been planned months before, while maps marking the boundary line between the two states were revealed only on 17 August, and the process was to have a long-lasting impact. Pakistan was later partitioned again when in 1971 East Pakistan became Bangladesh, but even this did not mark the final event in the Partition story, as the Kashmir region remains disputed.

This chapter presents a discussion of these two postcolonial moments – Hong Kong in 1997 and India in 1947 – and in particular, explores the way that both end of empire moments have a bodily impact on the citizens of the two locations. In analysing these two examples, it becomes clear that while conventional histories record formative moments, in living postcolonial history it is very difficult to limit the impact of an event to a specified date; to do so is to privilege official accounts, and thereby to deny the multiple histories that require attention from a postcolonial perspective.

Urvashi Butalia insists that Partition is not confined to its formal historical recording on a specific date, or even to one kind of telling. Butalia found that later communal violence in South Asia in 1984 following the assassination of Indira Gandhi triggered the retelling of Partition stories. The violence was reminiscent of Partition, and for many witnesses whose stories Butalia collects, the sense of separation between the two events is uncertain. Butalia chooses to arrange her material in a manner that shows, firstly, a need to acknowledge multiple versions and types of history rather than reliance on a single, conventional, accepted version, and secondly, a distrust of 'objective' histories altogether. Thus, there emerges in her work a need to acknowledge the equivalence of personal, oral histories when read alongside formal ones which claim objectivity, and with this need, an insistence on temporal uncertainty, and on the lasting and repeated impact of things.

In formal histories of world events, the dates of Partition and of the withdrawal of British colonialism in Hong Kong imply a sense of certainty: the end of one administration and the beginning of another. It is, of course, generally accepted that most historical dates are subject to some slippage, with the effects of any change being felt both before and after the formally recorded date. But colonial regime change elicits a particularly forceful impact before and after that specific moment. The partition of India, which created the new country of Pakistan in the vast wing-shaped territories at the North East and North West of the region, is a highly contested event which is rarely described as having any positive results. Indeed, in the worst analyses, Partition has been described as an act of revenge by the exiting British colonial regime (as is, for example, the assumption of an anecdote told to Butalia during her research: a woman claims that she overheard a British imperial army officer talking gleefully just days before about the impossibility of future social order after the mess created purposely by Partition (2000, p. 95)). The extensive and excessive violence and the scale of forced migration make the event a particularly memorable one. Hong Kong's handover marks a transfer from British to Chinese control, yet at the same time marks Hong Kong's difference from both administrative systems: while it moved from Capitalist to Communist Empire, Hong Kong maintained its uniquely capitalist and internationalist practices, as dictated by the handover regulations. However, neither event can really be understood as occurring cleanly at the moment of recording.

Because Partition was formally announced in principle some months before it officially took place, some movement began before the official date. Similarly, the effects were felt long after the new boundary was publically declared. One particularly telling example is the enforcement of the Abducted Persons Recovery and Restoration programme which was in place for ten years with the purpose of 'recovering' (often against their will) those women and girls who had been forcibly taken by members of the 'other' religion and had since married and in many cases had children in their adopted community. Similarly, it is important to recognise that for some members of society, Partition was always hazy and uncertain: days after all citizens were supposed to have relocated to the country corresponding with their religion (Muslims in Pakistan, Hindus and Sikhs in India), some members of the scheduled castes (the marginalized lower classes) continued as usual, working in their established jobs, unaware that Partition was taking place and that their livelihoods had to be relocated. The stories of wealthy members of society throwing the family jewels into deep wells and abandoning established residences tend to dominate the reported migration stories. Likewise, the handover of Hong Kong to China had an extended timescale in the public imaginary. It had been a long established event, necessarily, because of the 99-year territorial lease. Some fifteen years before the designated date there were attempts to renegotiate and extend the lease, but as China had never fully accepted the legality of the agreement, this was sure to fail. Celebratory arrangements were made for the handover, but at the same time there was a sense of nervous anticipation, not least because of the Tian'anmen Square massacre in 1989: there was some uncertainty expressed in Britain (albeit mediated by self-interest) about handing over Hong Kong and its capitalist inhabitants to what was seen as a brutal communist regime. This event in particular prompted the declaration that Hong Kong must be permitted to retain its capitalist identity for at least 50 years following handover. In this way, Hong Kong will feel for some time the ongoing effect of the end of British colonial government. Additionally, Hong Kong may be regarded as existing under a new colonial regime, so the end of British rule is not equivalent to decolonization: Rey Chow has insisted that China should still be regarded as imperial, rejecting suggestions that it is somehow less colonial simply because it is a Third World, communist nation (1998, p. xx).

This inter-imperial transfer complicates the notion that the middle of 1997 marked Hong Kong's postcolonial moment.

As well as the fact that the established dates do not mark an absolute moment of change, the idea of the postcolonial moment fits into wider debate over the legitimate application of the term 'postcolonial': does the 'postcolonial' describe the period after colonization, from colonization to decolonization, from decolonization onwards, and if so, is that period limited to a certain amount of time following the end of colonial rule, or does it last indefinitely?

The post(-)colonial

The question over hyphenation (postcolonial versus post-colonial) is in part a debate in relation to the accepted location on a historical timeline of the postcolonial moment. For Ashcroft, Griffiths and Tiffin, the use of a hyphen implies the need to situate the post-colonial period from the moment of colonization, meaning that all culture affected by the imperial process from the moment of colonization to the present day should be regarded as postcolonial – or, post-colonial (1989, p. 2). However, in this scenario the same uncertainty arises in relation to the term 'colonial' – as Childs and Williams ask, whose colonialism is regarded as the relevant one? The colonial regimes commonly addressed by postcolonial studies, the predominantly British and French nineteenth-century empires, succeeded among many others the Portuguese and Spanish empires in Latin America. To assume that British or French nineteenth-century colonialism is the only one of relevance is, for Childs and Williams and others, Eurocentric, and tantamount to a kind of colonial retelling of the territories in question. On the other side of this debate is the fear that, without limiting the postcolonial to those British and French empires that started to fold in the middle of the twentieth century, it is possible to consider everywhere 'postcolonial'. It seems inappropriate to consider the United States as a postcolonial territory because it was once possessed by Britain and France, or to consider Britain postcolonial, having been subject to Viking and Roman settlement in previous centuries. Both of these nations are more commonly regarded as colonizers or neocolonizers; to equate them with territories they have colonized is to distort the history of recent colonial encounters.

Nicholas Harrison notes that the terms 'postcolonial' and 'postimperial' originally referred to 'the post-independence period of former European colonies' (2003, p. 7). However, the neat process of change from the 'colonial' to the 'post-' implied by this is, Harrison insists, questionable, not least by the realization that 'to talk of a culture as "postcolonial" may then carry misleading implications concerning the cessation of imperialist influence and interference' (2003, p. 8). Clearly, hegemonic control may remain in force over former colonies, resulting in a continuing imperial influence. As Leela Gandhi has pointed out, the hyphenated 'post-colonial' indicates to many critics the opposite of Ashcroft's assertion, as it is used 'as a decisive temporal marker of the decolonizing process' while she notes that others see the period from colonization onwards as representative of the postcolonial condition, and thus 'it is argued that the unbroken term 'postcolonialism' is more sensitive to the long history of colonial consequences' (1998, p. 3). Gandhi also distinguishes between postcolonial theory which is known as 'postcolonialism' and the historical condition addressed by that theory as 'postcoloniality'. Postcolonialism is understood by Gandhi as carrying out a practical, real-world solution to the problems of colonial history. Gandhi suggests that at both the individual and the state level, the colonial encounter is repressed and actively forgotten in order to self-invent and begin anew. For Gandhi, repression is not the equivalent of 'emancipation from the uncomfortable realities of the colonial encounter' and so it is here that postcolonialism can step in and theorise the recorded histories in order to produce real resistance to the effects of colonialism (1998, p. 4). Perhaps this purpose, which in Gandhi's formulation really amounts to retelling histories, rewriting national stories, and regaining national identity and independence, is misunderstood by some hostile critics who label postcolonialism 'political correctness' (critics imparting these views are mentioned by Bart Moore-Gilbert (1997, p. 13); Peter Barry also refers to this tendency to view postcolonialism, feminist, Marxist and queer theories of literature as political correctness (2009, p. 191)). As an academic field, postcolonial theory or criticism is diverse, raising questions about whether there are in fact limitations to what might be legitimately studied from a postcolonial perspective, even in former colonies. Bart Moore-Gilbert describes 'a variety of practices, performed within a range of disciplinary fields in a multitude of different institutional locations around the globe' (1997, p. 5). It is this multiplicity that Moore-Gilbert sees as responsible for resistance towards postcolonial studies that has led some to fear that the field will implode (1997, p. 11).

The 'when' leads inevitably to the 'what' of the postcolonial. This is an ongoing debate, especially with the use of the internet which has grown dramatically since the last few years of the twentieth century. In order to circumvent uncertainty over what postcolonialism may address, Nicholas Harrison suggests postcolonial studies may be characterized as

> an attention to the history of colonialism/imperialism and its aftermath, [...] distinguished from traditional historical or political writing on the colonial or post-independence era by the particular attention that is paid to the role within that history of 'representation' or 'discourse'. (2003, p. 9)

It is this particular attention to representation or discourse which Childs and Williams engage with when they suggest that the 'when' and the 'what' of postcolonial studies might be better understood by asking how the theories interrogate their places and histories: as well as engaging with colonies and former colonies, to do so in a postcolonial way is to adopt a resistant attitude: postcolonialism must be seen as 'conceptually transcending or superseding the parameters' of colonialism, questioning it, and 'rejecting the premises of colonialist intervention' in order to 'mount a critique or counter-attack' (1997, p. 4). In this way, the 'post' in 'postcolonial' replicates the stance of the other 'posts', postmodernism and poststructuralism.

As unfixable as the theoretical field itself, the officially designated postcolonial moments in Hong Kong and South Asia are subject to much temporal slippage. In the sections below, I will discuss the relationships between both India and Hong Kong and former colonizer Britain, as conveyed in a range of official and unofficial histories, in literary texts and news reporting, to put to work the idea of the postcolonial.

'A borrowed place on borrowed time': Hong Kong

In the years leading up to 1997, the issue of migration was frequently perceived as either racially or socioeconomically motivated. The British government was accused of holding up immigration due to a fear of admitting large numbers of racial 'others' as British citizens or residents. Britain did not make it easy for Hong Kong citizens to migrate to the UK, putting in place a number of restrictions resulting in a policy that meant only wealthy, entrepreneurial Hong Kong residents could hope to gain British residency or citizenship. Laurie Fransman notes that out of a million application forms for British passports that were printed in preparation for the 1997 handover, only around 65,000 were filled in, blaming this discrepancy on a number of practical factors: the length of the form, complicated questions about tax, and people's fears that if they failed to gain a British passport, they may be targeted by the new Chinese government as unfaithful (1995, p. ix). But Fransman also refers to a more complex question of identity: while the British assumed that the small number of applications indicated that Hong Kong residents felt a sense of allegiance to China, Fransman argues that the complex social history may have left people with an uncertain sense of identity: were they British, Chinese, or was their nationality uncertain? And could even Hong Kong be defined as their home, when it was just emerging as a nation, and not even an independent one, as it changed hands from Britain to China? In this climate, Hong Kong residents had to negotiate racial, political and administrative definitions of national identity and for those privileged wealthy citizens able to make a decision on which nationality to adopt, balance their decision with the awareness that the application for a British passport was awkward and indicative of a half-hearted welcome by the former colonial power.

In Hong Kong, the imminent transition period from British to Chinese rule was interrupted by the Tian'anmen Square massacre. In Tian'anmen Square in Peking, in May 1989, hundreds of thousands of protesters including many students gathered in an attempt to express political dissatisfaction, pointing out that changes in the government resembled the kinds of sackings and manoeuvres under a dictatorship, expressing a sense that China's leaders were out of touch, and demanding an end to government corruption. The Chinese government reacted strongly to the protest march: the army was instructed to kill protesters, and reports claimed that tanks were driven over the hundreds or even thousands of dead bodies repeatedly until their bodies were reduced to a pulp, before bulldozers piled up the remains to be incinerated by troops with flame throwers (Rafferty, 1991, p. 5). This very brutal act of aggression against the body, coming as it did on the brink of the end of the British leasehold government of Hong Kong, raised questions over whether it was responsible to deliver Hong Kong to 'China's not-so-tender mercies', as Kevin Rafferty puts it (1991, p. 9). This question reveals, of course, the assumption that the colony is a territory in its infancy, and that the colonial ruler performs a parental role and is required to take decisions for the infant nation. Britain's eventual insistence that the long-term arrangement to cede Hong Kong to China could not be tampered with was not necessarily an act of postcolonial conscience; China was a powerful nation, insistent on regaining Hong Kong, and any notion of a renegotiation of the British lease had been ruled out some time before. However, the British government made it clear that Hong Kong would not simply become a Chinese district: instead, it would be permitted to retain its independent way of life for at least 50 years. This included retaining both its capitalist society, and at the same time, its real and symbolic independence from China, creating a buffer to soften the impact of any future events that Hong Kong may not support.

British colonial rule in Hong Kong had itself been enabled by a process of bodily intervention; it was by trading opium (a drug that subdues the body) through the British East India Company that a relationship was developed with China, leading to the eventual colony of Hong Kong. After two unsuccessful attempts to establish a trading port in China in 1596 and 1637, in the late eighteenth century the British East India Company set up what was intended as a permanent base, and began trading, buying items to export, including silks, porcelain and tea. However, the only thing that Chinese merchants were willing to import from the East India Company was opium, which was used in China as a medicine, smoked with tobacco or chewed raw, although it was prohibited. Kevin Rafferty has recorded the huge volume of opium imported into China, noting that 5000 chests were imported per year by 1820, rising to 20,000 chests by the 1830s and almost double that amount by the end of the decade, at a cost of a tenth of the government's annual revenue (1991, pp. 104–7). It is unsurprising that China eventually intervened to quell its citizens' developing dependency on the illegal drug. Newly appointed High Commissioner Lin Tse-hsu imposed a strict policy in order to excise opium from China completely, destroying supplies, threatening to set ships carrying the drug on fire, and imprisoning thousands involved in the trade, executing one prisoner each day. Britain's refusal to halt the trade in opium to China despite these heavy restrictions led to the Opium War (1839–42), and eventually to British colonial rule in Hong Kong. The British reacted strongly against Chinese aggression towards British ships and citizens living in the area and retaliated, demanding repayment for the ships and goods destroyed. After repeated attacks on Chinese ports and cities, the Opium War ended with two treaties securing British colonial presence in China. The Treaty of Nanking, signed on 29 August 1842, opened five ports to British trade (Amoy, Foo-chow, Ningpo, Shanghai and Canton). Another important step in enabling British colonial control of the area was the acceptance of an official British representative in China, when previously China had strongly resisted hosting a British diplomat. The supplementary Treaty of the Bogue allowed non-Chinese residents exemption from Chinese law, and together the treaties meant that Britain had a trading centre, a territory in which citizens could reside under British law, and that this territory was in contact with the rest of China through the new diplomat. As Rafferty writes, Hong Kong 'was obviously intended as a colony where foreigners could do business without interference from the Chinese' (1991, p. 120).

It was Chinese citizens who rapidly developed the land in Hong Kong, though, turning a quiet fishing region into a busy, permanently occupied community by quickly building and furnishing new houses and factories and setting up a large commercial centre. Tak-Wing Ngo has noted that in the colonial imagination, Britain was responsible for the supposed positive transformation of the territory, the 'barren-rock-turned-capitalist-paradise' (Ngo, 1999, p. 1). This view, Ngo insists, is contested by the nationalist interpretation, which sees Hong Kong as 'part of the modern history of China, characterized by invasion and humiliation at the hands of Western powers' (1999, p. 1). Neither of these portraits of Hong Kong, both of which reduce the location to a passive subject, is adequate, according to Ngo, who calls the image of Hong Kong as a 'concubine of two masters' a gross simplification of the history and development of the nation which emerged because of the autonomous acts of independent citizens of the territory. Some had entrepreneurial roles, as is commonly known, but there were others who must be acknowledged as active agents of Hong Kong's history: 'collaborators of the ruling regime, compradors of colonial businesses, anti-colonial radicals, marginalised industrialists, revenue farmers, landlords and social activists' (Ngo, 1999, p. 2).

Ngo argues that postcolonial Hong Kong has not simply shifted allegiance, but that it now reflects its complex history in its current multiple national identity (1999, pp. 10–11). As a colony, Hong Kong could never be regarded as wholly British. The British government conflicted with the national heritage of citizens, who were mostly Chinese, having left mainland China to live in Hong Kong, or who were the descendents of migrants from China. This differs somewhat from other British colonial regimes because Hong Kong changed rapidly following British colonization. Expanding rapidly from a small fishing community into an economic hub, it was so densely populated that, as Kevin Rafferty observed, it could not produce enough food or even enough drinking water for its inhabitants, so 'every day the people of Hong Kong depend for their very existence on lorries ferrying pigs and other livestock and green vegetables across the border from China; as well as a continuous flow of water through [...] two pipelines' (1991, p. 336). This relationship with China further complicated the situation, especially considering the fundamentally opposed political systems governing the two countries, with Communist China supplying necessities for life to thoroughly capitalist Hong Kong.

It is perhaps Hong Kong's powerful economic position that led to its steadfast refusal to define itself as a colony, the word 'colony' being replaced by 'territory' in official documentation, on the banknotes and in school books in the decades leading up to 1997 (Rafferty, 1991, p. 150). The refusal to recognize its colonial status, though, means that there is less impetus for contesting colonialism, and perhaps this is why there were fears that British colonial rule would be replaced by a Chinese one in 1997, rather than a more independent national identity. One of the most commonly voiced fears was that wealthy, capitalist Hong Kong would be forced by Communist China to adopt a socialist regime. Issues of economics, manufacturing and trade have dominated the studies of colonial and postcolonial Hong Kong, distorting the impact of colonialism so that Hong Kong's significant financial position is falsely understood as the direct and only impact of British colonial rule, opposed with the alternative, which would be the Communist system in China, which, whatever its problems and its merits, is inevitably demonized by capitalist commentators from the West.

For example, Tak-Wing Ngo describes how 'economic policies both advanced and constrained Hong Kong's development', by privileging trade while holding back industrialization in the middle of the twentieth century (1999, p. 8). Ngo states firmly that to consider the impact of colonialism in Hong Kong in purely economic terms is false, and this is an important point: to repeatedly present Hong Kong in economic terms is to repeat that colonial myth of barren-rock-turned-capitalist-paradise. Though it is important to consider the massive impact that trade and commerce in Hong Kong had on the territory, on China, and globally, to see Hong Kong simply in terms of its wealth is to dehumanize it. By examining the other effects of colonization, and specifically the impact of laws regarding personal rights and freedoms including those concerning sexuality discussed below, is to enable Hong Kong to be recognized more clearly as an independent entity. Hong Kong has a strong international identity even if it is now officially ruled by China, and even though it does still reside under the lingering influence of the 50-year agreement to retain the economic landscape that was developed under British colonial rule. This lingering influence is noticeable even in recent court cases related to gay relationships.

Queer Hong Kong

It is a bodily issue in Hong Kong that I would like to explore here, a debate that started before the end of British colonial rule in Hong Kong, and which has been repeatedly debated in independent Hong Kong law in very recent years: that is, the legal position of homosexuality and the specific laws relating to bodily freedoms in sexual relationships. There was a particular court case in 2005 which challenged existing laws on gay sexual relationships and sodomy more generally. Although homosexuality was decriminalized in Hong Kong in 1991, the age of consent for homosexuals was 21, while heterosexuals were recognized as consenting adults at age 16. The penalties for underage sex also differed: while heterosexuals faced a maximum of five years in prison for having sex with an underage partner, for gay underage sex there was a potential life sentence. It was this aspect of the law that was questioned in 2005 when a twenty-year-old man, William Roy Leung, challenged the law in a private case which he won on 24 August. He argued that the laws were discriminatory and stereotyped gay men as deviant. The High Court Judge for the case also explained that even though sodomy was illegal for heterosexual couples it was only the man who faced prosecution and a potential five-year sentence, while both gay men, if one was under 21, could be imprisoned for life – clearly, this was an unequal state regulation of the body. The sodomy law was not a dormant one: prominent gay activist Roddy Shaw stated in a number of news stories that 65 men had been arrested under gay sex laws in the five years prior to this case, 26 of whom had been convicted.

William Leung's legal victory was challenged by the Hong Kong government, who lost its 2006 appeal based on the court's ruling that sodomy is an act of sexual intercourse equivalent to sex between heterosexual couples, for whom sodomy carried a lesser penalty. Both the 2005/2006 case and the earlier decriminalization of homosexuality in 1991 have been conceived in terms of their relevance in colonial and postcolonial relations between Britain and Hong Kong. In 1991, Hong Kong was still a British colony, so it is unsurprising that British newspapers would discuss the change in the law from the perspective of Hong Kong as a colonial territory. However, even in 2005, a number of online news reports specifically discussed the issue in Hong Kong's context as a former British colony, implying that the anti-gay laws were an imperial hangover, and seeing changes as a postcolonial victory. Many governments outside the West, in contrast, have suggested that homosexuality itself is a foreign import. The initial changes to Hong Kong laws on homosexuality passed in 1991, along with the Bill of Rights passed a few months later, were seen by China as 'a British attempt to hamstring the incoming administration with unnecessary restrictions' (Vines, 1991). The decriminalization of homosexuality did bring Hong Kong more closely into line with British law, as was pointed out in *The Guardian* (Vines, 1991). Considering the force with which British law was applied in Hong Kong, perhaps it is unsurprising that any rejection of those laws remaining in force would have symbolic significance in the postcolonial context.

Christopher Munn has written about the unusually rapid implementation of British law in Hong Kong, with the intention of dominating the territory quickly and gaining the allegiance of later generations of Hong Kong Chinese (1999, p. 48).

Along with changes in the law, there was increased visibility in the lesbian and gay community in Hong Kong with the outgoing British colonial regime. Day Wong has traced the development of gay activism, beginning with the establishment of the Ten Percent Club in the late 1980s, and its formal registration in 1992 following the decriminalization of homosexuality, through to the growth of organizations in the 1990s. Wong proposes that the lesbian and gay movement in Hong Kong differs from those elsewhere, in that instead of building a community identity that differs from the heterosexual norm, Hong Kong gay activists protest for fair legislation and recognition on the basis of the 'normalness' of gay people. Spokespersons have emphasized that gay people are 'law-abiding, contributing and productive' Hong Kong citizens, 'who deserve to receive the same treatment as heterosexuals' (Wong, 2006, p. 196). This in turn means that gay organizations, groups and individuals publicly 'express a sense of pride toward their identity as Hong Kong citizens rather than toward their own sexual identity' (Wong, 2006, p. 202). This contrast with other gay movements can be understood as a result of Chinese pressure, exemplified by the very public statements at the time of the decriminalization bill, and restated when William Leung's court case was appealed, which repeatedly made claims that homosexuality was a foreign oddity and a perversion imported by the former colonizers. Such public statements may have stifled any alternative manifesto or approach by gay organizations and activists. However, at the same time, the expression of allegiance to Hong Kong rather than to an international, cross-cultural gay identity and community marks Hong Kong's intrinsic need to find its own national voice, and to restate that voice in all of its citizens' movements and groups. It expresses a desire to forge an anticolonial identity by ensuring that Hong Kong does not simply remain subject to its former British colonizers. One way of doing this is to reject a British or European-style gay culture. In this way, the nation cannot be accused of being simply that little pocket of Britain in the East as it had been perceived during the early colonial period. While resisting the British legacy, there is at the same time a need to resist China's control if Hong Kong is to develop its own sense of national identity. By expressing the strength and unity of its citizens, Hong Kong resists the kinds of fractures and divisions that could make it vulnerable to increased control from China. So the expression of a Hong Kong gay identity that is not in any other way distinct from the Hong Kong norm strengthens Hong Kong's international presence and its independence from both its former colonizer and its current ruling power.

There is an element of this anxiety in gay literature from Hong Kong. Nicholas Wong's 'I for Illness' (2008) is the story of Ian, a gay man who nervously conceals his sexuality, and is pathologized and marginalized by the need to be the unobtrusive 'Ian' and not the queer 'I'. Ian feels loneliness and desperation both at work and at a gay spa where his feelings are reinforced by self-doubt and constant rejection by other men. The story indicates that the body remains a significant factor in the negotiation of gay identity in Hong Kong. The protagonist's attempts at encounters with men are all instigated by touch rather than other methods of seduction (looking, talking). He exists in a kind of limbo that mirrors the country's hovering between two identities, increasing the fragmentation in his mind which leads to fantasies and enigmatic conversations with a man who may or may not really exist in a back room of the spa. The story makes direct reference to Hong Kong's independent status when Ian discusses the stock market since 1997, and the anthology in which the story appears is intended to question Hong Kong identity in the 50 years between colonizing states.

While Hong Kong is an interesting case because its postcolonial moment occurred so very recently, India provides a fascinating comparison in literature and in theory, in part because of its much closer postcolonial relationship with its former colonizer, the United Kingdom. While Hong Kong tends to be discussed in economic terms, this is not the case with India; there is a wealth of scholarship on colonial and postcolonial India, addressing among other issues education, language, literature, landscape, personal relationships and bodily encounters. The postcolonial moment in India is summed up by the brutal, bodily effects of Partition.

The Partition of India

The Partition of India, creating the separate territories of India and Pakistan, is recorded in official histories on the date 13 August 1947, at midnight, exactly 24 hours before the official moment of Indian independence. Tai Yong Tan and Gyanesh Kudaisya note that Partition has been understood in conventional histories as a fundamental postcolonial moment which is the focus of both celebration and tragedy, the combination of pain and joy often described in terms of 'the "birth pangs" of the "Nation"' (2000, p. 29). Such discourse is an implicit acceptance of colonialist perception of the colony as an 'infant nation', assuming that the country was 'born' only after colonial rule ended which reinforces Eurocentric notions that former colonies are only given meaning by colonialism. Even the image used here (of birth pangs) is limiting: a birth date implies that an individual is born completely and cleanly at the moment recorded on a birth certificate. Yet, the body that gives birth to this nation or infant has grown and changed to create it. The process of giving birth is a long one which can easily straddle more than one calendar date, and the motherly body continues to change after giving birth. In the case of Partition, an assumption that the two nations were 'born' at the stroke of midnight is flawed for two reasons: firstly, because the events of Partition were not restricted to a 24 hour period – far from it: the effects are ongoing even today, and secondly, because for the majority of those affected by Partition, their histories and memories do not correspond with such a straightforward linearity.

The plan to divide colonial India into two distinct territories of India and Pakistan on the basis of majority Hindu/Muslim populations was formally announced to the public on 3 June 1947. However, at this stage the precise location of the boundary between the two nations had not been decided. In the very final stages there was secrecy surrounding the new mapping of the subcontinent, but the boundary commissions had only made their decision on 12 August. In a recent history of Partition, Yasmin Khan notes that the boundary line was revealed on 17 August, just as British troops began departing Bombay (2007, p. 125), implying that revealing the boundary location was delayed in order to allow the British to withdraw from India without having to be burdened by the effects of Partition. Once it had been announced that India would be partitioned to create Pakistan, there was a need to rapidly decide on where the boundary line would fall. Cyril Radcliffe, a British judge who had never before visited India, was appointed to chair both the Bengal and Punjab Boundary Commissions. Yasmin Khan has claimed that Radcliffe had 'none of the requisite skills for drawing a border' (2007, p. 105); this border stretched 3800 miles and was intended to demarcate sensible territories based on statistical information related to the predominant religion of the populations, as well as relevant cultural, historical and geographical factors. All of this was to be done from within an office and without visiting any of the regions through which the boundary line was to pass. Travelling through 3800 miles may have been considered prohibitively time-consuming when the Border Commissions needed to publish their decisions in just a few weeks. Likewise, there may have been some practical intention behind the appointment of a chair who had never visited India, in that it was assumed decisions would be taken impartially. In the end, though, the result of such a process was a much disputed and an impractical border, which 'zigzagged precariously across agricultural land, cut off communities from their sacred pilgrimage sites, paid no heed to railway lines or the integrity of forests, divorced industrial plants from the agricultural hinterlands where raw materials, such as jute, were grown', leaving East and West Pakistan separated by a thousand miles, or a journey of five days by sea (Khan, 2007, p. 126). For many, the uncertainty of the border was itself instrumental in the brutal response to Partition by South Asian citizens.

Yasmin Khan claims that 'uncertainty about the precise location of the new borderline collided with the intensely negative attitudes ascribed to "Pakistan" and "India"' (2007, p. 111). Uncertainty surrounded Partition at every stage; even from the British perspective, there was an assumption that India may only be partitioned temporarily: Yasmin Khan has reported that Andrew Clow, governor of Assam, announced that Partition would be in place not permanently, but 'for some time to come' (2007, p. 89). The boundary was created uncertainly, and decisions were withheld meaning that local administrators could not prepare in advance for the implementation of Partition. Clearly, for the majority of citizens who were affected by Partition, the overwhelming feeling was one of uncertainty: Urvashi Butalia claims that the questions 'where were we headed? Where would we end up?' resonate through virtually every Partition narrative that she has heard in her extensive oral history project, as presented in her important work, *The Other Side of Silence* (2000). Flaws in the process and faults in the borderline have led to a frequently held position in accounts of Partition blaming the inadequacy of the boundary decisions for the violence that ensued, an opinion that has dominated questions over the legitimacy of the concept of Partition itself. Studies which emphasize Radcliffe's inexperience in South Asia and the rapidity of his decisions seem to suggest that a different boundary line could have led to a positive invention of two South Asian nations. Mahatma Gandhi was fundamentally opposed to the concept of Partition, calling it evil, a 'vivisection' of India (Tan and Kudaisya, 2000, p. 70). Literary representations have also questioned the legitimacy of partitioning what had once been a diverse and plural community. Literary texts present a Partition that was doomed to fail, no matter how much care and attention was paid to the specific borderline, no matter how many twists and turns had been worked into the division.

Partition in literature

A number of literary representations of Partition have focused on the impact on the mind and body of individuals. Literature is, like Butalia's recording of oral histories, an 'alternative archive of the times' (Fraser, 2008, p. xiii), and in the following sections including the one on Partition Histories, I aim to demonstrate that in addition to unofficial histories of the kind uncovered by Butalia, literary depictions of those histories offer valuable ways of rethinking the official history. The short story has been seen as holding a particularly important position in the retelling of Partition, because of its ability to convey 'individual fates' in the specific moment, in comparison with the novel where those voices may be lost amid what is frequently a long stretch of narrative time (Fraser, 2008, p. xiii). The best-known Partition short story is Saadat Hasan Manto's 'Toba Tek Singh'. When Tai Yong Tan and Gyanesh Kudaisya refer to 'cartographic anxieties' that followed the borderline decisions made by the boundary commissions, they could not more aptly describe 'Toba Tek Singh'. The story conveys the ludicrous nature of Partition through the disturbed psychology of insane asylum inmate, Bishan Singh. Living in a state of 'limbo' unaware of the date or even the year, Bishan Singh repeats 'the same mysterious gibberish: "*Uper the gur gur the annexe the bay dhayana the mung the dal of the laltain*"'. After overhearing discussions about plans to send inmates to the country where their families live after Partition, he takes to ending his solemnly delivered mantra with 'the Government of Pakistan' or 'the Government of Toba Tek Singh' (Manto, 1987, p. 14). Learning of the Partition plan, Bishan Singh asks repeatedly about his own home town, Toba Tek Singh. Not receiving a satisfactory response as to whether the town has been placed on the Indian or the Pakistani side of the border, he starts to lose a sense of his own identity, confusing himself with the town, and renaming himself Toba Tek Singh. Thus, 'cartographic anxieties' are raised by his inability to locate himself or his past, when the town that he understands as his home and his origin – his spatial context – suddenly occupies the same state of limbo that he had come to know temporally. The image clearly equates to the sense of tremendous uncertainty that accompanied the creation of a partition through South Asia and the resulting divisions that at times seemed as senseless as the asylum inmates' chatter. Singh's habit of naming himself directly parallels the amount of knowledge that he is provided with concerning the location of his home town. When given an answer to his question, 'Where is Toba Tek Singh?' – an answer that is not entirely satisfactory, but which does at least claim a modicum of decidability: 'in India ... no, in Pakistan' (p. 17) – he is once again referred to by his original name, Bishan Singh, suggesting a regained sense of identity. Any sense of certainty that he had experienced is lost, though, when officials try to push him over the border into India, to join a bus of inmates bound for an Indian asylum. Believing that Toba Tek Singh was in Pakistan, this town so much a part of himself that he had become interchangeable with it, he could not tolerate being taken to India, away from his home and himself. He remains in 'no man's land' between the barbed wire fences separating the two countries until it is impossible to separate Bishan Singh from Toba Tek Singh, the town from the man, and no-man's land from a mappable, nameable territory:

> Bishan Singh [...] collapsed to the ground.
> There, behind barbed wire, on one side, lay India and behind more barbed wire, on the other side, lay Pakistan. In between, on a bit of earth which had no name, lay Toba Tek Singh.   (p. 18)

Such undecidability is not only to be found in fictional accounts. Urvashi Butalia records the story of a child being held in a refugee hostel who said that her name was 'Sita-Hasina' – an impossible name, at once Hindu and Muslim. When asked, she named her father, whose name had a similar impossible duality. This child, because of her name that straddled both religions and both territories, 'defeated all attempts [...] to allow boundaries to be fixed for her' (2000, p. 205).

The response to Partition was extremely violent, which raises the question: how to 'disentangle rationality from madness, political intent from momentary insanity?' (Khan, 2007, p. 130). Is it Partition which is insane, or the violence that followed? Bishan Singh's body, when it collapsed in death in no-man's land, became a marker of the borderland. This defiant body opposes the body/land markers that Yasmin Khan describes, the 'macabre signposts' left visibly on display at the periphery of 'rightful' territories (2007, p. 127), dead bodies acting as warnings to those of the same religion as the dead that they were not to pass beyond. Bishan/Toba Tek Singh's body, adamantly placed between two territories and refusing to be pushed over the border (refusing to be subject to physical manipulation), marks instead a protest, a refusal to accept Partition. Partition is seen as an act of brutality towards India's 'body' in 'Toba Tek Singh'; newly created Pakistan is, according to one particularly confident asylum inmate, 'the name of a place in India where cut-throat razors are manufactured' (p. 11). For Tan and Kudaisya, the blame for Partition violence lay with

Cyril Radcliffe, who had made the final decisions over where the specific boundary line would lie: 'Radcliffe knew only too well that this had been a butcher's job, and not a surgeon's operation' (2000, pp. 93–4). Whether a good job (a surgeon's operation) or a bad one (a butcher's job) had been carried out, though, the image is a bodily one. The implication here is that a good job – a surgeon's operation – may have fixed an ailing South Asia, whereas the poor decisions ensured that the carving up would take place on a dead body, would be butchery. This is not quite the same as the idea expressed by Gandhi, who suggested that Partition itself delivered a fatal blow to India when he (in another fleshy image) referred to it as 'India's vivisection'. The connotations of experimentation in the term 'vivisection' retain the sense of culpability that Tan and Kudaisya lay entirely on Radcliffe, but for Gandhi, blame is attributed, not necessarily equally, to both the exiting British colonial government and the Muslim League who campaigned for a separate Muslim homeland.

Symbolically, Partition on religious lines equates to the separation of the body of Mother India, a brutal act that was replicated on the bodies of South Asian women especially violently when people fled to newly appointed religious territories, or when they refused to be exiled because of their religion. The idea that India was a body, carved up by Partition and left either dead or wounded, again assumes that Partition is a particular historical moment and that the violent disfigurements and killings inflicted upon individuals are comparable on a large scale with the scar which was carved into India's body at the moment the borderline was announced. Urvashi Butalia's retelling of Partition history once again insists that this image is too simplistic, when she describes the way that 'inside the bodies of women and children, the boundary' – and with it, the wound, the history – 'remained fluid' (2000, p. 235). Children of interreligious marriages, pregnant women, and even in many cases, women who had been abducted by men of the other religion and were thus considered 'tainted' by their own communities could not be easily placed on one or other side of the border, and thus their 'wounds' remained open. Certainly, a woman who had been abducted and raped may in many ways feel the ongoing wound, but perceiving children and unborn children as scars or wounds is more problematic. Nevertheless, this is the way that they were understood: in order for women to be readmitted to their original communities, they were asked to abandon their children, and to undergo abortions in order to make themselves 'pure' again. Abortion was illegal at the time, so mass state-sponsored abortion clinics were set up for women to be 'cleansed' (the operation was called *safaya*). Those women who could not abandon or abort their children were sent to live in ashrams (hostels), if, as was often the case, their families would not accept them with their children. Clearly, then, the ashram represented another way in which the bodily impact of Partition was ongoing and was not a singular or limited temporal act.

Salman Rushdie's portrayal of independence and Partition in *Midnight's Children* questions the notion of the 'gift' of independence, in the portrayal of the bodily impact on children born at the moment of independence who were endowed with magical powers. The children have physical or mental powers including telepathy, gifts for multiplying food, growing vegetables in the desert, transformation, transportation across space, size-shifting, intense beauty, sex-change, and for inflicting physical wounds by speech alone. Saleem Sinai, formally awarded the prize for being the first baby born on the stroke of midnight, is able to communicate psychically with all of the other midnight's children, and sets up a mental space where they can all meet, which he calls the Midnight's Children's Conference.

As adults, the midnight's children undergo a further bodily transformation, a forced sterilization preventing the inheritance of their powers by future generations. Indira Gandhi imposed a mass sterilization campaign in 1976 and 1977, coercing men to have vasectomies. In the novel, the fictional Indira was responsible for stripping the midnight's children of their magical powers by forcing both men and women born on independence day to undergo irreversible sterilization: 'testicles were removed from sacs, and wombs vanished for ever', and along with them, 'hope' (p. 439). India's motherly body, violated by Partition, is directly contradicted by the image of Indira Gandhi in *Midnight's Children*, as a distorted mirror image – 'Indira is India and India is Indira' (p. 427) – distorted, according to the narrator, in recompense for the deflected glory that he had received as the first midnight's baby. With Saleem in the role of 'mirror-of-the-nation' (p. 427), Indira's power in the novel is minimized. The personal battle between Indira Gandhi and Saleem Sinai represents a fundamental betrayal of the possibilities of independence. The novel insists that after colonialism, independent India's own leaders effected just as brutal and unjustified a bodily punishment on the children of midnight, the independence generation, with the sterilization programme. Here, Mother Indira as head of a violent, mass sterilization programme is a threatening, unmotherly bodily representation of India, and not a nurturing, motherly one. Divided brutally in the last act of the colonial government, the wounded, widowed motherly body turns on its own children.

Midnight's Children is also a novel of linguistic and structural inventiveness, with a digressive narrator in Saleem Sinai who is repeatedly called to account by narratee Padma, a pickle factory worker and adult Saleem's frustrated lover, whose non-standard English dialogue frequently interrupts to demand a standard narration and a sense of cause-and-effect: 'Arré baap! [...] Just tell what happened, mister!' (p. 425). Rushdie's most frequently cited contribution to postcolonial studies is his insistence on the empire writing back to the centre (Ashcroft, Griffiths and Tiffin's renowned postcolonial study *The Empire Writes Back* takes its title from Rushdie). This is achieved by appropriating the English language and shaping it to suit the speaker so that instead of mastering Standard English, the postcolonial writer creates it anew, owns it. Rushdie was not the first writer to reshape the English language for a postcolonial purpose, and he acknowledges a debt of influence in this to G.V. Desani, whose novel *All about H. Hatterr* was perhaps the first Indian novel to use non-standard, or 'rigmarole English' as a direct challenge to the notion of the literary canon, stating that in doing so, the text is knowingly 'staining your goodly godly tongue' (1972, p. 37). The novel was written in London during the years that independence and Partition were being debated by the colonial government and the Congress and League political representatives in India; and was first published in 1948. Its thorough questioning of English literature and the structure of the European novel, which was imposed as a literary standard by notions of canonicity, must be read in the context of Independence and Partition. Most notably, *All about H. Hatterr* is a rethinking of Shakespeare's status – frequent misquotations and misinterpretations of Shakespeare's plays insist that Shakespeare, having been exported as a dubious gift from the British colonial government to the Indian upper middle classes, is not relevant to an Indian context. The novel begins with a direct challenge to Shakespeare in India who is seen as an unwelcome intruder in a revised scene where the old king Hamlet's ghost is sighted:

> 'Halt!
> 'Approach ho, all's not well!
> (*He sees a figure of a feller*)
> 'Who art thou, fellow?
> 'Thou, with thy folio?
> 'How now, out in the Street o' Scribes, this hour o' the night, disquieting the graves o' the great?
> 'Be gone, I say!   (p. 29)

Thus, Shakespeare is the 'fellow' holding his 'folio', halted by India. This 'fellow' is at the same time Desani in London, called to attention by the London literati. In this way, Shakespeare is, on the crux of independence, handed back to Britain in a battered and bruised state. Misinterpretations are rife in the novel; Bannerji interprets Beatrice's 'I have a good eye, uncle. I can see a church by daylight' (*Much Ado about Nothing*, 2.1). She claims that she has insight enough to observe what is plain for all to see, while Bannerji interprets this as Shakespeare's (and therefore, everyone's) method of measuring the level of sight required to possess good vision, claiming that the Bard 'observed Life. He held an untarnished mirror to Mother Nature. He reported Truth faithfully' (p. 165). Rather than realizing that the line should perhaps not be taken as a literal indicator of strong sight, Bannerji explains that 'only rich and well-to-do people could afford glasses. If a poor man could see a church by daylight, without spectacles, it must have been assumed that he had a good eyesight. There was also a great deal of fog in Elizabethan England' (p. 165). Having been repeatedly misinterpreted by Bannerji, a staunch admirer of Shakespeare as the universal Bard, he is rejected by Hatterr: 'Hell, we have advanced since! [...] I am interested in *Life today*, not as it was in Elizabethan England!' (p. 165). Thus rejected and handed back to Elizabethan England by twentieth-century India, a ravaged Shakespeare is directly comparable with the body of mother India, which is at the same moment being handed back to South Asia by a departing British colonial administration, in pieces: Pakistan 'two Wings without a body' (Rushdie, 1995, p. 178) and India an inert body, stripped of its wings. The rejection of Shakespeare, though, is a just one, an act of independent thought and a taking back of the Indian literary voice, a writing back that happened long before Rushdie's.

Partition memories

Partition has remained a more dominant memory of 1947 than South Asian Independence from British colonial control (Tan and Kudaisya, 2000, p. 7). This is because of the extent to which its effects are still being experienced in South Asia. The ongoing Kashmir dispute is one post-Partition hangover, which has been described as 'one of the longest running disputes in the world', as well as 'the most bitter and intractable' (Khan, 2007, p. 98; Tan and Kudaisya, 2000, pp. 221–2). In Kashmir, the violence was (and is) prolonged, because the religious designation was even less straightforward to proscribe there than in other territories: while the ruler was Hindu, the majority of the population was Muslim, and after hesitating to select one country or the other for the borderline state to join, renewed calls for independence resulted in a long period of violent resistance and aggression. Tan and Kudaisya also note wider disharmony, claiming that what should have been a celebration of 50 years of independence will be remembered as an era of armed nuclear hostility between India and Pakistan, punctuated by nuclear weapons testing in May 1998 by both countries (2000, pp. 221–2). There are many other indicators of the ongoing effects: efforts to 'recover' the victims of violence and enforced migration went on long after they were practically useful to those victims in many cases. Women who had been abducted were intended to be 'recovered' from their new homes and taken back to their original region and to their family. The Abducted Persons Recovery and Restoration Ordinance became a Bill and then an Act, under which legal authority it created a working definition of an 'abducted person' which took no account of free will either at the time of the assumed abduction or at the time of 'recovery'. In practice, although there may well have been a number of women who were relieved to be recovered from positions of servitude within their abductor's household, there were a large number of women who wanted to stay with their new families. From an outsider's perspective, it might be difficult to imagine that a woman would choose to stay with a man who had once abducted and raped her and forced her into marriage, as was a common scenario. In reality, though, there were many reasons why this might be the case, as Urvashi Butalia points out: poor women were sometimes abducted by wealthy men meaning that their living conditions were drastically improved; women relied upon their new husband (and perhaps children) as their only family, and were assured of no welcome from their original communities having undergone abduction which carried with it connotations of having been 'spoiled' or sullied; unlike men, women did not participate in religion in any real sense (being barred from entering places of worship), so their original religion may have held only a vague meaning for them; and, women were unwilling to trust policemen and other officials who promised to give them safe passage because they had been abducted once and feared it happening again, and in many cases, women had been raped by the police (Butalia, 2000, pp. 119–20). As a result, the act of 'recovery' was in many ways as violent as the original abduction: some women were persuaded to abandon their children or to abort their unborn babies in order to ensure that they were accepted by their families. The 'recovery' operation continued for ten years before it was abandoned. Because many of the abducted girls were as young as six years old when they were taken, and a vast number were in their early teens, these ten years were formative ones for many, and the practices of recovery were flawed, if only because it was assumed that no woman could speak for herself. All interreligious marriages after 1 March 1947, when the first Partition-related violence in the Punjab started, were void as it was assumed that there could be no circumstances under which a woman would marry into a different religion, or choose to stay in the adopted country. The violence that is often assumed to have been restricted to the time immediately succeeding Partition in fact, according to Priyamvada Gopal, 'echoes in postcolonial India, in what are called the "communal riots" or "inter-community violence"' (Gopal, 2009, p. 69). In this sense, there can be no assumption of a straightforward linear narrative to describe Partition if its after-effects echo repeatedly in ongoing violence. For Butalia, the word 'partition' is 'so inadequate' (2000, p. 285) with its implication of a simple division, when placed in the context of so protracted and violent a cleaving.

The effects of Partition have inevitably led to questions over why India was divided in the first place. Some claim that the British policy was intended as a final act of 'divide and rule', intended to leave a weakened territory. For Yasmin Khan, the act was symptomatic of the British intention to 'cut their losses' (2007, p. 48) in the hurry to get out of India. For others, though, Partition had a positive meaning: Urvashi Butalia notes that many welcomed the move in relief that a plan – any plan – for a future independent South Asia had been decided upon (2000, p. 55). And on reaching the border, many of those who had been made to migrate felt a sense of optimism and patriotism (Khan, 2007, p. 161) which for them may have accompanied a sense that Partition was the right thing to do. Sara Suleri has claimed that on arrival in the new Pakistan, Muslims were pleased to have been granted what they had asked for (1991, p. 74) in a very positive representation of Partition compared to those which focus on the violence accompanying migration and division. There had been a sustained campaign by the Muslim League for a separate Muslim homeland alongside the broader desire for an independent South Asia, supported by the Congress party who wanted to retain a united, plural India.

And, indeed, there were some outcomes to Partition which have been understood as largely positive by those whose lives were changed for the better, as they understand it. From a feminist perspective, the new emphasis on women's activity and work in the public sphere necessitated by the rebuilding work following Partition meant a relaxing of the ordinary family roles. Instead of getting married, many women were required to work, in social work, for example. This must, of course, be understood in the context of exactly why there was a need for these women to undertake social work, as Urvashi Butalia explains: 'just as a whole generation of women were destroyed by Partition, so Partition provided an opportunity for many to move into the public sphere in a hitherto unprecedented way' (2000, p. 90). There was lots of healing to be administered after the brutal act of Partition. However, it is still important to recognize the increased sense of independence and societal participation that Partition brought for a number of women.

In the end, it must be conceded that Partition and Independence was part of a longer period of disharmony which included colonization. For one thing, Partition had a precedent: Bengal had been partitioned in 1905, in an act that was repealed in 1911 (Fraser, 2008, p. 57). And, aside from the general colonial context within which the event took place, the specific circumstances at the end of a long colonial regime meant that South Asia was damaged and liable to react aggressively to any further pressure. In the aftermath of the Second World War, in which 2.5 million Indian soldiers had fought, there was widespread hunger, a lack of resources, incessant strikes leading to a halted postal service, and no post meant that no bills – including taxes – were received or paid (Khan, 2007, pp. 16–17, 26, 84). The foundations of separatist violence had been laid by the colonial regime itself, according to Yasmin Khan who has described an enforced separation of religious communities made public in places like railway stations where drinking water taps were labelled 'Hindu' and 'Muslim' water (2007, p. 19). Electorates had been drawn on religious lines in 1909, which had resulted in a hardening of religious boundaries which had previously been 'more porous and less sharply defined' (Khan, 2007, p. 20), Hindus, Muslims and Sikhs having lived in 'relative peace and harmony' at earlier times (Butalia, 2000, p. 4). In addition to these distinctions, there was a pervasive acknowledgment of violence against the body as a legitimate punishment by the Whipping Act which was used by the colonial government to suppress riots (Khan, 2007, p. 29). Khan's implication is that South Asian sectarian violence in response to Partition was a direct result of colonial violence. Frantz Fanon has claimed that the first response to an unsupportable regime is to react violently – not against the regime, but against the easiest target: those in the same situation. What Fanon calls a 'fraternal blood bath' allows those struggling to demand independence to ignore the real obstacle before a process of reclaiming control can take place (1967, p. 42).

Partition histories

Conventional historical accounts of Partition tend to record one of two separate facets: histories of political intrigue, and histories of violence, migration and survival. For Urvashi Butalia, both of these constitute the public,
general histories: it is only by locating and telling the particular, those stories told inside the households in India and Pakistan, that Partition might
be more fully understood (2000, p. 3). Butalia's first purpose was to find
and 'make visible' women's histories of Partition, the stories that did not
exist elsewhere in dominant versions, in order to complete an 'incomplete
picture' – a task that she later discovered could not be concluded, because,
as she writes, everyone who makes a picture of Partition 'draws it afresh'
(Butalia, 2000, p. 100). Rather than intending to produce a postcolonial
retelling of Partition history, Butalia's approach acknowledges the awkward
status that history itself has in the postcolonial context by allowing that no
history can be complete or unbiased. Her purpose was, in the end, to place
previously untold histories, histories of women, children and scheduled
castes alongside existing histories. At the same time, she acknowledges the
stories yet to be told – stories of prisoners, lepers, eunuchs, mental patients,
those who she suggests 'truly live on the borders of society' and who were,
however inappropriately in some cases, expected to declare their religious
affiliation or to have it declared for them (2000, p. 259). And similarly, she is
aware that her histories are collected from one location only – the Punjab,
which has been discussed more than any other part of South Asia in recalling Partition because it was the province with the most death and the most
obvious geographical division (Butalia, 2000, p. 17; Khan, 2007, p. 7). In telling certain stories and pointing out those yet to be told, Butalia allows the
multiple histories produced to demonstrate the inadequacy of any one of
those histories, each one declaring its own particular agenda and making
its own choices about what to leave out, about what to expand upon. And in
the process of recording multiple histories, Butalia discovered that there
were 'no neat chronologies', 'no clear beginnings or endings', that retelling
the past was done 'within the context of the present' and from this position,
for so many, '1947 and 1984 [the sectarian violence following the assassination of Indira Gandhi by Sikh extremists] flowed into each other and
often it became difficult to disentangle what it was they were remembering'
(2000, p. 18).

The same kind of segregationist violence was enacted again, in riots
following the demolition of the Babri Masjid mosque in Ayodhya in 1992,
built on a disputed site which had once reportedly been the site of a Hindu

temple. Taslima Nasrin explores the communal rioting and violence following this demolition in the novel *Shame* (1994, first published in 1993 in Bengali, titled *Lajja*). The novel combines statistical and official information from news reports and formal documents with fictional accounts of violence done to individuals, as well as issues of migration and social disorder. At one point, Sudhamoy suffers a stroke and his wife realizes that she is 'completely helpless' (Nasrin, 1994, p. 69) as a significant minority surrounded by her Muslim neighbours. Their particular circumstances are supported by a section from a census reproduced in the novel showing Hindu and Muslim population changes across a number of provinces, noting in each record a vast increase in Muslim population (up to 89%) coupled with a very small increase or even a decrease in Hindu population in the same regions. Sudhamoy reflects on the injustice of separate laws, such as legal precepts regarding state ownership of what is classified as 'Enemy Property' (p. 129), the name given to a house left by a Hindu who had left the area which then automatically became state property. Muslim-owned properties remained in family ownership following the owner's migration. This conjunction of histories – fictional and factual – achieves what Butalia hopes for: a sense of multiple accounts of events, layered to offer a more representative picture. At the same time, the events described in the novel support Butalia's assertion that Partition violence is ongoing, that it is echoed in repeated examples of communalist violence.

When Indira Gandhi was assassinated by a group of Sikhs, the violent response involving brutal killings reminded many, according to Urvashi Butalia, of Partition. Partition stories 'no longer seemed quite so remote: people from the same country, the same town, the same village, could still be divided by the politics of their religious difference, and, once divided, could do terrible things to each other' (2000, pp. 4–5). This connection made in the public psyche between two periods of religious violence led Butalia to the awareness that Partition was not a completed period of history, but was in fact ever-present. This realization leads inevitably to the conclusion that any kind of history which records Partition in a restricted time slot is flawed, and insists on a presentation of history that takes into account multiple stories. Butalia's collection of oral histories of Partition is acutely sensitive to the nature of living history, to the idea that memory ensures that a historical event is not completed, but ongoing; memories are historical records that 'blur', that 'flow into each other' (2000, pp. 10), but which, for that, should not be seen as inferior to accepted textbook histories. Conventional histories claim an authority and certainty which is belied by Butalia's collected histories; these histories prove the continuing presence of Partition, and offer a necessary additional method of understanding the events set in motion by Partition.

The amount of authority that is invested by ordinary people in formally recorded histories meant that many people had considered their own stories unimportant. Butalia describes one man, Rajinder Singh, who had considered his stories too insignificant to tell to his own family. On telling them to Butalia for the first time, his family suddenly became aware of their importance once they were recorded on tape. Instead of asking Rajinder Singh to talk again about his experiences, though, they wanted to listen to certain sections of the tape over and again, as though by becoming recorded (by no longer being an oral history which is subject to change on each telling) those stories had gained prestige and authority, or a kind of factuality. The oral histories recorded by Butalia are also mediated, like all histories, by the tellers. However, instead of claiming an 'illusion of objectivity' (2000, p. 15) as a conventional history must, Butalia's histories openly acknowledge the way that they – like all histories – are constructed subjectively and are subject to change by being located in the moment at which they are told, and also in their spatial particularity. Space was a particularly influential aspect for Butalia, who soon realized that women's stories had been marginalized, and that in order to recover them, she would need to work in the margins – to speak to women in the literal corridors and back rooms, but also in the gaps between their male relatives' stories, to listen to women's speech but also to 'their silences, the half-said things, the nuances' (2000, p. 100). Butalia learned to listen to the silences which told of women's rape and abduction when her interviewees found speaking the words too painful. These silences exist, too, in literary representations, including Manto's 'Toba Tek Singh'. In a moment of clarity Bishan asks about his daughter, and the response is weighty with those gaps and silences that speak of potential violence done to this young woman: 'Your daughter Roop Kaur ...' – he hesitated – 'She is safe too ... in India' (p. 16). Manto's short stories followed a period of what Priyamvada Gopal has called a 'stunned silence' in response to the horrors of Partition (2009, p. 70). Where writers were able to respond to the violence, they did so by retaining those silences rather than speaking directly of the violence, as is clear in 'Toba Tek Singh'.

Butalia, while keen to represent multiple histories and to voice previously silenced stories, is at the same time sensitive to the flawed way in which some of the non-standard histories are used. Female suicide or the killing of women by their male relatives in order to spare them from conversion, rape, and forced interreligious marriage is retold as a story of male bravery and female heroism, and is thus used as a lesson in dutiful behaviour (2000, p. 65). For Butalia, such functions of history are problematic and insist once again that any notion of 'truth' is difficult to find: one must ask, whose truth is being told by such lessons? In recording and interpreting the stories that had been fractured, silenced, nuanced, and subject to change with each new telling, Butalia inevitably records those histories in a stable form. Thus, some of that sense of ongoing history must be lost in the process, and for the reader (and for Rajinder Singh's family) they are invested with a sense of authority and certainty which may not be appropriate for such personal and necessarily subjective histories. In order to ensure that the histories collected do not lose their potency or their ability to insist upon the nuanced and unfixed nature of the history of Partition, Butalia repeatedly insists that they be placed in a collective relationship with all previous and subsequent histories. In this manner, *The Other Side of Silence* must be understood as a key text in the debate over the way that history can be used – retold, reinterpreted – by postcolonial studies, if it is to remain effective and is not simply to impose alternative histories, any of which may be as flawed as a disputed colonial one.

The proposition that history really should be uncertain, or is somehow better because of its uncertainty, is no doubt a contentious one for some. Postcolonial studies set out in the first instance to correct problematic tellings of history and replace dominant histories with those told by the formerly marginalized and dominated voices. Should not the aim therefore be to produce a superior version of history? Why applaud the notion that history can never be told objectively or with a sense of completeness? Perhaps one reason for the need to retain a sceptical distance from history is made clearer by a closer examination of the very violent events that together make up the history (the multiple histories) of Partition. Partition violence was so brutal and cruel that it would be naïve to assume that there is any one perspective from which those events can be rationalized or explained satisfactorily in a historical account.

Yasmin Khan records the scale of the violence, the 'carnage' resulting in up to a million deaths, as well as the numerous instances of disfigurement, dismemberment and rape, and the events that demonstrated a clear intention to kill vast numbers of people, such as the examples of whole villages of people being hacked to death with farm instruments, imprisoned in barns and set alight, and lined up against walls to be shot in the manner of a firing squad (2007, p. 6). This slaughter, according to Butalia, 'sometimes accompanied and sometimes prompted' people's migration from one side of the border to the other (2000, p. 3). Where people were not killed, they were forced to undergo elaborate conversion rituals where, for example, Hindus would be instructed to undertake regular prayer, accompanied by ritualized beef-eating after cows, sacred to Hindus, were sacrificed in public spaces (Khan, 2007, pp. 68–9). There was particular violence against women; figures suggest that 75,000–100,000 women were abducted and raped. Men purposely impregnated the women of the opposite religion; women's breasts and genitals were mutilated or tattooed, their bodies and faces bitten, scarred, and branded with religious slogans, and rape was used as weapon, punishment, even 'sport', while some women were used as trade for their family's freedom (Butalia, 2000, pp. 3, 105; Khan, 2007, pp. 129, 133, 134). Specifically, the motherly body was a meaningful site for the enactment of violence and for the focus of nationalist discourse for Hindus. Manhood was proven by the ability to protect the motherly body of the nation: India 'needed men to protect the honour of the motherland', and:

> [i]t became important to establish the purity of Mother India, the motherland which gave birth to the Hindu race and which was home to the Hindu religion. The country [...] was imagined in feminine terms, as the mother, and Partition was seen as a violation of its body.)   (Butalia, 2000, p. 147)

After Independence and Partition, there was therefore a sense of 'shame' or 'inadequacy' that India had allowed a part of itself, its body, to be lost to the other nation – new Pakistan. Partition represented 'an actual violation of this mother, a violation of her (female) body' (Butalia, 2000, pp. 149–50).

The after-effects of Partition were many, and stretched out into the succeeding decades. For the women who had been abducted during the Partition disorder and violence, there were often just two possibilities: prostitution or recovery. Recovery was a problematic process, and, as Butalia has established, the results were so often highly unsatisfactory, which begs the question: why persist with such a difficult programme? For Butalia, the reason for the heavy-handed Indian abducted persons' recovery programme was more to do with ideas of national honour than genuine consideration for the women's welfare. By reclaiming women who had been taken to Pakistan, there was an associated recovery of national honour, 'honour that was staked on the body of Mother India, and therefore, by extension, on the bodies of all Hindu and Sikh women, mothers and would-be mothers' (Butalia, 2000, p. 151). For those recovered women who were not accepted by their original families, life on the street and prostitution was often the only possibility (Khan, 2007, p. 135). In more general terms, Partition led to mass migrations – it is estimated that around eighteen million people were uprooted at the time of Partition and in later years as a direct result, more, and more quickly, than any other recorded population movement before or since (Tan and Kudaisya, 2000, p. 230; Butalia, 2000, p. 3).

The Hong Kong situation is clearly very different, and less violent. In Hong Kong, the need to retain a sense of identity outside the colonial construct has led to a nationalist position which privileges a Hong Kong identity over any other, including an internationalist, queer identity; this is noteworthy because Hong Kong is in many ways such an internationalist place in outlook. The attempt to standardize national identities in South Asia, by allocating them according to religion and providing territory in which to contain those identities, has rendered South Asian identity somewhat in flux. It has extended the moment of independence – accompanied by Partition – so that it remains vital even in present-day disputes over territory, as in the case of Kashmir. For Hong Kong gay activists, there was a need not to be 'other'; for South Asians during Partition violence, there was a need to erase, to weaken, or to capture that which was other. Mass abduction, rape and impregnation of the 'other' female body – if she was not disfigured or slaughtered – recalls the combined fear and desire that constituted the colonial othering process enabling the manipulation of colonized bodies and territories. Edward Saïd's work has been fundamental to shaping the concept of the other in postcolonial studies. In the following chapter, Saïd's work is read alongside more recent considerations of the other in the works of Trinh T. Minh-ha and Rey Chow.

Part II

Postcolonial Theories

3 Otherness

From travelers' tales, and not only from great institutions like the various India companies, colonies were created and ethnocentric perspectives secured.

Edward Saïd, *Orientalism*

In drawing attention to the idea that colonial binaries were constructed in various ways, Edward Saïd notes that some promoters of imperial ideologies came from unlikely places. While it might be assumed that vast trading companies like the East India Trading Company would have a vested interest in producing and maintaining ethnocentric attitudes, it is not immediately so clear how or why scholars, translators, travellers and explorers constructed the same ideas. In *Orientalism*, a highly influential, foundational text for postcolonial studies, Saïd explores the history and development of Orientalism. This is a term that once simply identified the Orientalists, Western scholars who studied Oriental art, history, archaeology, languages and literature, but Saïd reconsiders this work to reveal the ideological basis on which it operated, and to describe how the figure of the other, the desired yet despised foreign other, was constructed. Orientalism, for Saïd, is part of 'the idea of European identity as a superior one in comparison with all the non-European peoples and cultures' (1995, p. 7). This chapter presents Saïd's ideas alongside Trinh T. Minh-ha's, whose films and theoretical writings provide new ways of thinking about the other. At the same time, her work reveals some of the ways in which anthropology or ethnology and associated documentary film-making – supposedly objective ways of studying living communities – operates in the same ways as the earlier Orientalist scholarship addressed by Saïd. In addition, this chapter discusses some of the work of Rey Chow, who has further questioned the way that even contemporary postcolonial scholarship cannot necessarily present the 'other' unproblematically. Chow considers issues of language and translation in relation to the way that the other is represented in the postcolonial text.

Defining the other

The idea that the colony is inhabited by the primitive other who must be controlled and then improved is the basis on which all ideas of imperial domination and control, as well as related activity such as missionary work, are founded. For Edward Saïd, the other is set up within a straightforward oppositional relationship between 'us' and 'them', in which force is used to control the unruly others because '"they" mainly understood force or violence best; "they" were not like "us" and for that reason deserved to be ruled' (1993, pp. xi–xii). Saïd explains how imperialism and colonialism are different but closely related terms, imperialism being the practice, theory and attitudes of a dominant metropolitan centre ruling a distant territory, following which, usually, comes colonialism which involves creating settlements on that territory. Both of these ideas involve more than just the desire to acquire territory and extract wealth, though clearly these are strong motivations. What comes along with this is a hierarchical ideological perspective which involves the notion that, as Saïd writes, 'certain territories and people require and beseech domination', because those territories are populated by 'inferior' or 'subordinate people', and this is often constructed according to physical categories so that the populations are named 'subject races' (1993, p. 8). It is this perception which leads directly to the construction of the 'self' and 'other' binary, where the other becomes a repository for all of the undesirable aspects of humanity: brutality, under-development, weakness, immorality.

The imperial or colonial mentality was manifested indirectly in many nineteenth-century British novels, and one of Edward Saïd's intentions in *Culture and Imperialism* (1993) was to make visible some of the hidden colonialist assumptions in canonical literary texts where those assumptions had only been implied. For example, Saïd responds to the way that Jane Austen portrayed the sugar plantations in Antigua in *Mansfield Park*. Saïd noted that for Austen, the plantations were simply the means by which Sir Thomas Bertram acquired his wealth and supported his estate in England. Aside from this brief reference to the colonial situation, there was no attempt made by the novel to address the response of the colonized natives and they were presented as being complicit or at least indifferent in the colonial relationship. This amounts to a false representation of the plantation workers and the native inhabitants in the Caribbean, for Saïd, and his strategy for redressing this is contrapuntal reading, which is a practice of reading which involves an awareness of both the wealthy lifestyle of the dominating centre and the context of colonial production which supports it. The term 'contrapuntal' is most often associated with music, and Saïd has developed his term in part from a number of essays that he has written on the structure of music. Contrapuntal music includes a counterpoint, a second melody in accompaniment to the main melody, almost like two voices speaking at once. These two melodies generally work in harmony to produce a more complex sound, though they are separate melodies and not simply the same melody produced by different musical instruments or pitched differently. The term also refers to the ways in which contrasting themes and structures may be combined to create a whole view, and it is the sense of contrast that Saïd draws out to apply to ways of reading.

To read *Mansfield Park* contrapuntally means being aware of both early nineteenth-century imperialist concepts of the plantations in Antigua and anticolonial revisions in work including C.L.R. James's, who demonstrated how the plantation workers in the Caribbean were not indifferent to the use of their labour by describing their uprisings. In this way it is possible to achieve a fuller understanding of the conflicting forces at work, and also of how the colonial situation was maintained despite the resistance of its workers. By reading contrapuntally, we can in the first place understand the problems with Austen's silent representation of plantation workers, but we can also understand how such representations remained unchallenged for so long, because they were based on deeply held notions of the other, the foreign other who was so different from 'us' according to the framework that implied even though 'we' might not tolerate being worked to death on an Antiguan plantation, 'we' should not apply 'our' way of thought to the 'other' who is so vastly different from 'us'. Of course, this reading of the other is limited to racial categories and fails to address exactly who was speaking from the imperial position in Austen's novel and others like it from perspectives of class or gender. Clearly, the imperial perspective is that of the privileged class while the working class British were similarly voiceless. And as a female writer, at a time when women were not able to own property, how far can Austen be expected to engage critically with a system of acquisition and distribution of wealth which would always remain distinct from her own life, from which she would remain othered? In this way, Saïd's conception of the other has been seen as too restricted, as a dual relationship which only addresses the binary of white, Western colonizer and non-white, non-European colonized. Saïd's contrapuntal reading needs to permit numerous strands in order to gain a more nuanced understanding of the othering process. This may be more difficult to accomplish when the relationship between self and other is seen in the limited context of one colonial territory, as Rey Chow has proposed in *Writing Diaspora* (1993).

Rey Chow has made an important distinction between the specific other and the general Other (which she has called the Big Other), as presented by Rousseau. Rousseau's Other is, according to Chow, a more fundamental aspect of the self, the self-sufficient, indifferent native, the savage part of the self that exists before the Lacanian separation which differentiates between the savage and the civilized. Chow returns to this original definition of the Other to attempt to correct the incompleteness of the other as it has been presented by postcolonial and anticolonial thinking. For Chow, Rousseau's Other is misapplied when it is forced on to a specific context like, for example, the Antiguan slave. By misapplying the idea of otherness to specific colonial contexts, perhaps our understanding of what that other really means is restricted to racial and specific cultural constructions. A confident comprehension of the way that the other is presented in any colonial context falls down when further aspects of identity are taken into consideration, such as class and gender and, as some very recent postcolonial thinking has pointed out, factors such as sexuality and disability as well as the influence of and access to technology. An individual may be othered by the dominant Western colonial culture but also by aspects of their own culture in various ways, implicating many different factors. Alterity is more fully comprehended using Rousseau's model which allows a comprehension of the larger problems of otherness which might not necessarily emerge exclusively from within anticolonial discourse.

Orientalism and othering

In *Culture and Imperialism*, Edward Saïd describes the way that numerous discourses were presented in British colonial education in India – 'anthropology, Darwinism, Christianity, Utilitarianism, idealism, racial theory, legal history, linguistics and the lore of intrepid travellers' – all carefully positioned to reinforce notions of the 'inherent superiority' of the English (1993, p. 121). All of this came on the back of nineteenth century and earlier pseudo-science which aimed to establish a hierarchy of races. Elleke Boehmer has discussed the use of Social Darwinism to prop up imperialism in *Colonial and Postcolonial Literature*. This is a debate that continues today – a recent Channel 4 documentary explored the idea that there are racial standard averages for IQ tests (Race and Intelligence, 2009). Nowadays science is understood as potentially partial: it is generally accepted that statistical data can be gathered and skewed in ways that suit particular arguments, and that so-called intelligence tests are culturally specific and privilege those who have been best prepared and trained for them, so cannot be used reliably to establish an average intelligence among one or other racial group. The hierarchical relationship which cast the native as an inferior other was based on Orientalist scholarship, or Orientalism. Saïd elaborates on the definition of the Orientalist as anyone who teaches, writes about, or researches the Orient by suggesting that in all of the varieties of Orientalist scholarship there is a basic precept, an 'ontological and epistemological distinction made between "the Orient" and (most of the time) "the Occident"' where this fundamental opposition between East and West is 'the starting point for elaborate theories, epics, novels, social descriptions, and political accounts concerning the Orient, its people, customs, "mind," destiny, and so on' (1995, pp. 2–3). Saïd suggests that academic and imaginative works on the Orient, since the late eighteenth century, have worked in tandem to produce a complete sense of the Orient and to create a discourse which has dominated all subsequent meanings of and engagements with the Orient. Saïd's *Orientalism* is an attempt to analyse the vast body of work written from the West about the East, and to demonstrate that the single aim in representing the East was to enable Western domination and restructuring of the Orient. Rather than a haphazard collection of representations in historical, geographical, and literary texts, and in colonial inhabitation, rule, and education, Saïd insists, Orientalism developed into something like a corporate institution for dealing with the Orient. Saïd identifies Orientalism as a discourse, in Michel Foucault's terms, that operated to enable European culture to manage all conceptions of the Orient. With the Orient established so firmly, European culture gained strength and from this the self and other binary opposition emerged. Saïd reminds us that the Orient as it has been presented is not an inert fact of nature. Yet at the same time, it was not an entirely fantastical construction. The West, Saïd suggests, was not powerful enough to create an imaginary Orient from nothing. The Orient was Orientalized in part because the powerful position of the West subordinated the East and this enabled Orientalist discourse. The unequal power relationship meant that, as Saïd wrote later in 'Orientalism Reconsidered', the Orient became Europe's 'silent Other' (2001, p. 202).

Though Saïd's concept seems to divide the world into two neat halves, Orient and Occident, *Orientalism* is not indiscriminate. The book is in fact concerned specifically with the Arabs and Islam, who constituted the Oriental for hundreds of years according to British, French and American imperialism. The concept can be applied far more broadly to other locations and peoples, especially once colonialism (as it is most commonly understood, occurring in the nineteenth and early twentieth centuries) is taken into consideration. Orientalist scholarship enabled British colonials to gather and use literary and legal documents and to rule with them. This included translation carried out by people like Abraham-Hyacinthe Antequil-Duperron and later William Jones who worked for the British East India Company. However, there was a marked shift from the scholarly to the imperial employment of Orientalism. Cromer, the first British Viceroy of Egypt, put his knowledge of Orientals to use in government, creating a 'sort of personal canon of Orientalist wisdom' (Saïd, 1995, p. 38). A body of so-called knowledge existed before colonialism began in earnest, which included the assumptions of both Cromer and Balfour that the Oriental was 'irrational, depraved (fallen), childlike, "different"' (Saïd, 1995, p. 40). 'Knowledge' that had previously existed as an attitude, an abstract, scholarly position (if an ideologically flawed one) was then applied by colonial regimes and at this point it began to have a direct material impact on colonized peoples and territories.

Saïd makes an important distinction between latent and manifest Orientalism, using the language of Freudian psychoanalysis. He distinguishes between 'an almost unconscious' latent Orientalism and a manifest Orientalism which is at work explicitly in writing on Oriental society, literature, languages, history, and so on. He suggests that whatever new knowledge is added to the body of manifest Orientalism, the underlying awareness of what the Oriental represents remains 'more or less constant' in latent Orientalism (1995, p. 206). This means that the concept is a very rigid one that, even with the oncoming of critical rethinking from postcolonial theory, has remained in place in certain circumstances. This is why Orientalism did not disappear when colonial rule formally came to an end, which happened in most places in the years following the end of the Second World War. Imperialism, enabled by Orientalist discourse is, in fact, ongoing, as Edward Saïd has described in *Culture and Imperialism*: contemporary American territorial acquisition and control of native populations has a direct parallel with imperialism, and postcolonial theorists have described this new imperialistic behaviour as 'neocolonialism', and at other times include it under the broader concept of globalization. Specifically, Saïd claims that American Orientalism derives from army language schools established during and after the Second World War, government and corporate global expansion during the postwar period, Cold War competition with the Soviet Union, and the missionary attitude towards Orientals (which term includes all 'others'). He has also noted that American Orientalist scholarship has 'dehumanized' the Orient by ignoring Arabic or Islamic art and literature in favour of a social-scientific statistical analysis (1995, p. 291). This is potentially more negative than earlier Orientalist scholarship. Saïd acknowledges that those earliest Orientalists were scholars with a deep interest in Eastern art and litera-ture, and whose translations of extensive texts and transcription of stories like *The Arabian Nights* – even if they were seen as evidence of Oriental 'superstition' by those translators – is preferable to the new manner of pre-senting 'facts', trends and statistics at the expense of analysing literature and art; to ignore art and literature suggests that it is either non-existent or without merit.

Latent Orientalism is so difficult to overcome that potentially, it is impossible for a Western academic to study the Orient without repeating Orientalism because, 'to be a European or an American [...] means being aware, however dimly, that one belongs to a power with definite inter-ests in the Orient' (1995, p. 11). This implies that a hierarchical relation-ship between East and West prevails in all Western scholarship. There are two problems with this suggestion. Arif Dirlik notes that the American or European institution is complicated: when he suggests that the postcolonial begins in a temporal sense when 'Third World intellectuals have arrived in First World academe' (Dirlik cited in Childs and Williams, 1997, p. 7) he draws attention to the non-straightforward position of the academic. Just as the Orient is altered by its colonial past, so the former colonizer is influ-enced by the colony. The very nature of the Western academic department is rendered complex by its constitution. There can be no 'pure' Western academic position from which Orientalist discourse might be repeated. Secondly, Saïd's supposition implies no concept of class. Marxist thinking in postcolonial studies can be employed to critique the assumption of sim-ple West/East power relations based on the 'definite interests' that the domi-nant class had in the Orient during the colonial period, but from which the working classes were clearly excluded. In 'Traveling Theory' Saïd more directly considers what happens when academic ideas themselves 'travel' in a manner that admits a destabilized position for the First World academic. There is, he suggests, a three- or four-stage pattern to the movement of a theory, which involves firstly an original set of circumstances in which the idea was conceived (and this might be in either an Eastern or a Western location); secondly a process during which the theory passes through the pressure of various contexts and into its new place or time; next is a set of conditions of acceptance or resistance during which the idea is introduced, and finally a partial transformation of that idea in its new context. Saïd implies that this fourth circumstance is not always present by referring to a three- *or* four-stage process in the theory's journey, suggesting that this transformation is not always required. In the temporal transfer of Orientalist scholarship from the period of colonization to that after decolonization, latent Orientalism in Western scholarship can transform so that it is critiqued rather than repeated. Theory normally 'travels' across national boundaries, and the nation is a further area addressed by Saïd.

The nation and the novel

Edward Saïd has suggested that in the tradition of Orientalism as a discipline, there is a 'partly conscious and partly non-conscious' awareness of national tradition, or even national ideology (1995, p. 263), a sense of national identity that influences the apparently objective study of the Oriental. This accounts for the representation of oriental culture and society as inferior, when it is placed in comparison to the Orientalist scholar's sense of pride in their own national ideology.

The concept of the other developed at a time when a number of Western European countries were engaged in developing a sense of nationhood. National or communal identity is often taken for granted as something easily identifiable. However, as Benedict Anderson has pointed out in *Imagined Communities* (1991), the nation itself is a very tentative concept, built on, as the title of his study suggests, imaginary connections between the members of that assumed group. Migration complicates an individual's national identity, of course, as Homi Bhabha has discussed in his introduction to *Nation and Narration* (1990). Here, Bhabha points out that the nation is unfixed and multiple, that it cannot be seen as 'other' in relation to 'what lies outside or beyond it' (p. 4) because the boundary of a nation is not simple, straightforward, or certain. Instead:

> The problem of outside/inside must always itself be a process of hybridity, incorporating new 'people' in relation to the body politic, generating other sites of meaning and, inevitably, in the political process, producing unmanned sites of political antagonism and unpredictable forces for political representation.   (1990, p. 4)

For Saïd, though, all nationalisms and not just postmigration ones originally develop 'from a condition of estrangement' (2001, p. 176), a need to expel feelings of exile and to create a sense of belonging. This would imply that Bhabha's notion of hybridity is a temporary process which is overcome by a more potent need for human connection and belonging, even uniformity. Bhabha has been criticized for presenting hybridity as if it is a positive thing for the individual who lives on that margin. There is certainly something attractive about Bhabha's process, though, which creates a boundary resembling an '*in-between*' space meaning that there can be no other that is not also part of the self. In a national sense, no nation can be seen as unique or homogeneous, supporting Benedict Anderson's suggestion that the nation can only imagine itself as whole. Anderson claims that the terms nation, nationality and nationalism are notoriously difficult to define. This is partly because the concept of the nation is such a recent one, yet civilizations such as the ancient Greek and Egyptian seem instinctively to be attached to nations recognized nowadays. Also, nationalism is considered an ideology which means it has different nuances from nationality. In response to this difficulty, Anderson proposes a new definition which directly challenges the stability of nation as a concept, when he claims that the nation is imagined. The nation is imaginary, according to Anderson, because members of a nation will never know, meet, or even hear of most of the others, yet there remains an idea of 'communion' (1991, p. 6). This imaginary comradeship or communion is deeply problematic when it creates a situation where millions of people are willing not just to kill but also to die, in the name of their 'nation'. Anderson goes on to explain that the nation is limited – it is never possible that a nation can encompass all of humanity when nations are contained by boundaries. These boundaries are, as Anderson states, elastic at times – India is a clear example of this: it supposedly became a complete 'nation' as a result of British colonial rule, and then at the end of that rule it was divided to create the two nations of India and Pakistan, which was later divided again into Pakistan and Bangladesh.

Perhaps it is easy to find problems with Anderson's argument: people living within the same nation might (sometimes) share a language, a government, a national media, and so they have the same reference points and in that way could be said to share something like a national identity which makes them more connected – even if they never meet – than somebody with a different language, government, or media. And indeed, Anderson notes the importance of language in developing a nation state. In fact, he suggests that the concept of nation emerged at the same time as print capitalism, which brought about a standardization of language: if texts could suddenly be printed in mass numbers for national distribution, it was imperative that everyone could understand them, and so it was important that all printers used standard spellings of words. And when a language becomes standardized, it invites a sense of national pride. The emergence of the novel accompanied the efforts of European nations to export their sense of national identity, so that the English novel, newly reproducible in bulk, was able to convey a sense of Englishness across the globe.

However, it is just as easy to counter these claims and to support Anderson's argument that a nation is imaginary if the common ground between members of a nation is so broad that it becomes almost meaningless. And how far can we say that, for example, all English-speakers form members of the same nation, when English is spoken in so many standard varieties and dialects in so many places, and the same can be said for other languages including French and Spanish. Similarly, do some countries evade nationhood and remain fragmentary if there are multiple languages spoken there, as is the case in Switzerland and Canada, for example? For Ernest Renan, it is wrong to confuse national identity with either racial or linguistic groups, and instead, Renan describes race, religion and language as unimportant in comparison with the more abstract definition of nation as 'a soul', as a combination of 'a rich legacy of memories' with a present-day 'desire to live together' and a culmination of a long past of endeavours, sacrifice, and devotion (1990, p. 19). It is such idealistic concepts of the nation which populate armies and which Anderson has objected to on the basis that people kill and die for that nation without any tangible sense of community.

In recent postcolonial thinking there has been a return to analyses of nationhood in an effort to define Britishness, Frenchness, and so on, albeit in a very different context. Nowadays, there is a need to acknowledge that there is such a thing as British cultural identity, not in order to promote its cultural superiority, but in order to ensure an equivalency between Western European and other cultural and geographical populations. The absence of an identifiable British culture, for example, had led to an assumption of neutrality in cultural and social practices and ideologies, and a related assumption of cultural oddness in cultures that differed from British practices. By acknowledging the cultural practices of, for example, Jamaican or Turkish people, these practices were seen as somehow different from the 'norm' and therefore strange or primitive. Instead, by acknowledging that British identity also comprises cultural practices, national groups can be understood as directly equivalent and compared on equal terms. Trinh T. Minh-ha has also considered the changing representation of national or racial categorization, explaining that at one time 'effacing it used to be the only means of survival for the colonized and the exiled', whereas 'naming it today often means declaring solidarity among the hyphenated people of the Diaspora' (1991, p. 14).

The other impetus for acknowledging the cultural diversity of Western European nation states was the growing tendency to create the West as a monolith. Edward Saïd has been accused of seeing the West as a vast, homogeneous mass rather than a collection of complex and diverse nation states, and in this way replicating previous colonial interpretations of Africa and South Asia as similarly homogeneous and simplified locations. For example, Ibn Warraq's *Defending the West* (2007) critiques *Orientalism* for this reason, though the study fails to acknowledge Saïd's measured analysis of early Orientalist scholars. Seeing the West as a monolith would be unhelpful for postcolonial theory: a reversal of colonial thinking (so that the West is seen as uniformly bad and evil where once the non-West was seen as uniformly primitive and immoral) is of little use: what is required instead is to question and critique colonial thinking and to rethink the relationships between nations and their citizens. However, as Trinh T. Minh-ha has written, even if it is not useful to construct a monolithic concept of the West, it is still useful to try to understand how and why the West has become monolithic to its others, and to acknowledge some of the ways in which this has come about by discussing notions of a 'Western ethos, about Western empires, European imperialism, or about the metropolitan West and its overseas territories' (1999, p. 48).

Saïd's other

Edward Saïd's work has sometimes been divided into two categories: academic and political, though it is difficult to maintain this distinction when all of the texts considered to be 'academic' (including *Orientalism* and *Culture and Imperialism*) show political commitment, and when the texts considered 'political' (for example, *The Question of Palestine* and *Covering Islam*) are, though sometimes conveyed passionately, constructed and researched in an academic manner. He was also a controversial figure, partly perhaps due to his willingness to step outside disciplinary boundaries and to use, for example, theory of music to formulate concepts related to colonialism and other historical and critical thinking. Perhaps he is considered controversial mainly because of his engagement with Palestine, which attracted criticism from different commentators for being either too politically involved or not political enough. This contradiction is an important one in understanding Saïd's position as an academic with a political agenda that is not limited or specific, but which aims to encourage a critical and a vigilant position in relation to ongoing regimes and discourses. Perhaps Saïd's position between a committed politics and academic thought is summed up neatly by his plea, in the concluding part of 'Orientalism Reconsidered', for a 'sharpened sense of the intellectual's role', without which, 'the critique of Orientalism is simply an ephemeral pastime' (2001, p. 215).

In an effort to convey the ongoing nature of Orientalist representation after colonialism, Saïd has discussed modern and contemporary film, and the continued representation of the Other, specifically the Arab, as 'an oversexed degenerate, capable, it is true, of cleverly devious intrigues, but essentially sadistic, treacherous, low' (1995, pp. 286–7). Trinh T. Minh-ha, well known for her film-making and her lengthy commentary in numerous interviews on her own films, has repeatedly stated that she has not been influenced by such representations and that her film-making is not, as has often been assumed by critics, a direct response to negative representations of the foreign other in Hollywood film. She has stated that before she left Vietnam and moved to America she had only a passing familiarity with Vietnamese film and had not seen any Hollywood films. It is interesting then, that she would choose to create radically challenging film on the subject of the West's others, that challenge both perceptions of those othered communities and film-making practices in general, especially documentary film.

Trinh T. Minh-ha's dissatisfaction with the 'other'

Saïd has noted that 'the Orient was routinely described as feminine, its riches as fertile, its main symbols the sensual woman, the harem, and the despotic – but curiously attractive – ruler' (2001, p. 212). This implies that the Orient was not actually feminine, that the other is not a feminine other, and in reversing Orientalist thinking to an extent excludes female experience of otherness. Perhaps this is one reason why Trinh T. Minh-ha has expressed dissatisfaction with the term 'other' as it has sometimes been represented by the West. Trinh has rejected the consignment of the Third World to a 'one-place-fits-all "other" category' (1991, p. 16). It is difficult to establish where the boundary between self and other should rest, in the context of globalization and the postcolonial diaspora: the centre and the margin merge so that there are 'margins within the center and the centers within the margin' (Trinh, 1991, p. 18). In this way, there are no regulations about who may represent whom; Trinh and Saïd agree on the point that it is unhelpful to suggest that only Africans may make film about African communities, only women may write about women, and so on. Trinh suggests that there can be no logical categorization to govern who can represent whom, asking whether such a boundary should be divided based on skin colour, language, nationality, geography, to say nothing of class, gender or sexuality. She also questions how such divisions can exist in relation to hyphenated identities and hyphenated realities (such as her own, as Vietnamese-American), and uses the example of racial reclassification in South Africa, where, following the end of apartheid, people were able to reclassify their racial identity, and did so in the thousands. For Saïd, a kind of 'possessive exclusionism' (2001, p. 215) determining who may represent whom is a problem which could undo the progress made by recent critical thinking; instead of imposing restrictions Saïd, like Trinh, calls for a greater crossing of boundaries in order to ensure a thorough questioning and dismantling of existing hierarchies. Trinh first states her objective to encourage boundary crossing in *When the Moon Waxes Red* (1991). In the introduction to this book, she discusses the way that the moon has been represented in separate critical and theoretical traditions, literary and cultural representations. Using the moon and moonlight as an image, Trinh points out the way that theory, ownership, hegemony, and so on, must always remain questionable: there can be no conclusive theory, no absolute ownership or insurmountable hegemony because there is always a transgression across boundaries, like the moonlight which shines on both sides of a geographical boundary. The moon, thus, cannot be conclusively theorized by anyone who chooses to attempt it because its light will always be accessible to anyone who can see.

Trinh's sense of otherness expresses a multiple and uncertain categorization and not a straightforward East/West duality. This multiple position occupied by the other involves, for Trinh, three identity categories that produce the othering that she experiences: being a non-Western or coming from the Third World, being a woman, and being a writer. Specific experiences led her to formulate the idea that the category of 'other' is unsatisfactorily broad and general: in *When the Moon Waxes Red*, Trinh describes the way that her written work was repeatedly rejected by those publishers who had actively sought Third World writers, when it did not match their preconceptions. Her manuscript was pushed further and further towards the margins by publishers who were seeking a formulaic representation of the Third World, and not a genuinely challenging text like hers, which questions the nature of academic writing by employing

metaphorical language and imagery along with an unusual style of presentation which, because of its particular use of secondary sources and
quotations does not always adhere to ordinary presentation conventions.
This is Trinh's most challenging contribution to the stylistic practices of
academic writing. Trinh weaves others' ideas with hers rather than using
the accepted method of referencing other scholars' work by including
quotation in quotation marks or an indented passage, and then commenting on and making use of, or developing the ideas presented to construct
a new argument. Trinh is not comfortable with the kind of transformation that Saïd's travelling theory describes, where the idea or source text is
employed for a specific purpose by the theorist who uses it in a new temporal or spatial context. This is why she uses a different stylistic method
that she calls speaking nearby or speaking *to*, rather than speaking *about*.
Speaking *about* someone or something, about another writer's idea or
about a story, involves, for Trinh, 'the conservation of systems of binary
opposition (subject/object; I/It; We/They)' which 'secures for the speaker
a position of mastery' (1991, p. 12). She is writing here about the way that
a story is retold, but the same principle is applied in her own academic
work when she places quotation in the midst of her own ideas without
making the expected full reference to that quotation. It is often presented
in a non-standard form: italicized, tagged on to paragraphs rather than
fully integrated, sometimes indenting multiple questions mid-argument.
The effect of this style is that the text on the page appears more like a conversation between many voices than a singular argument during which
support is employed from previously established sources. In speaking
to a text, story or scholar, the dualistic relationship between the speaker
and the other is broken down, and the impression produced is that the
other 'speaks-by-itself-through-me' (1991, p. 12) and the two are merged.
By extension, the other, for Trinh, is not as clearly identifiable as Saïd has
suggested. The other is not a repository for everything that 'we' dislike,
because there are too many similarities and too many connections. Trinh
has added to the term 'other' the prefix 'inappropriate/d', which renders
the other both 'someone whom you cannot appropriate' and 'someone
who is inappropriate' (2005, p. 125). This affords power to the other if they
cannot be appropriated, or controlled via either dominance or hegemony,
more power than Saïd allows the wholly demonized and vilified other.
The struggle for colonial domination and the colonial need to represent
remains, though: the other is 'inappropriate' (strange, unlike 'us') and so
there is a desire to appropriate and 'correct' them, to make them appropriate; this is an impossible desire in Trinh's terms.

Though she has written two renowned scholarly works, *Woman, Native, Other* (1989) and *When the Moon Waxes Red*, it is Trinh T. Minh-ha's films that really convey the full impact of her ideas. Her film scripts with stills from the films are available in textual form, along with interviews and other written pieces. It is interesting to note that though Trinh's films are only available in a very limited number of academic libraries and are not available to purchase commercially, her film scripts are available in books which can be found in most academic libraries and also to buy online. Perhaps there are reasons why it is more important for Trinh's work to be available in textual form. On the page, because of the way that the stills are presented alongside the script, it is clear to see the multiple angles from which images are presented: many subjects are presented on the page in multiple frames from separate angles and distances. Trinh's third film was *Naked Spaces: Living Is Round* (1985), filmed in a number of West African communities and featuring three female voice-overs, described in detail in a footnote accompanying the script. There is a low-range voice that has an assertive tone and quotes villagers' statements and sayings as well as quotation from African writers' works; a high-range voice that cites Western thinkers and expresses mainly Western logic; and a medium-range voice that speaks in the first person and relates personal feelings and observations (Trinh, 1992, p. 3). Though the three voices are, at the beginning, described as having distinct functions and purposes within the film, the boundaries blur as the film continues, so that sometimes the Western voice will repeat something that the African voice has said earlier, conveying Trinh's assertion made later in *When the Moon Waxes Red* that the centre and the margin reside within each other. Although the African voice in *Naked Spaces* is the only one that is meant to sound assertive, there is no sense that the film produces a simple reversal of colonial binaries where the formerly colonized is shown in a positive sense and the former colonizer appears negative. It is Trinh's intention to 'approach things indirectly' in order to create a resonance rather than seizing or grasping things (1999, pp. 33-4), and in this way avoiding any 'sureness of signification' (1992, p. 228) which could never, of course, be certain or sure as there is no single correct way to view a subject. The relationship is not a straightforward one between binary opposites of centre and margin or West and non-West, as the presence of three voices indicates immediately. The third voice is not so much a mediator between the other two voices. Instead, it appears to manifest when both supposed binaries are brought together and revealed to be part of each other. This speaks a denial of the binary process of othering by bringing together the explicitly colonial binaries as false creations of the colonizing process. By specifying African and Western voices, the reference to colonialism is clarified, though the film only very rarely and briefly dwells on particular colonial regimes; for example, the Western voice states that the Joola people of Benin are: 'renowned for having raised a fierce armed resistance to the French colonial administration at the start of the century' (Trinh, 1992, p. 41). The postcolonial context also remains in the background of *Surname Viet Given Name Nam* (1989), another film which straddles documentary and feature film categories and resists firm categorization, by including numerous reconstructed interviews with Vietnamese women, recreated using actors. The film brings together women's experiences of marriage and motherhood with state politics and glances internationally or comparatively, to show how women are exploited and demeaned at all levels. Though there is a clear colonial context for Vietnam, the film is more concerned with revealing the lives of women in contemporary Vietnamese society than in explicitly asking the women interviewed about their response to colonialism. At certain points, though, the women inevitably make reference to outside forces including 'French colonization, American presence, long war years' (Trinh, 1992, p. 67). The implicit references to colonialism in *Naked Spaces* continue in the way that the female body is conveyed. The ultimate colonial other, the veiled (or unveiled) woman, is a repeated emblem for the colonial othering process that was first conveyed by early imperial travellers in diaries and travelogues, including Mary Wortley Montagu's recollections of a harem visit where she was undressed and then veiled by harem women. Such letters and diaries were among the first supposedly documentary, or objective, studies of the Orient (or the other) made available to a Western audience.

Trinh and film

Trinh T. Minh-ha does not write standard academic texts. Her presentation style, her language, the structures of her texts and even their subject matter is not conventional for academic writing. Yet, she is a very highly regarded academic. With this apparent contradiction in mind, it is interesting to consider how Trinh has positioned her own work in relation to the dominant Western academy, and how she uses her particular position in order to critique dominant academic thought generally but also in order to construct a concept of the other which is not based on a duality of the kind that might be implied by Saïd's construction of the other, but which represents (at least) a triple identity, what she refers to as a triple bind, partly implied by the title of her widely read academic text, *Woman, Native, Other*. For Trinh, the position of other involves a negotiation between the three factors which make her 'other': her identity as a woman, as a 'native', and as a writer.

Edward Saïd's other is produced by the Western or the European gaze which, like the male gaze in feminist theory, affords authority to the gazer: the European is a detached and knowing watcher while the Orient is gazed upon. Trinh's film disrupts this Western gaze. Like Brecht's alienation effect which makes the constructed and unreal nature of theatre explicit for the audience, Trinh's film is constructed in such a way that the sense of realism conveyed by continuity editing is constantly disrupted. For Trinh, documentary is dehumanizing, exploitative like ethnology, so to move as far as possible from the hierarchical relationship between film-maker and subject, the interviews on which *Surname Viet Given Name Nam* is based are recreated, in part to avoid the exploitative relationship, but also to impose a sense of referentiality, which exposes the fictive nature of all film, all narrative, and all supposedly objective genres.

One of the ways in which Trinh disrupts realism is in the use of light. Lighting is ordinarily employed to create a realistic effect, or to convey mood: for example, deep shadows will be created when the plot requires drama or mystery, while false lighting is employed to mimic a summer's day, a sunset, candlelight, and so on. In *A Tale of Love* (1995), lighting is used in a way that makes the lighting as visible and prominent as the props and the actors. Bright streams of deep orange, blue, green and yellow light punctuate the set. As Trinh says, 'Neither being privileged, both actors and light become visible when the two cross each other's paths' (1999, p. 11). The character Kieu, sat on a futon, is a model and while the photographer moves her body around, bright strips of colour light up her face. In most of the stills produced alongside the film script in *Cinema Interval*, Kieu's mouth is shown in shadow while the rest of her face is lit with bold colour. Her appearance approximates the geisha (and, indeed, she calls herself a sex worker because her modelling requires her to be semi-naked), in a position of service, beauty and silence. This reading of the lighting implies that it conveys plot, but for Trinh, light conveys separate aspects of the narrative and is not subservient to a dominant narrative conveyed through directed actors. *A Tale of Love* is a kind of retelling of *Romeo and Juliet* but, instead of focussing on Shakespeare like many postcolonial retellings, Trinh is interested in the figure of Juliet and the nature of her relationship with Romeo. This story is opposed with the famous Vietnamese love story, *The Tale of Kieu*, written by early nineteenth-century poet Nguyen Du. Trinh notes that many Vietnamese people can recite the tale by heart, and describes how the story, which celebrates the female protagonist as a national hero, conflicts with patriarchal society which marginalizes women.

The idea that the European gazer is able to remain uninvolved, detached, as Saïd has noted, is something that Trinh exhaustively takes apart in her films, not just through the use of lighting but through all of her technical choices. Trinh objects to the fabricated reality created through documentary camera and editing techniques. One technique frequently employed to convey a sense of authenticity is the hand-held camera. A hand-held camera automatically suggests to the uncritical viewer that they are watching a genuine segment of reality, presented objectively and without ideological motivation on the part of the film-maker. This is clearly not the case: documentary film-makers have come between the subject and their audience by providing Western clothes for the naked native to normalize them, and on the opposite side of the scale, have thoroughly defamiliarized them by recording only the ritual-istic elements of native life: religious ceremonies, marriages and burials. This is something that Trinh actively resists, instead recording everyday interactions. Even on a small scale, documentary film-makers are highly selective about what is included in the frame, avoiding any signs of con-tact between the West and the community being recorded by refusing to film trains or cars, and removing plastic objects, such as toys and cook-ing utensils, even where those connections play a part of the inhabitants' daily lives. Yet, the untouched status of the native culture is belied by the very presence of the film-makers. Aside from inclusions and exclu-sions, the voice-over, editing and every aspect of presentation conveys the film-maker's ideology. In an effort to avoid possessing the subject and presenting it from her own particular perspective, Trinh makes use of a range of techniques which evade realism, foregrounding the pres-ence of the film itself, and of the cinematography and editing choices made. Her film uses:

> [j]ump-cuts; jerky, unfinished, insignificant pans; split faces, bodies, actions, events, rhythms, rhythmized images, slightly off the beat, discord; irregular colors, vibrant, saturated, or too bright; framing and re-framing, hesita-tions; sentences on sentences, looped phrases, snatches of conversations, cuts, broken lines, words; repetitions; silences; chasing camera; squatting position; a look for a look; questions, returned questions; silences.   (1991, pp. 56–7)

Repetition, in particular, is used as a transforming device which builds in nuances and differences so that repetition does not equate to reproduction, but instead is a 'production of the same with and in differences' (1992, p. 114). Of course, as Gerard Genette explains, there is no such thing as pure repetition; because of the context into which the repeated image or event is reproduced, each repetition is a response to its place in the narrative. Trinh uses repetition in this way especially in *Reassemblage* (1982), her first film. Snatches of conversation are repeated to help convey the musical quality of the Sereer language, and the subject is shown from a number of perspectives, repeating an image in order to explore various ways of seeing it. By announcing her own presence, placing herself within the film instead of at an assumed objective distance from it, Trinh achieves a more equal dialogue between filmed subject and film-maker, and works against an assumption of authenticity and objectivity which, for Trinh, can never exist. In fact, she states explicitly that 'there is no such thing as documentary', citing Alexander Kluge who claimed that the documentary is no more realistic than the feature film (Trinh, 1991, pp. 29, 39). Trinh's intention is to avoid what she calls an 'omnipresence' (1992, p. 113) that pervades many films, effacing the gaze of the film-maker in the objectivity that anthropological films attempt to convey.

Naked Spaces most directly attacks the notion of anthropological film. The subjective, mid-range voice (which is in fact Trinh's voice) stammers on the word 'anthropological' as is made clear in the printed script from the film: 'An anthropo … An anthropo … an anthropological shot: one that turns people into human species' (1992, p. 31). *Naked Spaces* also challenges the notion that documentary and feature films are distinct and that in terms of objective representation documentary film holds the higher position. This is achieved in the first place by conflating a documentary image with a poetic script. In the second place, it is achieved by questioning the notion of objectivity and by rejecting conventional documentary film techniques. *Surname Viet Given Name Nam* takes a further step away from documentary by performing previously published interviews. The printed editions of the scripts show that both films deal differently with the documentary question. *Naked Spaces* includes frames of different shapes and sizes carefully placed on the page, often repeating an image or showing a subject from a range of angles and distances. This compares with a much more mediated use of film stills in the *Surname Viet Given Name Nam* script. Here, the still is shown along with storyboard images and notes conveying the film-makers' carefully constructed frames.

Even the subject of *Naked Spaces* falls between drama and documentary: the published film script attributes to the Western voice a description of the funeral tradition in Togo:

> Funeral performances are referred to as plays; the house of the deceased being the stage, a group of skilful performers, the actors, and the villagers in attendance, the critical audience. Drums, flutes and horns are the voices of the ancestors. (Trinh, 1992, p. 18)

Rey Chow has also commented on the anthropological gaze in the context of mourning, with reference to the Chinese novel *Jia* (*Family*, 1931) by Ba Jin. The novel conveys scenes of mourning women with what Chow refers to as 'an unsympathetic anthropological gaze' which is 'quite typical of postimperialist systems of knowledge production' (2007, p. 567). The women's mourning is conveyed as farcical, wailing as tradition requires as new guests arrive, then halted as they realize what they can hear is in fact their guests departing. For Chow, the women's mourning ritual is represented in *Jia* as an 'exotic ethnographic find' (2007, p. 566). Anthropology has offered an imperfect anticolonial response, by attempting to 'rectify the master's colonial mistakes' (Trinh, 1992, p. 124), mistakes like casting Phillipino actors in films about Vietnam. However, this attempt to rectify previous problems by representing a culture authentically has led the field to insist upon rigid rules. Trinh is against imposing such rules, not just because they are restricting or even because such rules over how a film can be produced enable the kinds of hierarchical representation from the Western gaze, but more importantly, because they represent the filmed subjects as fundamentally different from and inferior to the Western viewer.

One example that Trinh provides is regarding rules over the music that can be used in anthropological film, which must be authentic in time and location to the subject in the frame: so, music performed by residents of Burkina Faso, for example, must not be used alongside pictures of Mauritania and in fact, the music must be shown being played in the situation on film and cannot be imposed non-diegetically. This might seem like a reasonable prescription, but Trinh reminds us that similar rules do not govern the way that subjects in European documentaries may be presented. She claims that the viewer can cope quite well with German classical music, for example, played over pictures of a British family. Of course, we could argue that European culture is more globalized: British families have more access to music produced elsewhere than the subjects of remote Third World communities. But if the intention of anthropological film is to produce complete authenticity, then the same rules should apply to all documentary, and not simply to documentary film about Third World communities. If they cannot be applied, perhaps documentary simply cannot produce authenticity.

The other point to remember about Trinh's exploration of the other through film is that this is not singularly the colonized (or formerly colonized) other. Trinh is also engaged in exposing the female other, and in *Naked Spaces* there is a critique of patriarchal African society as well as an exploration of the relationship between First and Third Worlds (Trinh's preferred terms, which approximately equate to Saïd's Orient and Occident when applied broadly). This is implied by the unequal conceptions of locating gendered beauty when the African voice states, seemingly contradictorily:

> It is beautiful because his fingers leave lines and his lines are visible
> If the woman plasters the walls such that from far away you don't see the different levels, we say the house is beautiful.   (Trinh, 1992, p. 21)

These quotations are taken from the published film scripts; publishing the scripts makes even clearer the contradiction that men's work is beautiful because of the imprint his hands have made while women's work is only beautiful if her efforts are invisible. Trinh conveys gender inequalities in Vietnam in a similar way. A visual parallel makes the contradiction clear in the film script of *Surname Viet Given Name Nam*:

> When he claps his hands, she has entertained.
> When she claps her hands, he has made a significant contribution – to his village, his town, his country. His fatherland, as they call it now.   (Trinh, 1992, p. 57)

The male/female inequality is also conveyed by the way that the film stills are presented on the page. For example, one page shows three large images of men in a warrior dance holding spears in very active poses. This is juxtaposed with a small picture of a woman in a passive pose with her face resting in her hand and a calm facial expression, glancing sideways. She is, though, in the way that her image is positioned on the page, seen as if she is looking away from the men and not towards them, to indicate more possibilities than a continuation of patriarchal culture. Even the title of *Surname Viet Given Name Nam*, derived from a saying, demonstrates the national oppression of women: a young woman is asked whether she is married yet, and she replies 'Yes, I am with husband, his surname is Viet and his given name is Nam' (Trinh, 1992, p. 51).

In her analysis of the other, Trinh explores the way that the native informant has been exploited by imperialist ideology. The native informant performs a mediating role in order to convey information to outsiders about the native culture and Trinh's work traces this figure in modern neocolonial relationships. In the process of recruiting a native inform-ant, the neocolonial produces a disciple, who can work for the neocolonial programme, 'asking the right kind of Question and providing the right kind of Answer' while also legitimizing the neocolonial project by lending it an authenticity, the 'seal of approval' of the other (Trinh, 1991, pp. 68–9). The native informant in this conception becomes an agent of the neoco-lonial and the native culture is not represented, but rather, infiltrated by the colonizer through the mediation of the native informant. The kind of knowledge that the native informant is expected to provide is, according to Trinh, always knowledge that the colonizer could anticipate, meaning that 'the other will always remain in the shadow of the self, hence *not-really-not-quite* "all-knowing"' (1991, p. 70). Rey Chow is similarly ambiv-alent about the native informant figure, specifically the native intellectual in a postcolonial situation, who will, she says, inevitably become 'a traitor to one's native culture' (2007, p. 570).

Rey Chow, language and the other

Chow explores translation, which is fundamentally connected to colonial and postcolonial thought. Edward Saïd suggested that in the colonial mindset, Islam was perceived as 'a fraudulent new version of some pre-vious experience, in this case Christianity' (1995, p. 59). This fraudulent new version – also expressed in broader terms by Saïd when he sug-gests that for the Westerner, the Oriental 'was always *like* some aspect of the West' (1995, p. 67) – resembles the colonial conception of trans-lation as an inferior copy. The colonies themselves were conceived as inferior translations of the 'mother' country. In the postcolonial context, Rey Chow has examined the representation of the other in the context of literature and translation. In 'Translator, Traitor; Translator, Mourner (or, Dreaming of Cultural Equivalence)' (2007), Chow suggests that in the postimperialist context novels like *Jia* represent one's own culture as other through the act of cultural reflexivity. Chow sees the narrator of *Jia* as a translator, in the sense that storytelling is a form of exchange during which the narrator/translator presents the story anew. This narrator/translator is 'intent on modernization' (2007, p. 569) and so disparages the traditional mourning scene as regressive. The figure of the translator is an important one for Chow in analysing the postcolonial context; she suggests that

> [b]y bringing to the fore issues of exchange, cultural inequity, and the reversal of temporally inscribed values normally conferred on original target languages/literacies in the process of translation, the figure of the translator thus helps sharpen the focus on problems of unevenness that are inherent to postcolonial intercultural encounters. (2007, p. 570)

Rey Chow notes that in the representation of the other from Asia or the 'Far East', the European intellectual 'must speak in absolute terms, making this other an utterly incomprehensible, terrifying, and fascinating spectacle' (1993, p. 33). But it is also an original European concept of the absolute other that Chow returns to in order to reinvigorate the postcolonial concept of the other which she suggests has become too limited and simplistic, confined to racial categories. Yet, the broadening of the concept of otherness has not always been welcomed by academia: Chow notes that the emergence of postcolonial thinking was not welcomed by feminist theory; many theorists experienced a kind of melancholia on learning that the woman is no longer the only other (1998, p. xviii). A diversified alterity also indicates clearly that otherness 'is hardly a unified essence', which has led to numerous hybrid notions (1998, pp. 3–4). Hybridity is most frequently associated with the condition of the postcolonial migrant, and the migrant is explored in the next chapter.

4 The Postcolonial Migrant

> Everything she valued had been upset by the change; had in this process of translation, been lost.
>
> Her language: obliged, now, to emit these alien sounds that made her tongue feel tired, was she not entitled to moan?
>
> Salman Rushdie, *The Satanic Verses*

In *The Satanic Verses*, Hind Sufyan, a Bangladeshi migrant living in London, bemoans the loss of her identity in the process of leaving her home and settling in a new place. This loss of identity is accompanied primarily by a loss of language, which further marks her detachment from everything she valued and understood. She is typical of the literary migrant who must unwillingly forsake their native tongue in order to speak a strange one inexpertly. Language has been a focus for critical attention in postcolonial analyses of migration within and outside literature. Colonial literature conveyed the ineffectual speech of the native, an impression reversed in an act of anticolonial literary revolt by writers like Chinua Achebe, who wrote the dialogue of his 'native' characters as a complex and contemplative language, in comparison with a fractured and awkward English spoken by the colonial authorities and their representatives. Rushdie's novel is one example of a literature of the postcolonial diaspora which takes as a major theme the difficulty of fitting into a new location when language creates a barrier. Each colonial encounter and each instance of postcolonial migration has involved a linguistic negotiation. This chapter will pay particular attention to the act of migration and especially its impact in terms of language, and will examine Frantz Fanon's analysis of the Antillean colonial context, Homi Bhabha's theories on migration, diaspora and hybridity, and Paul Gilroy's discussion of the black diaspora.

The Sapir–Whorf hypothesis

The idea that identity is lost with language in the act of migration seems to support the Sapir–Whorf hypothesis, a concept with origins in Edward Sapir's early twentieth-century theories of linguistic determinism. Sapir claimed that language and identity are fundamentally connected, and that language controls thought and identity. Benjamin Whorf took this idea further to claim that language does not just constrain thought, it shapes thought. According to this theory, people who speak different languages perceive the world differently. This implies a fundamental and permanent disjunction between different linguistic groups, and intractable problems for the migrant who must shape not only their language but also their world-view in order to function coherently as a postcolonial migrant. However, at the same time, the total reliance on language as a measurable manifestation of identity seems flawed. If the Sapir–Whorf hypothesis was entirely accurate, then a migrant who mastered the language of their adopted location would at the same time master its world-view and then achieve a sense of uncomplicated belonging. In the context of colonialism, this must always be a more problematic relationship because the spectre of colonial power cannot be sidestepped by an expert command of the colonizer's grammar. For Fanon, mastery of the colonizer's language by the colonized individual involves an adoption of the ideology associated with that language, but for most individuals, this remains complicated by an ongoing relationship with origins and the language of home. Fanon explores this problematic at length in *Black Skin, White Masks* (1986 [1952]), which has become a major text for postcolonial studies.

Fanon on language

In the first chapter of *Black Skin, White Masks*, 'The Negro and Language', Fanon states that 'to speak means [...] above all to assume a culture, to support the weight of a civilization' (1986, pp. 17–18). If a speaker is able to assume a culture by learning its language, then they become a member of that culture and adopt its ideology. This is expressed as a potentially dangerous position in Fanon's further claim that to speak a language is to support the weight of a civilization – this weight may be a heavy burden to bear in the colonial and postcolonial context. Fanon is writing about the specific situation of the French colonies in the Caribbean, the Antilles islands which form the majority of the West Indies. France had a particular approach to its colonial subjects in the Antilles; there were opportunities for Antilleans to study and work in France. This differed from the British colonial administration which placed more obstacles in the way of migration and naturalization in Britain. At the same time, though, the French policy demonstrates the belief that the French colonial ideology was superior, and the assumption that black Antilleans would inevitably choose to leave behind their language, place and culture in order to adopt a superior way of life in France. It is in this sceptical sense that Fanon uses the word 'civilization', a word which has been used by colonialism to claim permission for undertaking all kinds of violence. The French colonial believes that when the Antillean learns to speak French with native command the impact on his personality is wholly positive, while the black man perceives at some level that something about him is fundamentally flawed: 'The Negro of the Antilles will be proportionately whiter – that is, he will come closer to being a real human being – in direct ratio to his mastery of the French language' (1986, p. 18). For Fanon, colonial education and the dominant colonial ideology created a situation where the Antillean believed himself to be French, European, white, and not black like the African. The Antillean even perceived definite distinctions between his own skin colour and those of Africans where those distinctions were minimal or even absent. At the same time, then, the black Antillean believes himself to be not-black because of his European attitudes and his French language ability, while the colonial perspective reminds him that whiteness is synonymous with humanity. If his black skin, something that does not actually change with his grammar, makes him less of a human being in imperial eyes, then there is a serious disjunction between perception and reality which is not just a colonial prejudice, it is also a colonial racial prejudice which has been acquired by the black colonized subject. This is at the centre of Fanon's examination of mental illness or psychopathology in the colonial Antilles.

At this point, it may be useful to address Fanon's language which is conspicuous because of his use of the word 'negro' and his habit of discussing 'the negro' in masculine terms. Firstly, the term 'negro' will be an unfamiliar one for contemporary readers because it is no longer considered appropriate. The term 'negro' came to be associated with quasi-scientific racist ideologies, Social Darwinist ideas that suggested different races could be placed on a continuum of human development (where white Europeans represented the most advanced, and black Africans the most primitive) and that different races had inherent characteristics in terms of personality, morality, intellect, and so on. The term 'negroid', used in order to maintain these racist classifications and to endow these ideas with assumed scientific merit, was found in advertising, cartoons and other popular media as well as in pseudo-science. It identified the wildly exaggerated body of the black man or woman, often depicted in a highly sexualized form, or as animalistic and stupid. The term 'negro' (and sometimes 'nigger') was used in English translations of Fanon's work, translated from the French 'negre'. Fanon often used 'negre' ironically to respond to those who used the term pejoratively: this is clear when the words 'negro' and 'nigger' are repeated in a bombardment of insults and stereotypes at the beginning of 'The Fact of Blackness', Chapter 5 in *Black Skin, White Masks*.

Regarding gender, it is true that Fanon observed in the main the situation of black men and discussed black boys in colonial schools. In his introduction to *Black Skin, White Masks*, Homi Bhabha excuses Fanon from charges of sexism, saying that he uses the word 'man' to mean 'human', inclusive of man and woman. This position is not borne out by the fact that in *Black Skin, White Masks*, Fanon fails to make himself aware of the situation of women. This is displayed in his consistent use of masculine language: he, him, the man, and in his 'grossly reductive' description of white women and their sexuality (Sharpley-Whiting, 1998, p. 10). African-American feminist bell hooks calls Fanon sexist and patriarchal, and in addition, he has attracted criticism for his portrayal of the Algerian woman in 'Algeria Unveiled'. According to Ann McClintock, Fanon expresses patriarchal sentiments in his description of Algerian women's militancy in the revolutionary battle to imply that 'Algerian women are not self-motivating agents, nor do they have prior histories or consciousnesses of revolt from which to draw' but rather, 'women learn their militancy only at men's invitation' (in Gibson, 1999, p. 290). T. Denean Sharpley-Whiting collates these diverse feminist critiques of Fanon, and repudiates them collectively by reading his work in context. Sharpley-Whiting responds to the accusation made by Marie-Aimée Helie-Lucas that Fanon is 'myth-making' in his description of Algerian freedom fighters, by claiming that Fanon's work was based on experiential evidence and that both 'Algeria Unveiled' and 'The Algerian Family' are exemplary in this way, placing Fanon among 'the twentieth century's most progressive male modernist thinkers' in bringing together ethnicity, gender and sexuality (1998, pp. 73, 56). Fanon in these works showed that the French colonial missionary project in Algeria, which aimed to unveil the Algerian woman and claimed to be a feminist liberation movement, was in fact merely a controlling mechanism. Sharpley-Whiting similarly responds to Egyptian feminist Mervat Hatem's claim that Fanon was a conservative who saw women as defenders of tradition through wearing the veil by pointing out that when he discussed the female freedom fighters he did so in terms that presented the woman in a position of equality with the Algerian man. Describing rape as a form of colonial oppression and terrorism which had an impact on Algerian men as well as women is not necessarily evidence of a masculinist outlook; Fanon's supporters insist that this demonstrates his fundamental belief in the central and equal position of women in public, political Algerian society. On the other hand, Fanon does not make this point explicitly, so the question remains over why he described women's experiences through the gaze of the male-dominated society.

Fanon has also been criticized for the way that he engages with sexuality; Sharpley-Whiting refers to Fanon's homophobic 'revulsion' when one man describes another as sexually attractive. There is, to a good degree, an assumption of heterosexuality as normality in the way that Fanon expresses this. Fanon goes on to say with horror: 'Imagine a woman saying of another woman: "She's so terribly desirable"' (1986, p. 201). But this is delivered explicitly as an indignant response to Michel Salomon's racist assumption of the black man's 'aura of sensuality'. It is this assumed 'aura of sensuality' – something that Salomon claims to invoke either 'attraction or revulsion' in the white man – that in fact sparked Fanon's revulsion. He shows emotional, personal involvement with Salomon's text more than a prescriptive view of sexuality, expressed as it is through language which is at once a confession of his views and a way of admitting the offence he has taken at Salomon's work.

To return to the discussion of language, Fanon describes three aspects of the complex relationship between language and identity for the Antillean in the French colony. In the first instance, the colonized Antillean must acquire the language – and with it the identity – of the colonizer. Fanon suggests that this is a factor of life for all colonized people:

> Every colonized people [...] finds itself face to face with the language of the civilizing nation; that is, with the culture of the mother country. The colonized is elevated above his jungle status in proportion to his adoption of the mother country's cultural standards.   (1986, p. 18)

This 'jungle status' is attributed to the colonized by the colonizer. A programme of intense, ideologically motivated education was put in place in the Antilles, and this, in conjunction with the fact that the former slaves had been taken from Africa and separated from any original sense of place or identity, meant that people grew up to feel as if they lived in an extension of the European motherland. Black Antilleans in the army would identify themselves as European when placed between the Europeans and the Africans in the Senegalese infantry regiment. It was mastery of the French language which afforded power in the army, where Antillean soldiers would perform interpreter roles, conveying orders to the regiment.

Confident command of the French language was put to the ultimate test when the Antillean left the colony and went to live in France. Creole was the common language of the Antillean, which developed from the French patois spoken for specific purposes of trading and working in earlier generations. Though Creole is nowadays recognized as a language in its own right and is experiencing a resurgence in the Caribbean, where it is being taught in schools alongside French and English, at one time it was ridiculed, especially in France where Fanon suggests it was considered 'a halfway house between pidgin-nigger and French' (1986, p. 20). A deep-seated fear of speaking incorrectly leads to a modification of both language and behaviour when the Antillean moves to France. Self-conscious of the potential language crimes he might commit, he will demonstrate hypercorrection:

> The Negro arriving in France will react against the myth of the R-eating man from Martinique. He will become aware of it, and he will readily go to war against it. He will practice not only rolling his R but embroidering it. (1986, p. 21)

Fanon has already established that language and identity are fundamentally connected, so this 'war' against the self demonstrates the ease with which psychological problems can develop from migration. The Antillean migrant is careful to use only the French language in order to demonstrate the distance they have travelled from their origin. As a result, Fanon suggests, the black man who has lived in France for a length of time returns radically changed: 'he answers only in French, and often he no longer understands Creole' (1986, p. 23). To an extent, the community is party to this change and considers the returned man as master of the French language and culture, as embodied proof that the Antillean can equal the French. Hailed as an oracle by the community, high expectations are placed on him and one revelation that he has not seen or done something that the community expects and values about France renders him a joke forever. The newly returned Antillean is placed in a precarious position of cultural representative, and as mediator between the colonizer and the colonized, a position that Fanon suggests is replicated in all contexts of colonial migration.

Fanon's migrations

Fanon's tendency to produce emotive responses to writings about race and to provide personal anecdotes in order to support his ideas points to his own position as migrant. His theories are now applied globally, a recognition that is problematic for some, including Homi Bhabha, who resents the use of Fanon's work outside its intended remit. He suggests that Fanon's work was never intended as a supplement to Marxist thinking, and that the use of Fanon's ideas to bolster general and unspecified calls to end exploitation of all kinds is unsatisfactory. In his foreword to *Black Skin, White Masks*, Bhabha makes a distinction between socialism and Fanon's theories, though, suggesting that Fanon is employed by socialism to convey ideas of generalized 'resistance' or moral outrage when, in his opinion, socialism as an organized movement does not adequately address questions of gender or race but subsumes them into a broader class struggle which does not recognize the nuances and categories in a global society. However, Fanon's main concern in *The Wretched of the Earth* is to reject capitalism and hierarchical structures in any guise, seeing the emergence of 'tribal dictatorship' in newly independent parts of Africa as equivalent to previous colonial or 'bourgeois dictatorship' (1967, p. 147).

Commenting on Fanon's work on Africa, Henry Louis Gates Jr notes that Fanon is sensitive of his dislocation from the Third World, and observes that he underwent the same transformation from European to black West Indian in France that he has observed in others. He goes on to suggest that many Algerian revolutionaries are 'irritated by the attention paid to him in the West as a figure in Algerian decolonization: to them [...] he remained a European interloper' (1986, p. 264). This is again attributable in part to language; when Fanon worked as a psychiatrist in Algeria and Tunisia, he did not understand the language and conducted his consultations through an interpreter (Gibson, 1999, p. 264). However, Fanon's position as migrant contributed to his position as a global theorist, in line with his vision of a kind of universalist humanism: concluding *The Wretched of the Earth*, he suggests a rejection of specificities, European or otherwise, in order to embrace new challenges for the human condition, mankind, collaboration between men and the improvement of humanity (1967, p. 252). His migrations also enabled him to theorize that position in the context of Algeria Bhabha has implied in *The Location of Culture*, where he insists that

> Fanon's vision of revolutionary cultural and political change as a 'fluctuating movement' of occult instability could not be articulated as cultural practice without an acknowledgement of this indeterminate space of the subject(s) of enunciation. (2004, p. 55)

Fanon and psychopathology

As a psychiatrist, Fanon's concern with language and identity was in the context of psychopathology. Fanon's proposition is that the uncertainty of identity arising from the mastery of a new language has a direct impact on the psyche. He also asserts that this is a direct result of the unstable sense of identity formulated in the colonial West Indies, which differs from the colonial encounter in other places, where there was an existing, long-established language and culture; the Caribbean was, of course, different as the colonization of that territory involved bringing African slaves from all over the continent to work on plantations, and the descendents of those slaves formed the communities but had only a ruptured history to look back on, and the new common language of Creole, developed in the context of slavery. There is a contrast with other colonies, such as India. Initially, India was governed using existing laws, enabled by expert Orientalist translators like William Jones (discussed in Chapter 3 of this book). After Macaulay's Minute of 1835, an official edict which insisted that all education should thenceforth be conducted through the medium of the English language and using English literature, the aim was to instil a notion of British superiority and to ignore South Asian literature, art and history in favour of the study of European alternatives. The English education process thereby operated in a resistant relationship with South Asian history and culture. For the black Antillean, in the first generations after the Atlantic slave passage, there was no single, solid cultural position from which to resist French education, meaning the black West Indian schoolchild grew up with a white European sense of self which was contradicted by black skin and a distant yet shared heritage with the black African. This was compounded by an unequal relationship between races, based on a prejudice that Fanon defines as an inferiority complex developed in the black Antillean and a sense of dependency upon the white European expounded by the colonizer. For Fanon, psychoanalysis offers an opportunity to address socially motivated pathologies in both black and white people.

In tone, *Black Skin, White Masks* does not always read like a political manifesto, an academic study, or a psychological enquiry, though it is to a certain extent all of those things. Fanon discards a rigid methodological framework in favour of an uninhibited observational style. In so doing, he implies that established methods are counterproductive if they demand working within rigid frameworks in order to address a new question. He also rejects rigidity in terms of writing structure, employing a personal, poetic style from the beginning of the book, when he outlines the vicious circle that he wishes to eliminate:

> There is a fact: White men consider themselves superior to black men.
>   There is another fact: Black men want to prove to white men, at all costs, the richness of their thought, the equal value of their intellect.
>   How do we extricate ourselves?   (1986, p. 12)

The first three chapters deal with black people in 'the white world' as a result of migration, usually enforced by a heritage of slavery. Having observed black psychology in Martinique, he explains that identity is so seriously affected by the colonial encounter that 'it is in fact customary in Martinique to dream of a form of salvation that consists of magically turning white' (1986, p. 44). For women, he explains, this takes two forms: for black women there is a desire to 'turn white' but for the 'mulatto' who believes that she exists between black and white culture and skin pigmentation, there is an additional fear of 'slipping back' into black skin and black identity (1986, p. 54). Fanon describes his surprise and sadness when black women he meets deny their black skin and identity in favour of a European identity that they perceive as separating them entirely from the idea of blackness which they have learned from colonial stories, a blackness constructed of 'tom-toms, cannibalism, intellectual deficiency, fetishism, racial defects, slave-ships, and above all else, above all: "Sho' good eatin"' (1986, p. 113). Again in this example, language, or an assumption of the black person's inferior command of language, is oppressive.

In a chapter entitled 'The Negro and Psychopathology', Fanon draws a distinct parallel between the white European and the black Antillean, suggesting that in Europe the structure of the nation is paralleled in the structure of the family, so the family represents the nation in microcosm. This results in the child replicating his parents' values and customs and repeating those principles in order to maintain the stability of that society (1986, pp. 141–2). Fanon goes on to state that, if the child has a normal family, they will grow up to be normal, yet if they grow up in a family of criminals, the child would either grow up a criminal, or grow up insane. The same does not apply to the black child, though: 'a normal Negro child, having grown up within a normal family, will become abnormal on the slightest contact with the white world' (1986, p. 143). This is because his actual body is in conflict with the way that he has been taught to think about his body, and also because of the way that the white world perceives the black individual in the early and mid-twentieth century: as somebody to be feared or derided. Fanon employs the idea of *collective catharsis* to account for the psychology of the black individuals he meets who have not had any specific negative experience in the white world, but who are yet burdened with a pathological racial identity. The sense of burden is employed contentiously by Fanon who may again nowadays face charges of intolerance or bigotry – in the same way that he has been accused of homophobia and misogyny in response to his treatment of women and sexuality – when he refers to a particular anecdote in relation to an amputee:

> The crippled veteran of the Pacific war says to my brother, 'Resign yourself to your color the way I got used to my stump; we're both victims.' [Chester Himes, 1945]
>
> Nevertheless with all my strength I refuse to accept that amputation. I feel in myself a soul as immense as the world [...] I am a master and I am advised to adopt the humility of the cripple. (1986, p. 140)

Fanon suggests that there is no hope for the disabled man, that the impenetrable barrier between him and the world of power is inevitable whereas the only impediment for the black man is opportunity. Opportunity is constrained by the dependency complex, the notion that the white man is acting from a position of authority, safe in the knowledge that he is doing what is best for the black man, who is in need of the white man's superior knowledge and guidance because of his unassailable dependency. The only response to this dependency complex is a destructive, or self-destructive, one: 'the Negro is a toy in the white man's hands; so, in order to shatter the hellish cycle, he explodes' (1986, p. 140). A symbolic explosion, or elsewhere, a rebirth – 'Blood! Blood! ... Birth! Ecstasy of becoming!' (1986, p. 125) – allows Fanon to negotiate a hopeful outcome despite the pressure that existed between races in the mid-twentieth century, in a context which included racial segregation in the United States and apartheid in South Africa. He ends *Black Skin, White Masks* with a message of positivity. He asserts his independence and his power, saying, 'I am not the slave of the Slavery that dehumanized my ancestors' (1986, p. 230). He calls for an equality that puts aside and therefore defeats the past, claiming that both the black and the white man must surpass their ancestors and communicate anew. This requires work, effort of an intellectual kind – at the end of the book he pleads with the reader to become a person 'who questions!', the imperative tone indicating that an ability to question equals a power to change.

Bhabha and hybridity

If 'cultural difference emerges from the borderline moment of translation' (Bhabha, 1990, p. 314), the borderline is above all a linguistic one. The nation itself is connected with a language, a 'unisonant discourse' (1990, p. 315), which is disturbed by migrants (and minorities, and colonials and postcolonials: the particular kind of migration undertaken is as ambivalent as its effect). These migrants reveal and also embody 'a shifting boundary that alienates the frontiers of the modern nation' (1990, p. 315). This idea of the shifting or ambivalent boundary, and of a sustained sense of ambivalence in general, is fundamental to Bhabha's concept of hybridity as a mechanism by which the alienated subject is enabled to challenge oppressive authority (2004, p. 162).

The postcolonial concept of hybridity has been developed at length by Homi Bhabha. Although the term has been defined and disputed by others, including Robert Young who highlights the term's origins in colonial racist discourse (1995), it is Bhabha's definition which has been most prominent in shaping current thinking. Hybridity is a response that destabilizes colonial fixity and rigidity. Bhabha insists that hybridity does not assume a comfortable coming together of colonizer and colonized or any other binary oppositions. The concept is not employed in order to reduce tension, which might have the effect of justifying colonial interventions, but instead it intends to increase tension. This increase in tension is required in order to create a crisis for systems of authority which depend upon their ability to ascribe a kind of sense to colonialism. One method by which colonial authority has been normalized is through the idea of cultural relativism. Cultural relativism accepts cultural differences by showing that different practices, laws, moral ideas, and so on are 'normal' in their separate cultures. However, cultural relativism can only be understood if cultures remain entirely separate and do not affect each other. For Bhabha, the ability to see cultures as fully separate and to insist that specific practices are fundamental features of a particular, isolated culture have been used to justify colonial interventions: if a particular culturally isolated group practices (or is rumoured to have once practiced) something that the colonial authority recognizes as immoral, then the colonial power can claim that they are justified in intervening to prevent that supposedly normalized cultural practice through their civilizing mission. A linguistic example would involve the adoption of common words by both colonizer and colonized: pidgins and creoles arise due to the contact of different linguistic groups. An English-based creole will use some English words and others developed according to the situation and the other linguistic characteristics of the group. In the Caribbean, the two languages – English and Creole – will operate separately, although some speakers are able to speak both. Between the two languages is an area that is not distinct from either but within which the third space operates: those speakers who can speak both languages inhabit that third space: Jamaica Kincaid, for example, in her memoir *My Brother*, notices that her brother speaks to her in Standard English while he uses Creole with others. Similarly, when words are shared by speakers of both languages, the sense of certain separation between them is broken. Colonial intervention is rendered questionable by hybridity, as colonial authority rests upon rigidity and certainty.

In *The Location of Culture*, Bhabha claims that imperialistic control over culture can be transformed by hybridity. In practical terms, this might mean articulating cultural authority through 'forms of "native" knowledge' (2004, p. 164), for example, perhaps, by employing native languages, texts, and laws, to govern a native people. Bhabha's concept of hybridity can be applied to the use of South Asian laws in India by the British colonial authority. Although the British colonial regime intended to exercise total authority over India and decided that the most effective means of doing this might be through the use of existing laws which colonial translators accessed in Sanskrit documents, in fact their position of authority was challenged by this. Bhabha does not employ the concept of hybridity to contexts like this one in order to suggest that the colonial project was less harmful or in any way to justify it. He employs hybridity in order to challenge the colonial position, to expose its weaknesses and to render questionable and flawed any attempt at justifying colonial interventions based on cultural concepts. He writes:

> The voice of command is interrupted by questions that arise from these heterogeneous sites and circuits of power [...]. The paranoid threat from the hybrid is finally uncontainable because it breaks down the symmetry and duality of self/other, inside/outside. (2004, p. 165)

Bhabha draws attention, too, to the places where hybridity can be found: not just at the peripheries of geographical borderlines, in texts and laws drawn from multiple sources, on maps that reveal the influences in the naming of locations, but also inside, within, for example, the body of the 'coloured' South African who reveals a 'difference "within"', and inhabits 'an "in-between" reality' (2004, p. 19). The 'coloured' South African is used by Bhabha in response to Nadine Gordimer's literary representation of relationships between black, coloured, and white South Africans, and in this sense reveals the space between black and white which is not absolute but reveals one instance of their conjunction, their hybrid state, which undermines any sense of absolute or 'pure' cultural contact: the very presence of a 'coloured' population or individual belies any sense of absolute separation between black and white cultures. The hybrid space is also revealed, in the South African body represented in the domestic literary text, to be present not just in formal and public spaces but also in very domestic ones, which renders them 'unhomely' (2004, p. 19): terrifying and yet familiar because they represent both the homely and familiar, and at the same time the way that the homely can become unhomely, that the homely can be taken away and rendered terrifying. One domestic image Bhabha uses to represent the hybrid is the stairwell. The stairwell as a liminal space with its 'hither and thither' movement 'prevents identities at either end of it from settling into primordial polarities' (2004, p. 5). The stairwell connects two supposed opposites (upstairs and downstairs and all the potential class and race opposites that they might contain) and, where they are connected they are necessarily made a part of each other. Thus, notions of 'purity' in any context are rendered untenable by hybridity. Of course, this is the sense of hybridity as applied to the colonial context and not to the postcolonial diaspora. Migrants in the colonial context include colonial agents and military forces. Hybridity has an ongoing impact on the subjects of colonized and formerly colonized locations that might be most visible when those subjects migrate away from the colonial location and towards the metropolitan centre.

When hybridity is encountered in the context of the postcolonial diaspora, it has a somewhat different authority to challenge, and Bhabha discusses this in response to *The Satanic Verses* and the visible presence of the Indian migrant in London:

> The migrant culture of the 'in-between', the minority position, dramatizes the activity of culture's appropriation beyond the assimilationist's dream, or the racist's nightmare, [...] and towards an encounter with the ambivalent process of splitting and hybridity that marks the identification with culture's difference. (2004, p. 321)

Hybridity means that the migrant cannot be assimilated and made invisible in London, but neither are they ejected in a racist othering process. Instead, the migrant reveals the hybridity of Britain as a culture made up of multiple cultural identities, and this multiplicity exists within the individual.

The process of migration, Bhabha argues, means that it is difficult to clearly identify concepts like nation, peoples, authenticity and tradition, but at the same time this 'makes you increasingly aware of the construction of culture and the invention of tradition' (2004, p. 248). Culture is not something that can be scientifically identified, or that an individual must rigidly adhere to, and this position is consistent with Paul Gilroy's similarly ambivalent engagement with black British culture and some attempts to fix cultural identity rigidly, whatever that might entail for the black British woman who is not, after all, 'purely' Jamaican, for example, if she was born in Britain to Jamaican parents, and has an earlier African heritage. Even more clearly than the example of British colonial employment of local languages and laws, the black British identity reveals the impossibility of locating a pure culture in a postcolonial context and after any instance of migration. For Bhabha, this is a 'transnational' phenomenon which he connects with the 'translational' to again insist on the imperative function of language in identity formation after migration, but also to point out that in migration, what he terms a 'cultural translation' takes place. Just like a text which is translated and therefore reveals the traces of both original source and translated target language and culture, the individual who migrates is translated into a new place and operates through a new language, becoming a translated individual bearing traces of both locations and languages.

The translational phenomenon has an impact on the nation as well as on the migrant:

> Once the liminality of the nation-space is established, and its 'difference' is turned from the boundary 'outside' to its finitude 'within', the threat of cultural difference is no longer a problem of 'other' people. [...] The national subject splits in the ethnographic perspective of culture's contemporaneity and provides both a theoretical position and a narrative authority for marginal voices and minority discourse. (Bhabha, 1990, p. 301)

In this extract from 'DissemiNation', Bhabha points out that the nation-space is an ambivalent one, constructed from multiple identities. If this is the case, the nation can never be perceived as whole or pure, but always as a hybrid space. The concept of otherness or 'difference' is not about protecting borders to keep the nation 'pure' of outside influences; instead, it becomes necessary to accept that the nation is constructed from otherness, in the contemporary, global, postcolonial context where communities are affected by colonial and postcolonial migrations. Because of that, he suggests, there is a position for minority voices. For Bhabha, once the concept of the migrant is established, once the nation has been changed by its incorporation of migrants, even, perhaps, once the nation has been changed by its migrating citizens (including colonial agents and British convicts transported to colonial Australia, for example), there is no longer a straightforward relationship between self and other. The other is within the self literally because the self – the nation as a whole – is constructed from multiple individuals and ideas, some of which are 'other', and also because the relationships between nations are altered by migration. This extends today into globalization and neocolonialism: in what sense can a British company or organization really be said to be British, for instance, when its products or suppliers or customer service representatives are located elsewhere?

Questions of cultural theory

As Leela Gandhi has pointed out, postcolonialism is not unique in its desire to rethink imperialism: Marxist thinking is especially prolific here. Postcolonial theories have developed alongside other intellectual concepts and the intersections between postcolonial theories and philosophy can be traced back to the Kantian notion that man is enabled by the Enlightenment into adult rationality, a position that Gandhi notes simultaneously sets up the hierarchical relationship between an imperialist adulthood and the 'childish, colonised Other' (1998, p. 32). The particular kind of dialogue continued between postcolonial theorists and Western philosophy is frequently an area of attention. While both Frantz Fanon and Paul Gilroy develop their work in the context of material reality in concrete social contexts, Bhabha responds to and extends theoretical concepts from a more abstract position. Bhabha uses Derrida and Freud, Fredric Jameson and Jacques Lacan, and has been criticized for doing so by some who see this as employing Western thinkers and European theoretical models in a way that potentially re-colonizes the postcolonial within Western systems of thought, rather than rejecting those positions in favour of the development of a new theoretical model. It is perhaps important to point out straight away that Derrida in particular was committed to exploding phallocentric (male-centred) and logocentric (implying a notion of a unified centre and a guaranteed meaning) and, by extension, Eurocentric systems of thought, in his philosophy. But in any case, Bhabha's concept of hybridity itself refutes this criticism: hybridity would point out that there can be no purely Western theoretical form, and neither can a non-Western theorist be expected to operate entirely outside of Western intellectual thought in a postcolonial context. When Bhabha applies a theoretical framework that could be loosely termed Western, he challenges and adopts that theoretical position and in doing so, reveals its hybridity. Bhabha compares interdisciplinarity with cultural difference, suggesting it too is hybrid, and 'never simply a question of the admixture of pre-given identities or essences' (1990, p. 314). However, it might be insufficient as a response to those critics of Bhabha's use of Western theories to use his own theory stubbornly against them. So perhaps it is more important to remain alert to the origin of theories and to the way that they are used in order to maintain a committed response to colonialism. Likewise, it is important to be aware of the encounter which has created a context where an Indian intellectual feels the most appropriate theoretical model to use is one with largely Western origins. More broadly, Bhabha insists on the continued use of theory, suggesting that it is damaging and self-defeating to assume that theory is an elite language available to the privileged, and that 'the place of the academic critic is inevitably within the Eurocentric archives of an imperial or neocolonial West' (2004, p. 28). Such a position would imply either that there is no place in academia for the non-European, or that theory must be set aside by black intellectuals until all black citizens have the basics required to sustain life, a position that bell hooks has rejected in her essay 'Postmodern Blackness'. Hooks is talking about an American context, and writes in response to those who suggest that while black people are unemployed and living on welfare, it is the responsibility of the black intellectual to address those fundamental needs even if that means abandoning the abstract, the postmodern, the theoretical. She insists that it is racist and myopic to assume that black intellectuals have no position within the specific academic debates which are often considered more abstract, and to assume that black engagement with these fields will have no impact on the 'real life' of black Americans.

This is an ongoing debate which is still applied vocally in postcolonial studies because of the specific focus of postcolonial thinkers on the marginalized and unrepresented, but Bhabha insists on what he calls a commitment to theory, a phrase which is also the title of the first main chapter of *The Location of Culture*. Bhabha's main point is that theory itself raises such questions. He asks: what should theory actually be committed to? Radical theories which include Marxism and feminism as well as postcolonialism share a sense of activism and a desire to reveal the voice of the marginalized, and these theories create the theoretical questions about what those theories should do. Thus, 'the function of theory within the political process becomes double-edged' (Bhabha, 2004, p. 38). Radical theory does not function outside real world concerns, but neither is its function simply to solve an identified social problem. Theory has a commitment to reveal inequalities; to stop theoretical work and redirect attention towards practical activity would mean that even if one social problem could be fixed, others might remain dormant. Bhabha's view actually reflects what has taken place within postcolonial studies: instead of standing still, it has deepened, to reflect multiple aspects of identity and continues to grow to consider the impact of technology, globalization, the body, queer identity, and to encounter multiple textual forms.

Gilroy's conviviality

Paul Gilroy approaches the migrant condition through the conception of a black Atlantic world. This involves both the interconnected diaspora status of black people worldwide, and the interconnected nature of black and white histories, and where histories are connected, the ensuing construction of modernity is likewise connected. This is an important distinction from previous thinking about the impact of black people as somehow separate from European modernity. Gilroy works to undermine the often-repeated false insistence that national, racial or ethnic groups were, both at the time of colonization and afterwards, entirely distinct. The concept recalls the triangular Atlantic passage involving European travel to Africa, where black people were taken as slaves to the Caribbean, so that goods produced by slaves could be shipped back to Europe. The points of this triangular route across the Atlantic are re-enacted by black intellectuals who travel, literally and metaphorically, between the Caribbean and America, Europe and Africa. This travelling has given rise to what W.E.B. Du Bois first termed 'double consciousness', an awareness of being both inside and outside the 'West'. Gilroy works with examples taken largely from black British history and culture, and crucially, he has considered the culture of black Britain as something that develops alongside global black diaspora rather than as a discreet cultural entity within Britain. He explains that Black Britain draws cultural inspiration from other black populations, especially in America and the Caribbean. The creative processes are adapted to British experiences and meanings, and during this process, 'Black culture is actively made and remade' (1987, p. 154).

Gilroy expresses his discomfort with the term 'diaspora' in its most usual postcolonial form which tends to focus on national identity. Nationality is an inadequate category for representing the black diaspora because of the complex national identity that is understood by a British-born black person: though one individual might identify themselves as British and of Jamaican heritage, their ancestral migration connects them not only with Jamaica and Africa, but also with an earlier Europe that instigated that first migration, and also with America where other black individuals share similar histories. Gilroy's ideas have pushed postcolonial studies to rethink concepts of nation and diaspora and to reconsider the binaries through which black and white cultural encounters – and by extension, all colonial encounters – have been presented. In *The Black Atlantic* (1993), Gilroy addresses the etymological and cultural development of the term diaspora, and makes an explicit connection between black and Jewish diasporas, suggesting that both black nationalist thought and modern Zionism share aspirations and rhetoric. He shows how the two diasporas share themes of dispersal, exile, and slavery and notes that writing about Jewish culture and policy has been instrumental in the development of his thinking about identity in the black Atlantic diaspora:

> the concept of diaspora can itself provide an underutilised device with which to explore the fragmentary relationship between blacks and Jews and the difficult political questions to which it plays host: the status of ethnic identity, the power of cultural nationalism, and the manner in which carefully preserved social histories of ethnocidal suffering can function to supply ethical and political legitimacy. (1993, p. 207)

Gilroy points to the awkward ways in which contemporary diaspora black culture has been addressed, identifying two separate approaches. The first, which he defines as an ontological essentialist approach, intends to 'correct' black culture by 'recovering and then donating the racial awareness that the masses seem to lack', as demonstrated by its not-quite-black-enough hair styles, clothing and lifestyle choices (1993, p. 32). This approach assumes a uniform black culture when such a thing is clearly ridiculous remembering that, taking Britain as an example, black people are not only divided by things like class, age, gender and politics but also by their ethnic backgrounds: Gilroy is suspicious of an approach which implies that people of diverse Caribbean and African backgrounds, with various religions and languages, whether or not they have been born in Britain, have identical cultural identities. The alternative approach Gilroy terms 'libertarian' and 'strategic'. This second analytical position recognizes the 'polyphonic qualities of black cultural expression' (1993, p. 32), while presenting race as a social and cultural construction. In other words, it does not see race as a fixed or essential aspect of identity, but sees it instead as a way of approaching identity that has its foundation entirely within the specific society in which it is perceived. Gilroy is more positive about this approach, seeing merit in its focus on the impact of black creativity on society and on black identity. However, he remains dubious about its potential to fully address the contemporary experience of black diaspora because it invites an approach which ignores race, and in its idealism might not fully acknowledge the ways in which race is sometimes seen as a primary signifier of identity. To diminish the importance of race in identity constructions in this way is to assume that race is never an issue in society. Gilroy sees potential in both approaches, but a problem in the unresolved conflict between them, and seeks a third way to approach black diaspora identity.

Gilroy includes a chapter on black music in *The Black Atlantic*, an area that he has also explored in earlier works and in his most recent *Darker than Blue* (2010) where he discusses the impact of globalization and technology on rap and hip hop. Here, Gilroy notes that the global export of rap as an emblem of American culture has been accelerated by digital and internet technologies which enable people to create and distribute their own music videos worldwide, outside the control of corporate media and music distributors. Gilroy's strategy of demonstrating theory through relevant, 'real-world' examples, in conjunction with his experiences of teaching in a city polytechnic, perhaps demonstrates why many postcolonial scholars and students embrace Gilroy's work while they are more resistant towards Bhabha. Both deal with hybridity, but Gilroy's writing is more accessible and perhaps more persuasive, in part because his examples are taken from popular culture. Gilroy explores cultural conjunctions in music, music's 'doubleness', its 'unsteady location simultaneously inside and outside the conventions' (1993, p. 73). Music is not just a product of modern society, but it also directly challenges traditions and can be read as modernist, too. Edward Saïd has also used music (see Chapter 3 of this book), employing the terminology of classical music to theorize a postcolonial way of reading as 'contrapuntal', or plural. This connection provides a point of comparison between the two theorists: while Saïd attempts to rethink abstract, broad academic thought and ways of producing meaning and thinking through musical terminology, Gilroy approaches black British music to rethink the way that academic and other intellectual and social systems have tried to represent black diaspora identity. However, Gilroy is aware of the problematics of using music to convey identity. He states that 'the hybridity which is formally intrinsic to hip hop has not been able to prevent that style from being used as an especially potent sign and symbol of racial authenticity' (1993, p. 107). Racial authenticity is an essentially exclusive way of categorizing identity, which counters Gilroy's major position that identity is not so straightforward, a position that he sees as entrenched within the academy as well as in society in general. Gilroy claims that English and African-American versions of cultural studies share conceptual problems because of their nationalistic focus, which 'is antithetical to the rhizomorphic, fractal structure of the transcultural, international formation', the Black Atlantic (1993, p. 4).

The rhizome has been addressed most famously by Deleuze and Guattari in *A Thousand Plateaus* (1987). The rhizome is related to but different from a root, which for Deleuze and Guattari forms the comparative object. The root implies a certain and fixed origin, while the rhizome is multiple and can form connections in many ways: a potato is a rhizome, for example. Once planted in the ground, the potato develops multiple chits which develop into a stem and underground side shoots, from which new potatoes grow. A tree has a root, and the spread of root below the tree is replicated in the tree above, which creates a very different image from the potato plant. Deleuze and Guattari apply this comparison to language and to the book, to claim that language is not fundamentally connected to experience like a tree is to its root, and that a book is not an image of the world, but instead, both language and the book evolve separately from the world rather than in a relationship of mimicry. Gilroy's interest in roots and rhizomes developed in response to Du Bois's theory of double consciousness, first presented in *The Souls of Black Folk* (1903). Du Bois fostered a thorough immersion within and understanding of Western culture in order to enable him to demonstrate the place that blacks occupy within that culture. Gilroy extends Du Bois's insistence on a 'twoness' in the black American to the experience of post-slave populations worldwide.

Gilroy rejects the certainty implied by the notion that black and white histories and experiences are fundamentally separate. He is equally ill at ease with the terms that have been developed as a way to explain the coming together of black and white experiences and bodies, like creolization, métissage, mestizaje, and hybridity. In these terms he sees a dangerous implication of 'pollution', and claims that as they stand, they are inadequate for explaining the ways that people have influenced each other. Gilroy's attempt to address these inadequate terms involves the use of perception words – 'stereophonic', 'bilingual', 'bifocal' (1993, p. 3) – words that imply an equal conjunction of separate yet complete ways of hearing, speaking and seeing, and words that are ordinarily associated with more abstract or objective fields. These replace the more familiar terms like métissage and creolization which have come to be associated with undesirable mixed bloods or mixed languages; like bloods, languages are also considered through notions of purity and impurity. There are ongoing debates about the English language between those who celebrate language change and others who lament what they consider to be a degeneration of the language as it adapts.

In *After Empire* (2004), Gilroy posits 'conviviality' as an alternative to hybridity, a term that recognizes the fluidity and multiplicity of race and identity relations and which offers a less rigid alternative to Bhabha's concept which tends to rest on particular encounters. Gilroy defines conviviality as 'the processes of cohabitation and interaction that have made multiculture an ordinary feature of social life in Britain's urban areas and in postcolonial cities elsewhere' (2004, p. xi). Though the term sounds somewhat celebratory and idealistic, this is not the case – Gilroy insists that he is not suggesting racism has been replaced by tolerance and harmony. Instead, the term points to a general fluidity of racial and cultural boundaries, an absence of certainty which has accompanied racial and cultural integration. In a society which has been multicultural for generations, there is inevitably an impact on all members of that society. Contemporary Britain is not the same as Britain in the 1950s when the first groups of immigrants from the Caribbean and South Asia arrived in large numbers. Gilroy's term is an attempt to recognize this in discussions of race in Britain and at the same time it allows a reassessment of the term 'identity'. Conviviality is alert to the unpredictability of identification.

Gilroy demonstrates the historical and ongoing presence and impact of black people in world history and culture through a discussion of various media contributing to a positive representation of blacks, noting that black styles, musics, dress, dance, fashion and languages have all been valued and incorporated in British life. Once again, language is present in this list. Contemporary English language, especially in youth culture, is clearly influenced by what Gilroy might term black language: this is supported by a research project run in 2003–7 by Paul Kerswill and Jenny Cheshire at Lancaster University which investigates how white adolescents' innovative use of 'black' or 'Asian' pronunciation leads to the possibility of nonmainstream English speech forms entering mainstream English. However, the black voice had a hesitant beginning in British and contemporary global popular culture. Gilroy explains that in the immediate post-war period, black people were admired as musicians, while they were excluded from mainstream society: a band leader could perform in a venue, but would be unwelcome there as a customer. This can be compared with the BBC's Caribbean Voices programme. A similar kind of welcome was extended to black voices within this contained context, though it was led by a Caribbean voice (Una Marson's), which distinguishes its scope from more possessive encounters like the musical ones Gilroy describes. In both examples, more mainstream acceptance was a result of entrance into British culture via something of cultural and artistic value.

Gilroy intends to claim back the term 'culture' from ethnicity, to address the idea of culture in more sophisticated ways. One alternative to a focus on ethnicity is an exploration of class, though Gilroy warns that questions of race and class cannot simply be fused within a broad socialist agenda because the category of class is not a straightforward one nowadays, when the working class is no longer unified in the way it was once perceived to be. Gilroy suggests that there are multiple new categories which complicate class relations (previously understood as a response to a clear division between the working and the ruling class). These new categories include 'housewives', 'black youth', 'trainees', 'the middle class' and 'claimants', which for Gilroy, despite the variations between these groups, can be positioned as a potential class, named 'surplus population' or 'surplus labour' (1987, p. 35). This 'surplus labour' is maintained as a necessary by-product of capitalist society, the acceptance of which perpetuates an unhealthy society relying on the real threat of unemployment to retain competitiveness between individuals for jobs, and keeping pay low. Such a society problematizes 'housewives' instead of recognizing that – male or female – there is a role for childcare and work in the home that should be enabled by one partner earning a living wage. It justifies a 'middle class' instead of recognizing that this is an exploitative element of the working class, enabled by a capitalist system. And it expects that 'trainees' somehow should expect to be incapable of supporting themselves financially, thus justifying their marginal position outside the rest of the workforce, while assuming that 'black youth' is a category that can be wilfully excluded from the workforce. Gilroy posits three routes through which black culture has challenged capitalist discourse:

1. A critique of productivism: work, the labour process and the division of labour under capitalism.
2. A critique of the state revolving around a plea for the disassociation of law from domination, which denounces state brutality, militarism and exterminism.

3. A passionate belief in the importance of history and the historical process. This is presented as an antidote to the suppression of historical and temporal perception under late capitalism (1987, p. 199).

This challenge has come from a number of fields, including music.

Gilroy and music

Perhaps a good way to put Gilroy's assertion to work in a recent context is through a reading of the music video to Dizzee Rascal's 2009 song 'Dirtee Cash'. 'Dirtee Cash' is a cover version, or, more accurately a re-interpretation of 'Dirty Cash', by a dance music act called The Adventures of Stevie V, released in 1990. The video was premiered in a special programme on Channel 4 and 4Music on 21 October 2009. Dizzee Rascal has suggested in the media that the song is primarily about debt, greed and spending money you do not have. But the video extends these general statements of dissatisfaction with society and economics, and I would like to explore how the video conforms to Gilroy's three statements about the production of anti-capitalist statements in black expressive arts. Gilroy states first that black expression provides a critique of the labour process and the division of labour under capitalism. Dizzee Rascal's new lyrics refer to naïve understanding of economics in contemporary Britain: he says that everybody believes they can be famous, seeing life as a movie, and giant lottery balls are held aloft. Each of these images expresses individualism and the unrealistic expectation that immense wealth can be acquired without effort. He also makes reference to the rat race, a middle-class version of the same idea, where people engage in a cycle of something that they think of as work, without any consciousness of how they contribute towards society as a whole. When he suggests that he is, himself, left paying for this lack of contribution, he could be referring to national wealth created by both black and white working-class people, or making a more specific comment on the recent banking crisis and the rescue of the banks by taxpayers' money. A placard carried through the procession announcing that lending money is a thrill makes a further reference to the irresponsible banks and the resulting fragility of the capitalist economy.

The prominence of police figures in the video conveys the second part of Gilroy's formula, a critique of the state and the law operating as an object of domination, state brutality, and militarism. The procession itself with a marching band has echoes of a military parade, though a disordered one. A group of marchers wear striped prison overalls stencilled with the word 'people', the first 'e' in 'people' replaced by a £ symbol, indicating perhaps the harmful power of money as well as state domination caused by capitalism. A policeman is shown in a compromising position with a woman, followed by a more direct statement of police corruption when in extreme close-up he removes the identifying numbers from his uniform, a tactic adopted by corrupt and brutal police in order to carry out unauthorized (or ignored) violence. The police have red ribbons tied around their sleeves, which seem, when combined with the Margaret Thatcher figure who also wears a red armband, to make an approximate reference to the swastika armbands worn by the Nazis, to suggest a general fascist system supported by the law. The swastika is, though not actually banned in the UK, heavily restricted in its use and often censored, so it is likely that the makers of the video were advised not to use the swastika and instead used an approximation of the symbol. Red armbands have been more commonly associated with the socialist military including the Russian and Chinese communist armies. These systems have also been considered totalitarian, so the armbands may symbolize a general control operating within the British capitalist economy. It also potentially suggests the specific kind of 'liberal' capitalism supported by broadly socialist systems like the welfare state and the National Health Service which operate to mediate a rigid capitalist system which would require a more aggressive adherence to individualism. The red rags tied around the policemen's arms in this context indicate a kind of patching up of capitalism through socialist systems, like the kind put in place to support the failed banks, which was actually a form of nationalism, swiftly reworded to avoid any socialist reference and called 'recapitalisation' by the government, bank leaders and media.

The video makes frequent references to history, and these seem to express a belief in the importance of history and to plead against the suppression of the historical, the third aspect that Gilroy has suggested. The video begins with the words 'Lest We Remember' held aloft, constructed from burning wood, expressing regret about a disdain for history. The words recall the common phrase 'Lest we forget', frequently used in military remembrance including statues, displays and speeches, but which also has specific connection with Rudyard Kipling and his poem 'Recessional', composed for Queen Victoria's diamond jubilee in 1897. The poem is pro-imperial while it laments an inevitable end of empire. This connection could be understood as a direct anti-imperial message, though the use of the phrase in reference to the First and Second World Wars suggests that its place in the video is intended to condemn the neglect of history. This seems likely when the burning words are connected with the other images of destroyed history in the video, particularly the burning books: old copies of Penguin classic books are burned on a pyre, including the collected works of Shakespeare. It is tempting to see this as a statement intended as a reference to rewriting the literary canon, yet Marx's *Das Kapital* is also burned, and the message seems to be one of neglect of the lessons that history can teach. The video ends with the burning of William Blake's anti-industrial, anti-exploitative poem 'Jerusalem', which questions the existence of Christian good in an England which permits the 'dark satanic mills' inside which human bodies are worked like machines. The video is alert to the inequality of contemporary Britain, and shows the image of a newspaper being trampled underfoot – the paper is named Ye Olde Big Issue in reference to the magazine which is produced and sold by homeless people in Britain in order to create a link between those disenfranchised people and the world of work and earning. The antique title and look of the newspaper in the video indicates an ongoing sense of inequality which connects contemporary capitalism with an industrial Victorian era of exploitation. Rascal states, too, in a further direct expression of the value of history, that he has not forgotten where he came from.

5 Native and Nation

Ethnocentrism is the tyranny of Western aesthetics. An Indian mask in
an American museum is transposed into an alien aesthetic system […]
It has become a conquered thing, a dead 'thing' separated from nature
and, therefore, its power.

Gloria Anzaldúa, *Borderlands/La Frontera*

As Anzaldúa's comment suggests, postcolonial theory also has to take into
account the ongoing relationship between indigenous cultures and settler populations. A focus on diaspora and migration can obscure other
effects of colonialism on postcolonial locations, where colonial adminis-
trations leave various imprints on the native populations and their land-
scapes. This chapter considers concepts of the native – native cultures and
languages, native informants and expressive forms, and native theories
and conceptual frameworks – in order to build a picture of the postcolonial
work that addresses the state and status of the culture and inhabitants of
colonized or formerly colonized locations. The term 'native' was originally
used by colonizers simply to identify the indigenous inhabitants of a colony
in contrast to settlers or colonial governors. However, colonizers started to
load the term with their attitudes towards the indigenous population, so
'native' came to mean also childlike and savage. In contemporary scholarship, the term is usually used to refer to indigenous Americans, Canadians,
Australians and Maori, whose cultures have felt the significant impact of
vast settler populations. In this sense, 'native' is often an indicator of resistance to domination. However, it is also used to refer to other populations
living under colonial control. Where it is used in this sense, the colonial
associations of savagery and naiveté are always to be borne in mind.

Ngugi and English in Africa

In a recent article (2008), Ngugi wa Thiong'o notes that George Lamming's
work is a constant argument with both Shakespeare and the English language, an argument which Ngugi has also taken up. Though Ngugi is quick

to point out that he is not hostile to either Shakespeare or the English language, he is eager to demonstrate how both have been used to maintain inequality in colonial contexts, and particularly in colonial education, where both produced and reproduced cultural dependency on the mother country. Though Lamming's work made direct reference to the experience of Barbadians whose ancestors had arrived in Barbados as slaves (migrants of a particular, enforced kind), Ngugi claims that the statement of resistance and human liberation can be applied to all peoples and all contexts where oppression has quashed imagination. Ngugi's recent essay offers some insight into the motivation which compelled his earlier works, including his plea for the abolition of the English department in African university education.

In *Homecoming*, a collection of essays first published together in 1972, and a later book *Decolonizing the Mind* (1981), Ngugi wa Thiong'o questions the assumptions that English literature and the English language are appropriate for African university education, African literature and African politics. The aim of *Homecoming* is to alert the African to the lack of change in African education, politics and social organization since the end of colonial administration. In the introductory note to the collection, Ngugi states that the inherited colonial past is still operational, with the exception (an inadequate exception, he suggests) that the roles previously held by white European colonials – as landowners, company directors, and so on – are now held by indigenous Africans. In order to genuinely shape the future of African countries after decolonization, there is a need to thoroughly reshape and rethink the structures left over from colonialism. Replacing colonial capitalism with indigenous capitalism is not enough; replacing English literature with African literature written in English is not enough; instead, Ngugi's call for an Africa which is 'culturally and economically free' (1972, p. xviii) implies a separate culture which rejects all foreign intervention, past or present. This approach is sometimes termed nativism, the idea that, following decolonization, in order to thoroughly throw off colonial subjugation it is necessary to resurrect the pre-colonial culture, laws, practices and art forms and to reject anything influenced by the colonial system. This assumes that pre-colonial alternatives are lying dormant and unchanged. And, as Ashcroft, Griffiths and Tiffin point out, some commentators have suggested that it is undesirable to return to a pre-colonial system which was perhaps more patriarchal than the postcolonial one and so offers far fewer opportunities for women (2000, pp. 159–61). This, of course, rests on the assumption that the colonial system has improved living conditions for women: as we will consider later in this chapter in relation to *sati*, or Hindu widow-burning, the question of the colonizer saving the colonized woman from her own culture is a complex one.

Perhaps the most frequently cited essay from *Homecoming* is 'On the Abolition of the English Department', which was in fact a response to a paper presented by the Acting Head of the English Department at the University of Nairobi in 1968 in an effort to renegotiate the role and scope of the department. The response is written by Ngugi and two colleagues, Henry Owuor-Anyumba and Taban Lo Liyong. Ngugi and his colleagues question the role and status of an English Department in an African context and the assumption that, by continuing to administer the department as an English department, English literature and the English language are imperative factors in African culture and consciousness. The essay suggests that the English language might have official purposes, but that English literature and culture is out of place (quite literally) in Africa. Ngugi offers compelling evidence as to why African languages, literatures and cultures deserve to take the place of English literature in the African university, by surveying the ongoing tradition of oral literature; by pointing out that the languages used in Kenya include Kikuyu, Luo, Akamba, and Arabic and Hindustani in addition to those represented in the 1968 curriculum (English, French, and Swahili); by acknowledging the significant body of Swahili literature which is not studied as well as the vast field of modern African literature, including literature of the African diaspora in the Caribbean. And, in order to directly address the ongoing colonial influence, Ngugi claims that rather than privileging English literature, there are many other European literatures which should also be studied, listing French, Russian and German literature, including American literatures as European diaspora writing in the same spirit with which he considers Caribbean literature as literature of the African diaspora. The piece concludes with a direct challenge to notions of literary hierarchy, stating that university reading lists are decided based on flawed notions that there is a universal definition of 'undisputed literary excellence' (1973, p. 149). Ngugi asks from whose point of view such a value judgement can be made, bringing his appeal back full circle. It is important to state that Ngugi was not calling for a rejection of English literature, but for a reassessment of its position in the African university, considering the weight of competing African and worldwide literatures and languages.

In *Decolonising the Mind*, Ngugi extends his enquiry around English language and literature in Africa to consider whether the English language is a relevant vehicle for the expression of African life. In the first section of the book, 'The Language of African Literature', Ngugi questions the commonly held assumption that the English language is an appropriate language for African writers. He cites Chinua Achebe's question, in the talk he gave at the University of Massachusetts in 1975 (titled 'An Image of Africa: Racism in Conrad's *Heart of Darkness*'), over whether it is right to abandon the mother tongue for a foreign language, and his decision that, because he has been 'given' the language, he intends to use it. The idea of using African forms, style, grammar and idiom to enrich the English language in African literature is repellent to Ngugi, even if the resulting English language is a different one, an African English, 'altered to suit new African surroundings' as Achebe presented it, a position that Salman Rushdie has also assumed in more recent writings about the ability of South Asian literatures in English to alter the English language and thereby to own it, to use it as a subversive force for change (2003, pp. 163–5). Ngugi's insistence that African languages should instead be used by African writers is based to a large extent on the colonial practices of enforcing the use of English in Kenyan schools by corporal punishment and by forcing children who were heard speaking Gikuyu to wear humiliating signs around their necks with inscriptions such as 'I am a Donkey' and 'I am Stupid', a long-established method of enforcing the use of English in appropriated territories. As a result of these practices, Ngugi writes, 'In Kenya, English became more than a language: it was *the* language, and all the others had to bow before it in deference' (1981, p. 11). With this in mind, he made a decision to write and to deliver plenary addresses at conferences and speeches at universities in Gikuyu instead of English, and even to write in Gikuyu, then translate his work into English. Simon Gikandi has noted that this was a fairly short-lived practice fraught with anxieties, and that eventually Ngugi started to use the English language again as Gikuyu was impractical for an exile and academic in America. Having begun to use English again in his daily life, he set up *Mūtiiri*, a Gikuyu journal at New York University and intended to use his native language to publish. However, Gikandi has suggested that although the journal was far-reaching, scholarly, and challenging, at the same time there were 'vindictive' reasons for producing it:

> He wanted to prove that an African language could perform certain linguistic, philosophical, and scientific functions as well as European languages [and ...] the journal seemed to function under the anxieties created by its conditions of production and distribution. (Gikandi, 2000, p. 195)

In *Homecoming*, Ngugi addresses African culture more broadly, considering questions of the role of Africa in the international acquisition of wealth in

'Towards a National Culture', and calling for a new African social structure based on an African socialist model of collective labour as opposed to an imported capitalism which requires exploitation and ruthless greed. Ngugi's argument even in this essay is supported by a response to the literature that was employed at the service of colonialism: his reading of the Prospero–Caliban relationship argues for the development of an African culture not based on that of the European colonizer who, like Prospero, feared a confident native with knowledge of their own history. The Department of English at Nairobi University was renamed the Department of Literature in 1968, and since that time it has incorporated two departmental sections, teaching literatures in English and in French. Though the department's name change did not and still does not meet Ngugi's demands, the modules offered on the undergraduate degree programme today reflect the changes that he had hoped to make, and include numerous modules focused on oral literatures including Eastern African Oral Literature, on theories and genres of oral literature, on modern African literature, on literatures from various geographical regions in Africa, on Latin American literatures, and there are also modules which focus specifically on European, American, Canadian and Japanese literature. The only modules with references to English in the title are patently not the kinds of English literature that would have formed the basis of literature studied in the 1960s: instead, they are titled Indian Literature in English Translation and Anglo-Indian Literature. Another area where issues of native literatures, languages and theories are strongly debated is the somewhat different context of America and Australia where white settler communities have displaced indigenous communities. This is the focus of the next section.

Indigenous concerns: a different kind of nativism?

Distinctions can be drawn between US and Canadian native theory and literatures, in part as a result of the separate legal histories between natives and non-natives in the two countries. And, of course, while native writers in the US tend to identify themselves as Native American, the identifying term Native Canadian used in Canada creates a further sense of separation. Native American literary criticism or theory has been traced to a beginning point at the 1977 Modern Language Association (MLA) conference in Arizona, which brought together Native American writers and scholars in academic debate, for presentations, and to launch books and journals. A similarly high-profile event founded the field in Canada in the late 1980s;

a group of native writers in Toronto formed the Committee to Reestablish the Trickster, a network which supported publication, performance and workshops of native arts and forms of cultural expression, and brought recognition and focus to writers and artists who had not previously operated as a collective. Native American theorists have, from the 1990s onwards, employed poststructuralism and postmodernism as methodologies which, with their intention to question dominant modes of representation, have been considered appropriate for Native American literature which aims explicitly to talk back to the centre. Elvira Pulitano notes a resistance to the uncritical use of Western theoretical methodologies, though; some have called for new critical methods to be developed from within native thinking rather than adapted to native contexts from outside. However, Paula Gunn Allen, a prominent Native American writer and scholar, has claimed that there is a close connection between Native American experience and broader questions of postcolonialism, which would support the employment of postcolonial and poststructural theories, noting that 'for American Indian people, acculturation and colonization have created personal crises that are not easily resolved' (1980, p. 18).

Cheryl Suzack (2005) refers to the powerful ways in which theorists like Julia Emberley and Helen Hoy have applied postcolonial and poststructural theories to Aboriginal women's writing in a Native Canadian context. The political intentions of Native Canadian literary theory parallel the general commitments of postcolonialism elsewhere: these include the reassertion of a political, cultural and intellectual voice for Aboriginal people, an examination of the impact of colonialism, and a reassessment of colonial histories. Gerald Vizenor, a prominent Native American academic, whose published work also includes poetry, haiku, plays, novels and life-writing, forges postcolonial and Aboriginal concerns in the image of Christopher Columbus, representative of discourses of discovery and enlightenment and symbol of the myth that justifies the appropriation of land and of the stories belonging to the peoples of that land (Vizenor, 1992). There is a need to revise representations of the native, too: Louis Owens notes that by portraying the 'Indian' as an intuitive, non-intellectual, non-rational other for the Anglo-European, the Native American becomes an abstraction. Killing of Native Americans was carried out in vast numbers in the process of manifest destiny which Dee Brown has addressed at length in *Bury My Heart at Wounded Knee* (1970). Manifest destiny was the assumption that it was God's will that the Native American die out (or be killed) in order to make way for the European settler population, whose destiny it was to inherit America. This kind of killing, among the worst in the history of violent land acquisition, is moderated when the Indian is understood as an abstraction, as, in fact, 'something intuitive Americans kill within themselves' (Owens, 1988, p. 89). This is dangerous because in the process the violence of that history is somehow justified.

Paula Gunn Allen has examined Native American literary forms as well as stories, and makes a direct comparison between contemporary literature, which has a recurring theme of alienation, and traditional literatures, which, she suggests, do not engage with the concept of otherness. This implies a system not built on binaries which has, with the impact of the American colonial process, created a sense of otherness and alienation so strong that it 'becomes theme, symbol, character, and structure', indicating 'the extent to which it shapes the lives of the writers and of their communities' (1980, p. 4). People known as 'breeds', those with both native and white heritage, are emblematic of this impact; they are 'a bit of both worlds, and the consciousness of this makes them seem alien to Indians while making them feel alien among whites' (Allen, 1980, p. 5). The notion of purity or authenticity within the individual body is conveyed in literary works through 'tonguelessness', the inability to speak (Allen, 1980, p. 11), which is countered by the voicing of native experience through literature and theory. In this sense the claims for nativism, in practice and in theory by developing authentic native theoretical models instead of applying Anglo-American ones, has a certain resonance. This is made even more apparent when theorists draw attention to the ways in which native literatures have had themes and theories imposed upon them. Robin Riley Fast notes that although the concept of the border is one that has been enabling in Chicano/a (Mexican-American) writing, the same is not true of Native American literatures, even though the border remains a prominent theme. This is because the border represents something very different for Native Americans: the border is not a liminal or an abstract space but a very real and externally imposed barrier that surrounds the Reservation. There is no sense of borderline negotiation associated with the reservation boundary. The imposed border becomes internalized when it is applied to 'breeds', and is sometimes deliberately reinforced as a method of defending cultural integrity, another instance of nativism which includes debates over the guarding of native spiritual traditions to ensure that they are not shared with outsiders.

Another argument for the creation of a native theoretical methodology comes from the acknowledgement that concepts such as the split subject, which, though common to both postcolonial and native contexts, are very different in meaning and symbolism. Bhabha's split subject is the postcolonial migrant haunted by two cultures, tongues, and ways of thought.

The comparative concept in Native American thinking is a wholly positive one, and it is also specifically contained within a notion of the splitting of gender boundaries rather than geographical or linguistic ones, as Tara Prince-Hughes has explained:

> In many Native American cultures, two-spirit traditions have allowed individuals to express alternative gender inclinations by adopting the work, behavior, and dress of the other sex. The presence of two-spirits signifies the health and balance of their societies, for they are thought to combine powerful male and female forces harmoniously within one person.   (1999, p. 32)

The harmonious nature of this kind of split subject and their thorough acceptance and belonging within the community might adhere to some of the more idealistic postcolonial debates, but there are many more voices in postcolonial studies which would dispute the harmonious nature of a human splitting or duality (Gandhi, 1998, p. 136; Harrison, 2003, pp. 70, 74; Moore-Gilbert, 1997, pp. 129–30), and this suggests that notions of splitting cannot be easily transferred between the spheres of native and postcolonial thinking.

It is important to consider debates over orality and textuality in the context of Native American and Native Canadian thinking, too. Gerald Vizenor has, in his literary works, attempted a blending of tribal and non-tribal worlds which involves combining European epic forms with Native American oral narratives. He has also made use of the Western academy by incorporating French philosophical models relating to mythology including the work of Roland Barthes and Jacques Derrida. Multiple frames of reference are employed because for Vizenor, there is no simple method by which to translate Native American oral narratives, especially into the English language. Vizenor insists that English is incompatible with tribal and oral expressions; he describes it as 'a language of commerce and technology, a language without much place, without much spirit of place'. By contrast, he says, 'Tribal languages are concrete' and demonstrate 'a symbolic connection to place', because of their long history of having been spoken in the same place for thousands of years, giving them a dramatic connection with the earth (Bowers and Silet, 1981, p. 48). Vizenor makes a convincing point in some ways: English is a new language in America and, in its American history has been associated with technology and commerce. But his ideas raise other interesting questions about whether there are other languages which are more appropriate for translating Native American narratives, and more generally, about how far languages retain memories of place, and adapt as they move, and whether languages can remain fixed for thousands of years. To return to the points of connection and of departure between Native American and Canadian literatures and theories, Cheryl Suzack has prioritized an awareness of the distinction between scribal and print cultures, rather than oral and textual cultures, arguing for a recognition of pictorial representations (stories and ideas represented through images) as a fundamental part of Native Canadian expression. Similarly, Mudrooroo has questioned the legitimacy of telling native (Australian Aboriginal) stories through European forms. For Mudrooroo, there is a clear parallel between Australian Aboriginal literature and Native American literature: both groups of writers, he suggests, belong to a 'Fourth World' of 'indigenous minorities submerged in a surrounding majority and governed by them' (1995, p. 231).

Mudrooroo

Mudrooroo's is a prominent voice in postcolonial thinking about the Aboriginal experience. An activist for Australian Aboriginal rights, a novelist and academic, Mudrooroo's position has been contested by questions of his own 'authenticity', accusations that his Aboriginal identity is a false one, adopted so that, according to some, he could claim specialist knowledge of a culture and a literary – or, more accurately, an oral storytelling – heritage (see Chapter 1 for a fuller discussion of Mudrooroo's biography). Sander L. Gilman suggested that 'Australian academic Colin Johnson transformed himself into the Aboriginal critic Mudrooroo', describing this as a construction of a fictional ethnic identity and locating this within a society (Australia) seeking authenticity (1998, p. 23). Ivor Indyk has called Mudrooroo a 'master of appropriation' (1993, p. 854), a term which is also alert to the activist appropriation of European forms and vehicles that Mudrooroo has undertaken in order to create a space for the Aboriginal voice in Australian and global literary and cultural studies. It is unfortunate that such questions have, for some, taken precedence over Mudrooroo's contribution to academic thought. Mudrooroo questions the appropriateness of European – or 'white' – forms including biography, autobiography, and the novel, for telling Aboriginal stories to a popular market. Forms of Aboriginal life-story had a very different function traditionally, and detailed the lives of 'the Dreaming Ancestors, such as the Wandjina in the Kimberley region and the Djanggawul and his two sisters in north-eastern Arnhem Land'. Gillian Whitlock describes the ambiguous reception of Sally Morgan's *My Place* (1987), a bestseller which employed the Western literary conventions of detective fiction and quest narratives in order to make aboriginality accessible (2000, pp. 157–8). And the novel presents further difficulties: Mudrooroo contrasts the solitary practice of writing a novel with the community focus of the aborigine. Because of the intrusion of English into Aboriginal culture, Mudrooroo sees much Aboriginal literature as, above all, a white form, and considers that a return to native languages is essential in order to tell authentic Aboriginal stories, even where those stories document contact with white European languages, literary forms and cultures (1995, p. 231).

For Graham Huggan, Mudrooroo's literary work offers a method of resisting dominant culture through an engagement with colonial mimicry. Mimicry is a key postcolonial term which broadly refers to an ironic imitation, a mimicking of white colonial practices and languages in a manner which is empowering for the colonized, including Native Americans who 'deliver themselves from their oppressors by mockingly reproducing them in their own colonial mode' (Huggan, 1998, p. 94). For Bhabha, mimicry does not involve harmonization between colonized and colonizer. There is instead an ambivalent space between mimicry and mockery. His image of mimicry as 'camouflage' (2004, p. 128) draws attention to the sense that the resemblance is always partial and carried out for the purposes of defence or even attack. In a reading of Mudrooroo's *Master of the Ghost Dreaming* (1991), Huggan draws attention to a moment of mimicry where the Aboriginal imitates European missionary appearance: the women paint a resemblance of a European missionary woman's white lace blouse on their bare breasts, and the men paint on their naked chests a military uniform complete with painted lapels, buttons and pockets. For Huggan, the Aboriginals' appearance and the ceremony described in the text, 'through a process of interculturative adaptation' (1998, p. 101), or mimicry, creates its own agenda. In this way, mimesis, an uncanny method of identification which engages with the way in which people are represented by others (while mimicry does not engage so directly with representation but instead is concerned with identity and performance and appearance more generally), becomes a method of empowerment for the Aboriginals in the text, and, of course, for Aboriginal writing and identity when the text is read and interpreted.

Textuality and orality

Walter Ong's *Orality and Literacy* (1982) makes direct comparisons between oral and literate cultures and the corresponding ways of understanding the world which Ong suggests contrast as a result of the separate modes of storytelling, interaction, and recording information. Though Ong's study is not intended to privilege either orality or literacy, in its chronological markers it does assume that orality is a phenomenon largely of the past (exemplified through his discussions of Greek drama, for example) which has been replaced by textual (chirographic) forms. The focus on 'literacy' and the idea of learning to read and to be literate reinforces the implied assumption that literature is intellectually superior to oral expression and knowledge organization. Ong was a theologian who also studied literature and his approach to oral literature and culture was not informed by politically committed literary theories. Orality remains under-theorized: both Ato Quayson and Karin Barber have raised objections to the way that orality is presented in literary and cultural scholarship, even within postcolonial studies. Barber has claimed that postcolonial criticism of the 1980s and 1990s eliminated African-language expression from view. One product of this view has been the overemphasis of what Barber calls 'one sliver of literary and cultural production' (1995, p. 3): textual literatures written in English. Excised from view are other literatures, oral traditions, and expressive forms which straddle the traditions of literary and oral forms in any language. If postcolonial theory intends to privilege the native voice over a colonial one, then this 'sliver' of representation is wholly insufficient. Quayson notes a tendency to express the literary (or textual) at the expense of orality within oracy-inspired literature, which is exemplified in the title of a book which intended to collate and re-present all theories, practices and contexts of the postcolonial, *The Empire Writes Back*. As Karin Barber has pointed out, the act of writing is explicitly privileged by the title as the only potential method by which the margins can subvert the centre. The authors of this book, Bill Ashcroft, Gareth Griffiths and Helen Tiffin, do address oral narrative, although briefly, and with a constant eye on the textual. They show that Western linear textual narrative has been seen as a privileged form of literature in contrast with oral, cyclical narrative which is considered to be primitive and less skilfully crafted: for example, they suggest that features of African orature in novels, when read from a European literary perspective about the conventional structure of the novel, have been read as simple, or even imitative reproductions of European styles (2002, pp. 180–2).

Quayson attempts to moderate the bias for the written word in a 1995 essay titled 'Orality – (Theory) – Textuality: Tutuola, Okri, and the Relationship of Literary Practice to Oral Traditions' through an exploration of specific oral cultures, including the Yorùbá, which he describes as 'far from homogeneous' and 'in a constant process of transformation' (1995, p. 101). He conveys a rich and diverse field of oral genres in the Yorùbá culture, and insists that this points to the logical conclusion that the meaning of each particular genre only makes sense within its context of production. This is not a claim to exclusionism or essentialism, but an awareness of the impact of context on the oral genre produced. And the context of production is, Quayson insists, not limited to the context of performance, the very specific occasion and location at which the oral performance takes place, but includes all contextual aspects – the socio-cultural context of the performers, the gender and power relations between them, the relationship of the form to other oral narrative and poetic forms, and also the broader context of Nigeria. We might also want to add, more specifically, the colonial and postcolonial encounters and literary traditions that may have encountered and influenced Yorùbá oral forms. Quayson reads Amos Tutuola's and Ben Okri's well-known postcolonial literary texts in order to foreground the presence of oral genres in their textual works, in an effort to reverse the trend of fore-grounding the literariness of African texts. He suggests that Tutuola's narratives reproduce folktale formulae, while Okri's *The Famished Road* brings together traditional concepts and contemporary contexts. The narrator of *The Famished Road*, Quayson explains, exists at the mercy of spiritual and real-world realms, events, and perceptions, and in this way the narrator does not experience the enabling rite of passage which should characterize the traditional folktale. Instead, Azaro the narrator is an *abiku* (ghost-child), 'comprehending different realms simultaneously and utterly powerless to change the order of things' (1995, p. 112). If the narrator is forced to comprehend the two realms of existence simultane-ously, he must perceive their impact on each other, and it is the real-world events that in fact constitute his rite of passage. According to Quayson, Okri expresses an ambivalence towards the traditional form and this takes the form of, firstly, a fascination with the possibilities of orality, and secondly, a sense of its inadequacy in the context of a 'post-colonial real-ity that is cosmopolitan, in-between, and riddled by multiple identities' (1995, p. 114). Quayson concludes by stating the need to recognize both the ongoing process of orality and the need to pay as much theoretical attention towards orality as towards literature. Questions of orality inevi-tably lead back to the use of oral narratives in colonial interactions with natives in order to glean information about native culture, the kind of interactions that set up the ambiguous position of the native informant.

The native informant

The native informant figure originated in anthropological writings, and was a term used to describe a native member of a community who could communicate with foreign investigators to help them to learn about (or, inform upon) their culture, and who was perceived as a 'blank' on which the West could 'inscribe' cultural identity, as Spivak suggests in a very textual image (1999, p. 6). Because of this connection with anthropology, as Edward Saïd has pointed out, early anticolonial and postcolonial scholarship which tackled the subject of the native and attempted to reveal native or subaltern reactions to the colonial project was seen as inferior:

> The temptation for metropolitan audiences has usually been to rule that these books, and others like them, are merely evidence of native literature written by "native informants", rather than coeval contributions to knowledge. (1993, p. 312)

Saïd disputes this view by demonstrating that this category of works consigned to the work of the ethnographer's native informant included formative texts for postcolonial studies, such as C.L.R. James's *The Black Jacobins*, Ranajit Guha's work with the Subaltern Studies Group, George Antonius's *The Arab Awakening* (1939) which is an activist history of the Arab nationalist movement during the First World War and the following years when the Middle East was partitioned, and Syed Hussein Alatas's *The Myth of the Lazy Native* (1977), a study which refutes a claim made by the Malaysian government that Malaysia's slow economic development at that time was due to the inherent laziness of the Malaysian workforce, positing instead that the fault was with British colonial and later neocolonial administrators and investors whose policies held back economic development. Although Saïd has described the importance of these texts and others which aim to reveal the native or subaltern perspective, his position raises two issues which require some comment: firstly, Saïd complies with the view that ethnography is a questionable pursuit. Trinh T. Minh-ha has also discussed the shortcomings of anthropology at length. It is important to remember that anthropology has been used at the service of colonialism and has later repeated imperial assumptions about inherent cultural differences. Even when attempting to undo colonial prejudices, anthropologists have, according to postcolonial commentators, been guilty of nativism, an equally false representation of indigenous populations which has attempted to expel all signs of contact between the indigenous culture and the rest of the world. So Saïd's views are representative of the general postcolonial wariness of an anthropology that has demonstrated either imperialist or nativist positions. The second point arising from Saïd's comments is in regard to the native informant as an individual. According to the description above, the native informant emerges as an untrustworthy figure; as the word implies, an informant must inform on, or betray, somebody – for a native informant, the betrayal is against the informant's own community. Spivak too notes the problematics of the native informant figure, as it functions alongside a Northwestern European norm in its many manifestations, including the 'postcolonial informant', a somewhat distinct position.

Gayatri Chakravorty Spivak's *A Critique of Postcolonial Reason* (1999) is in part an examination of the native informant figure in literature, history, culture and philosophy, but as she indicates in the preface to the book, her intended aim of tracking and analysing this figure through the four spheres was quickly thrown into relief by her realization that the colonial subject was becoming detached from the native informant, and that a postcolonial subject had been appropriating the native informant's position. The book becomes, in response to this problem, an effort to consider the production and the use of postcolonial thinking. It asks where postcolonial knowledge comes from (whether it comes from a native or native informant figure or not), what relationship that knowledge has to the postcolonial native cultures, and how knowledge is reproduced in literary, historical, philosophical and cultural writings.

Spivak differentiates between the native informant in its original guise as the servant of colonial ethnography, and modern figures who, she claims, masquerade as native informants but are in fact 'self-marginalizing or self-consolidating' migrant or postcolonial figures (1999, p. 6) who might be charged with the role of nativists. The native informant in Spivak's formulation is – as a result of the distinction that she makes here – necessarily the dependent subject of colonialism or of neocolonialism: in this text Spivak is also alert to neocolonial practices and their replication of colonial ideologies even where they claim a distinction. Spivak's native informant is not the one generally found in postcolonial literature who is a positive figure with a wider frame of reference due to their hybrid status. Whether as an ethnographical tool or as a literary figure in masquerade, though, Spivak insists that the native informant remains 'needed', while at the same time 'foreclosed' (1999, p. 6). It is in response to this need for the native informant and the impossible position of the foreclosed native informant that Spivak seeks to engage with the native informant figure and to establish its role and employment in contemporary postcolonial thinking by tracing its representations through philosophy, literature, history and culture. Another reason for Spivak's interest in the figure is her preoccupation with the role of the postcolonial intellectual – that is, the scholar of postcolonial studies, but also the academic who might be categorized as culturally postcolonial because of their national or cultural heritage; Spivak reminds those who are suspicious of her academic practice – her use of particular, Western models of theory – that she *is* the native that she is supposedly stifling:

> Benita Parry has criticized Homi Bhabha, Abdul JanMohammed and Gayatri Spivak of being so enamored of deconstruction that they will not let the native speak. She has forgotten that we are natives too.   (1999, p. 190)

As a native and an intellectual in the Western academy, Spivak's engagement with the native informant figure is always fraught by her own position in relation to the texts, histories and subjects of her writing. As a result of this, she constructs *A Critique of Postcolonial Reason* as a main narrative accompanied by a lengthy set of footnotes which frequently dominate the page. This structure ensures that Spivak's own position is never an authoritative one: like Trinh's assertion that the critical voice can avoid an undesirable domination of the story or the subject by speaking *to* rather than *about* the subject, Spivak's text is an exercise in deferral because the footnotes position Spivak as a questioning reader of her own text as well as providing a location for optional, tangential theoretical and contextual material. For example, Spivak refers to a problematic translation of a passage from the *Gitā* providing an existing alternative and noting that this translation too can be questioned: the reader is enabled to make their own decision about the appropriateness of these or other potential translations (1999, p. 44 n.53), and Spivak states directly that in certain sections of the book the footnotes seem to overtake the main text.

The perspective of the native informant is '(im)possible' to engage with for Spivak, because of its origin in a very particular, exploitative use from ethnography – the native informant is:

> a figure who, in ethnography, can only provide data, to be interpreted by the knowing subject for reading. Indeed, there *can* be no correct scholarly model for this type of reading. It is, strictly speaking, "mistaken," for it attempts to transform into a reading-position the site of the "native informant" in anthropology, a site that can only *be* read, by definition, for the production of definitive descriptions. It is an (im)possible perspective.   (1999, p. 49)

Spivak defines '(im)possible' in her discussion of the function of rhetorical questions in relation to storytelling in *In Other Worlds* (1987). She explains how a cook asks the rhetorical question 'What's there to tell?' which is obstinately misunderstood in order to enable that story to be told. Rhetorical questions are not meant to be answered so the question is at once impossible to answer (because it is posed rhetorically) yet possible to answer because there is, in fact, a story to be told, invited by the question. This (im)possible status is attributed to the native informant who similarly has a story to tell, and a uniquely informed position from which to provide information, yet who can never truly tell their story because the moment they become the native informant their story is mediated by the control of the dominant, imperial audience.

The native informant has been created by anthropology to resemble a corpus of data and not an individual with agency; the native informant cannot then become the reader and read themselves. Other figures can do this: those colonial and postcolonial subjects who might masquerade as native informants but who have a knowing intellectual position in relation to their own history and culture, and will not be able to simply convey data for an ethnographic reader – that 'data' will always be mediated by awareness of the postcolonial context. The native informant is the servant of anthropology who can communicate with anthropologists but who is always subject to an anthropological reading. In contrast, the postcolonial migrant may have cultural knowledge of the same ethnographic group, but in addition, they have been shaped by migration and they are knowingly resistant to being produced by a dominant reading. In this sense the native informant is a naïve figure, in the sense that they are subordinated by the imperialist ethnographic gaze, while the postcolonial migrant is not. At this point, it might be useful to engage with some of Spivak's examples of the native informant figure and then to compare those figures with the postcolonial migrant whose self-marginalization yet belies their agency and their ability to evade anthropological positioning.

Spivak's example taken from philosophy is her engagement with Hegel's reading of a translation of the *Gitā* in his *Aesthetics: Lectures on Fine Arts* (first compiled as a collection posthumously in 1835 from lecture notes and published in English translation 1975), where he concludes that, because of his assumption of the 'nature' of Indian poetry, the relationship between form, content and meaning is somehow accidental rather than planned, whereas European literature reveals an expert realization of self-knowledge when the relationship between these three moments are perceived. Thus the relationship between form and content, which Hegel observes to be so similar, is rendered in Indian poetry as 'extremely monotonous, and on the whole, empty and wearisome' (Spivak 1999, p. 44). The native inform-ant figure perceptible in Hegel's reading of the *Gitā* is 'an implied reader "contemporary" with the *Gitā*' who is assumed male and has a life span of approximately 'two centuries' (Spivak 1999, pp. 49–50), commensurate with the amount of time that the text is assumed to have taken to produce, as it is generally accepted to be the product of multiple narrators and tran-scribers over a long period of time. This ahistorical assumed reader, the native informant who can be called upon to aid understanding of the *Gitā*, is clearly an impossible figure because of both the elongated life span and the ahistoricity, the separation of that figure from any historical context or any shifting influences over the two centuries that the text spans. Hegel's reading relies upon the assumption that a native informant can exist who is contemporary with the production of the *Gitā* and therefore 'reads' it as it is being produced, and can be called upon for information from the philo-sophical–anthropological reader (Hegel) who rereads the *Gitā* in order to make a comparison between Indian and European narrative construction, and the relationship between the three factors present in all art accord-ing to Hegel's conception of art: form, content and meaning. Philosophical engagements with a native informant are impossible, Spivak suggests, because in the imperial and postcolonial context there can be no 'function-ally completely frozen' native informant, of the kind required by philoso-phy in order to construct a universal, equal 'mankind' that can survive the 'fearful abyss of Nature' and achieve 'the sublime' (1999, p. 30).

Applied to a literary context, Spivak suggests that Mary Shelley's *Frankenstein* attempts to foreground a native informant figure in the monster. Spivak explains that the novel, written in the epistolary tradition, employs multiple narrative frames, one of which belongs to the monster who describes his attempt to learn to be human through reading, involv-ing reading *Paradise Lost* as if it was a true history rather than a narrative poem. Spivak connects this kind of learning with Caliban's, calling it educa-tion through eavesdropping. The monster's eventual admission of guilt and his intention to immolate himself recalls Caliban's submissiveness at the end of *The Tempest*, and in this way *Frankenstein* is revealed as an expression of the master–slave narrative that, like *The Tempest*, upholds the superior posi-tion of the master. However, what rescues the novel from this conventional subjectivity for Spivak is the monster's extension beyond the text: he drifts away on an ice raft so his death is deferred to a position outside the narrative bounds: 'the monster can step "beyond the text" and be "lost in darkness"' and thus 'Shelley gives to the monster the right to refuse the withholding of the master's returned gaze' (1999, p. 140). Frankenstein is a story of an eventual subaltern freedom, yet the monster is revealed as an impossible native informant who, like Shakespeare's Caliban, cannot tell his story because he exists only as a piece of data to be read by other, anthropological-type readers: he can never speak within the bounds of his text within which he is constructed as subject to his master and the mediator–readers of his narrative. The British imperial engagement with *sati* (Hindu widow-burning) in colonial India renders the Hindu widow similarly silent, placing her in a similarly impossible position as native informant, as Spivak describes in her chapter on history (discussed further below): the woman is lost between native patriarchy and imperialist ideology. In their manoeuvres to save the *sati*, the British construct the woman as object, and so she is only ever present in historical narratives about *sati* as a silent subject or a silent object, and is never able to speak within these constraining gazes.

In the final chapter of *A Critique of Postcolonial Reason*, 'Culture', Spivak moves on from texts and representations of previous historical contexts to consider the present: 'our culture' and 'our world' as she ambivalently puts it (1999, pp. 312, 313). Here, she examines Japanese fashion designer Rei Kawakubo, whose designs have included those dubbed 'Hiroshima chic', an evocative term that reveals Kawakubo's positioning by those who represent her, talk about her, as at once Japanese and yet also not straightforwardly Japanese but Japanese from an external perspective, the bombing of Hiroshima being the modern world's most resonant and traumatic image of Japan. And this is how Spivak describes Kawakubo's representation: she is internationally acclaimed because she is perceived as 'different', as authentically Japanese, yet she is 'the-same-yet-not-the-same, different-but-not-different' (1999, p. 340). Her most well-known clothing range is a collection of clothes for women called *Comme des Garçons* (like boys) which commentators have interpreted as indicating a feminist position. This range includes puff-ball skirts and sleeves, layered garters, clothes chopped up to reveal fleshy holes cut in the shape of generous curved lips, and satin bras worn on the outside of thick ribbony layers. These clothes are described as somehow entirely different from European design, leading some to suggest that Kawakubo is dismissive of European fashion. Spivak observes, though, that her clothes are worn by a global subject and do not in any sense represent the assumed Japanese native informant as the cosmopolitan fashion commentators suppose

> the thoroughly transmogrified (im)possible perspective of the native informant (a Japanese worker, an inhabitant of Chinatown [...]) would see, if it could, nothing but the appropriation of its trace in the interstices of the powerful texts of the master's radical discourse.   (1999, p. 342)

Kawakubo's fashion does not directly represent an experience of Japan for the European or American observer who attends her fashion shows in Paris or New York because such a position is (im)possible to convey.

Spivak distinguishes the native informant from the postcolonial informant, a figure who can speak about the native culture from a position of both intellectual agency and specific cultural knowledge, but who does so, according to Spivak, in a flawed way unless such a representation is produced as an interruption, or, broadly, in the manner of deconstruction, as she describes in the appendix to *A Critique of Postcolonial Reason*, in a short chapter called 'The Setting to Work of Deconstruction'. It is this postcolonial informant who Anastasia Valassopoulos locates in Ahdaf Soueif's *The Map of Love* (1997), both in the author's position as a postcolonial intellectual, working in literary fiction rather than in the American academy (which is where Spivak had suggested the postcolonial informant is usually found), and in the narrative world itself: while the contemporary Egyptian woman Amal reads and translates her ancestor's papers and diaries, in this process she reevaluates the colonial presence in Egypt. Amal is not a native informant: she is not an Egyptian subject to British colonialism, but a postcolonial member of an elite, global community who can, with the benefit of her intellectual position, look back on her colonial heritage and speak about it in the manner of a postcolonial informant or, in Valassopoulos's terms, a '*creative* native informant (2004, my emphasis). The postcolonial informant can maintain contact with their native culture, but for Spivak, such a position is taken at the risk of achieving only nativism, to, at worst, 'take advantage of the aura' of 'identification with those distant objects of oppression' and 'play the native informant uncontaminated by disavowed involvement with the machinery of the production of knowledge' (1999, p. 360). This impossible position perhaps accounts for Ngugi's struggle to resist the English language once he took on the role of postcolonial migrant academic at New York University, while it accounts for Spivak's insistence on the relevance of deconstruction (and the deconstructionist position in relation to prior Western philosophical models) for the postcolonial migrant intellectual, in order that their role as native is not subsumed under a nostalgic nativism. The distinction between the native and the postcolonial informant is to an extent determined by their agency, which is in turn dependent on socio-economic class or status: the native informant was in many cases a subaltern figure; the postcolonial informant cannot be the subaltern, according to Spivak's conception.

Spivak's concept of the subaltern

The term 'subaltern' was first used outside a military context (where it denotes a lower-ranking officer) by Antonio Gramsci. Gramsci applied the term in his political writings to refer to working-class people who were subordinated by hegemonic power and therefore disadvantaged politically and socially. In postcolonial theory, the subaltern includes marginalized social groups such as peasant labourers, rural workers, and working class, peasant, or lower caste women, all of whom share a marginal status and lack a political voice. The adaption of the term for a postcolonial context was first undertaken by the Subaltern Studies Group founded by Ranajit Guha, and explored in a series of books published between 1982 and 1989 edited by Guha, with later books associated with the group published as recently as 2005. Gayatri Chakravorty Spivak was involved in the group, and her essay 'Can the Subaltern Speak?' (1988a) established her voice prominently in the debate. Spivak extends the subaltern figure from Gramsci's specific definition by recognizing that the category includes 'subsistence farmers, unorganized peasant labor, the tribals, and the communities of zero workers on the street or in the countryside' (1988a, p. 288) and by addressing the figure of the subaltern woman. 'Can the Subaltern Speak?' is a consideration of the subaltern subject, and at the same time an exercise in questioning the role of the academic in any representation of that subaltern subject. Spivak situates these questions in a consideration of a range of theories of power, notably those by Marx, Michel Foucault, Gilles Deleuze and Jacques Derrida, with specific reference to Freud and to the Subaltern Studies Group. Spivak states that the first aim of her essay is to question the place of the investigator while remaining aware that there can be no satisfactory position from which an academic can speak for someone who they have defined as subaltern. A second intention is to consider the manner in which Western discourse has encountered the third-world subject. Like Trinh T. Minh-ha, Spivak rejects disdainfully the assumption of objectivity, or transparency, which is Spivak's preferred term. While Trinh addressed ethnography or anthropology, Spivak suggests that notions of transparency, based on the intellectual's assumed ability to transcend the material, are at work in much Western literary and cultural theory in the work of even progressive thinkers like Foucault and Deleuze.

In response to the assumption put forward by Foucault and Deleuze that the oppressed, or the marginalized, who Spivak repositions as the 'silent, silenced center' (1988a, p. 283), can speak and know their conditions when they are in a position of solidarity and if they have been 'given the chance' to form such an alliance, Spivak asks, and asks repeatedly, 'can the subaltern speak?' If they must be first represented by somebody who can enable them to form such a union, is their ability to speak not moderated by being 'given the chance' to speak by this external representative? Spivak claims that the subaltern must be unrepresentable, and so, if the subaltern is made representable, this proves that 'there is no unrepresentable subaltern subject that can know and speak itself' (1988a, p. 285). And the question of gender further complicates the subaltern figure. For Spivak, it is possible (and necessary) to address the subaltern subject in scholarly work, and the most reliable method for doing so is not to assume that the intellectual is exempt from ideological bias, but to be critical of the position from which the intellectual speaks and to remain alert to the method by which the intellectual speaks *to* that subject by 'unlearning' female privilege. This method evades the establishment of an essential or universal female subject which can be positioned as privileged and thus excised from questions of socio-economic and political context.

In order to demonstrate the complicated nature of the female subaltern position, Spivak engages with the practice of *sati*, or Hindu widow-burning, and its outlawing by the British colonial government in India. The subaltern subject identifiable in this situation is the Hindu widow who was expected by custom to immolate herself on her husband's funeral pyre. She had no voice with which to speak in her own community, yet she did not gain a voice when the British imperial governors decided to abolish the practice as she was silenced by the imperial voice. Spivak details the many ways in which the women's voices were absent from the whole question, from the examples of their mistranscribed names in police records to the nativist argument that 'the women actually wanted to die' (1988a, p. 297). If it is impossible to locate a woman's voice in a situation epitomizing the female subaltern experience, Spivak implies, then the inevitable conclusion must be that the subaltern cannot speak. Spivak elaborates on her position in an interview conducted in 1993, where she explains that 'in the case of the woman, the idea of subalternity, because of the woman's limited position to narrate, becomes contaminated' (Landry and MacLean, 1996, p. 289). Spivak responds to those who have misinterpreted her essay and accused her of saying that the subaltern cannot *talk*, by insisting that even if the subaltern can talk or utter in the context of their oppression, their utterance requires interpretation by a privileged interpreter and in this act of mediation and interpretation the subaltern is revealed as being unable to speak: 'even when the subaltern makes an effort to the death to speak, she is not able to be heard, and speaking and hearing complete the speech act' (1996, p. 292).

God Dies by the Nile

This displaced figuration of the subaltern woman between tradition and modernization is given a brutal rendering in Nawal El Saadawi's *God Dies by the Nile* (1985, first published in Arabic in 1974). The narrative is situated in rural Egypt and portrays the interdependent lives of agricultural peasant labourers and corrupt landowners and religious leaders. Much of the story concerns one family, a somewhat disjointed group of the nieces and nephews of matriarchal figure Zakeya. It is later revealed that their family structure is so unorthodox because of a sustained attrition of the family carried out by the mayor, who forces generations of the family's women to work for him as domestic – and sexual – servants, and arranges for the men to be sent away, through military service or unlawful imprisonment. The subaltern status of this family is established clearly and straight away: at the end of a day working in the fields, Zakeya and her brother Kafrawi, having just discovered that their niece Nefissa has disappeared, are shown to be completely powerless; in their fear, they sit, 'as immobile as the mud huts buried in the dark' (p. 7). The fragments of family are emblematic of a scattered consciousness imparted by the system of government which works to keep the working people superstitious, naïve and timid. The text conveys this scattered consciousness through sudden shifts in focalizer. It is reflected too by a general lack of knowledge about the specific circumstances of life moderated by an instinctive awareness of an unspoken threat; Kafrawi is accused of a crime he has not committed and when running away from the police, he runs from uncertainty, 'just putting enough distance as he could between himself and something he feared, just going without knowing where to go' (p. 60). This kind of latent knowledge is apparent throughout the text: Zakeya is finally able to identify that she is being punished by a particular person: she wrongly assumes that this is God, though, as she is unable to comprehend that her religious leader is corrupt, assuming instead that he (who symbolizes God) is the source of her ills and thus that God is the problem and must die. There is broad unrest, too, in the form of workers' resistance: they question why they must remain in debt to the local landowners when they have worked all year. While the Sheikh considers that hunger has made them blind (p. 127), the text implies that hunger, the result of their corrupt government, in fact made them able to see that corruption for the first time.

The women are, as Spivak suggested, doubly silenced, as they are subject to violence within the family home, and they have to perform physical labour outdoors and in public while their religious leaders insist that the female body should be hidden away. Family violence is encouraged: fathers are advised, 'Don't you know that girls and women never do what they're told unless you beat them?' (p. 21). The same conversation between father and sheikh recurs in the novel as successive daughters refuse to leave their family to work in service for the mayor, and the repetition of this conversation reveals the cycle of sanctioned violence against the subaltern woman. The beating of women is ingrained in society by those in power and put to work in order that the dominant patriarchs may control women and satisfy their own lust. Under the guise of religious duty, the women are repeatedly disenfranchised, and the patriarchal control and abuse of women always has an economic factor. There is an organized circle of fraud which operates because the community is encouraged to remain superstitious. Women are specifically targeted by religious representatives and encouraged to travel to a mosque near Bab El Hadeed in Cairo and to give their money (or food if they have no money) in exchange for incantations and charms which their local sheikhs have told them will cure insanity or depression, or any number of societally caused ills. When Zeinab is instructed to take her aunt to the city to cure her mental instability, the oracles insist that if she really wants to help her aunt to recover, she must go to work in the mayor's house. There, the mayor convinces her to have sex with him, which she does, believing that this was an act of worship: 'now she could leave herself in the hands of God, deliver her body and soul to Him, fulfil her vow, and savour the relief of having done so' (p. 99). In a society where men claim the authority of God, women reflect on their lives in the language of submission and claim no ownership of their own minds or bodies, being unable to do so because of their doubly silenced subaltern status. Even the fiercest female characters in the novel are constrained by their status within society: Fatheya is shown to be intellectually and psychologically superior to her husband Sheikh Hamzawi, yet still she had been forced into the marriage against her will. Her 'impudence' (p. 27) is rendered meaningless by her inability to make any choices about her own life, reminiscent of Spivak's example of the *sati*, whose only 'choice' is to die or to fit in to the British imperial idea of the colonized Hindu woman. The novel resists patriarchal dominance in a number of ways, though. The text is structured so that the method of focalization disrupts the male-centred narrative; although men instigate all of the main events of the plot, almost every chapter begins with a woman's perspective, her voice remaining that of Spivak's silenced subaltern because there is no hearer to conclude her speech act within the narrative world. There are multiple female focalizers, conveying a society-wide gender position rather than an isolated scenario. The final act of resistance is Zakeya's brutal killing of the mayor, which is entirely unexpected by the corrupt mayor himself:

> The mayor saw her come towards him. 'One of the peasant women who work on my farm,' he thought. When he came close he saw her arm rise high up in the air holding the hoe.
>   He did not feel the hoe land on his head and crush it at one blow. For a moment before, he had looked into her eyes, just once.   (p. 137)

In this final act there is desperation but also resistance, a violent resistance which is the inevitable result of the violent patriarchal society.

The White Tiger

In contrast with the rural peasant women depicted in El Saadawi's novel is the subaltern figure of Balram Halwai, a limousine driver employed by a wealthy family in Bangalore in Aravind Adiga's *The White Tiger* (2008), winner of the Man Booker Prize in 2008. *The White Tiger* is an exploration of the urban servant in the global city, and reflects upon the impact of globalization on the class of workers. On the one hand, there is a sense of disconnection from history, a vague and disappearing sense of tradition, and an erosion of community as new city jobs are created in the wake of globalization. The novel is structured as a modern epistolary narrative, as a series of emails written by Balram and addressed to Wen Jiabao, Prime Minister of China. It might be assumed that the subaltern is given the ability to speak when globalized India offers the opportunity to communicate by email, and not just to anyone, but to prime ministers. However, there is no indication that Balram's emails are read or even received by Wen Jiabao, and, as Spivak reminds us in her interview with Landry and MacLean, in order for the subaltern to speak, the whole speech act must take place: the subaltern must speak, and the intended hearer must hear. The novel conveys the extent of the subaltern's silence through his repeated effort to speak, and the heavy silence from the powerful side of the conversation.

In the sense that Balram Halwai's voice is in contention with the elite Indian voices who express a 'bourgeois nationalist' (Spivak, 1988b, p. 3) response to colonialism, he is a subaltern figure according to Ranajit Guha and the Subaltern Studies Group's definition of the term. Balram is repeatedly reminded of his subject status by his employers, members of the Indian urban elite who have the privilege of representation. While he drives Mr Ashok and his wife Pinky Madam, he is subject to a series of questions: 'how many planets are there in the sky?'; 'who was the first prime minister of India?'; 'what is the difference between a Hindu and a Muslim?'; 'What is the name of our continent?' (Adiga, 2008, pp. 9–10). Balram's answers, which he himself understands to be imprecise, are not provided on the page, but they are ridiculed by his employers who go on to discuss his 'half-baked' status while he remains with them in the car:

> "That's *really* what he thinks the correct answers are [...] The country is full of people like him [...] And we entrust our glorious parliamentary democracy" – he pointed at me – "to characters like these." (p. 10)

Ashok's opinion strikes Balram painfully, who agrees with his employer's assertion that he is 'half-baked', that he has had minimal schooling to begin the process of intellectual development but had it cruelly halted. But the two men have different responses to the phenomenon: for Ashok, the answer seems to be that men like Balram should not have a political voice, that members of his underprivileged class are ruining democracy. Balram's response is to lament his lack of education and to try to change it: he does so by taking the modern capitalist route of entrepreneurship. To be an entrepreneur, as the common capitalist myth has it, the individual does not need to have the attributes like education or class or caste position demanded by careers offering equal wealth and privilege; instead there is only the need for a capital investment and a spark of ingenuity.

Indian author and essayist Pankaj Mishra has called Balram Halwai 'a shrewd member of globalising India's lumpen proletariat' (2008) rather than a subaltern figure. The lumpen proletariat is a term most often attributed to Marx, who used it to define a group who occupy a social position considered below the proletariat, or working class. This includes beggars, prostitutes, the chronically unemployed, petty criminals, and others who might be considered debased or degenerate. Although Balram is, at the beginning of the novel, in regular employment and therefore a member of the proletariat in a Marxist analysis of society's structure, he undertakes a series of underhand activities in order to earn money, such as siphoning and selling his employer's petrol, taking money from corrupt mechanics who pay him a proportion of the inflated prices they charge his employer, and secretly using his employer's car as a taxi. In undertaking such activities, Balram is creating a barrier between himself and his employer. Rather than accepting their contrasting social positions, Balram positions his employer as the enemy who is stealing the wealth of the country that should be distributed more equally. However, in the type of activity he undertakes he is revealed as the debased, degenerate lumpen proletariat in the sense that Mishra suggests, because instead of employing recognized methods for renegotiating pay and conditions of employment, such as political protest and union organization, these are corrupt and criminal activities. Yet, because they are presented by Balram as entrepreneurship, the implication in the text is that entrepreneurship is based on criminal acquisition of an unequal share of the country's wealth.

The act of murder in *The White Tiger* is comparable with the similar climactic event in *God Dies by the Nile*, but something about their purpose in the two texts is unequal. Shankar Gopalakrishnan, an Indian political economist, has questioned Adiga's representation of the Indian subaltern, suggesting that he reduces the class to a group of 'oppressed crazies' (2008). *God Dies by the Nile* clearly and directly charts the descent into insanity of Zakeya, as a direct result of sustained patriarchal oppression. When Zakeya kills the mayor, the absolute knowledge of the cause of her life of pain and misfortune is clear to her: 'I know it's Allah', she says, and she is certain that she has killed Allah, and 'buried him there on the bank of the Nile' (p. 138). Of course, she is wrong: she has killed the mayor, who pretended to represent Allah to the peasants who worked on his land. Zakeya's act is the ultimate instinctual response of the oppressed, and her insanity is conveyed in imagery that shows it as a deep bodily wound: her powerful body that enables her to work in the fields is contrasted with the effects of her misery and insanity shown by her 'tightly closed lips' and her 'eyes staring into the darkness' which are present both at the very beginning of the text and at the end, unchanged after she has slaughtered the landowner with her hoe (pp. 4, 138). Zakeya has her choices imposed on her; Balram promotes the myth that he can negotiate his own destiny, enabled by his urban location and his globalized context: he has access to books that he reads in the market, to the detritus of his employer that he takes to sell and to earn money for himself. He eventually has access to email, via which he can have a (one-way) conversation with the Chinese prime minister.

Ankhi Mukherjee posits *The White Tiger* as an example of the deterritorialization of contemporary South Asian novels written in English, suggesting that the importance of the novel is its rendering of minority lives through a major language. This deterritorialization, or globalization, given the seal of authenticity when Adiga won the Man Booker Prize in 2008 for the novel, is another aspect that separates it from El Saadawi's novel, written in Arabic and read here in English translation. El Saadawi's Zakeya remains unchanged despite her act of killing, her lips fixed closed and her words ignored. The subaltern figure in Adiga's novel uses the tools of globalization and deterritorialization to express the changing position of the subaltern in global capitalism. The result is, in Mukherjee's analysis, that globalization has at least created a space from which the literary market is open to the fictional native subaltern voice.

Part III

Reading Postcolonial Literature

Introduction to Part III

The aim of this section is to offer postcolonial readings of selected novels commonly studied on postcolonial literature modules. The chapters address three separate concerns common to postcolonial literature: writing within the colonized location; postcolonial retelling; and migration. Each chapter brings together a number of novels in order to compare texts across different geographical regions or historical periods.

Chapter 6 compares three texts which reflect on the conditions of colonization. *Heart of Darkness* is written about the imperial presence in the Congo, reproducing the way that the colonial binary opposes black and white races, colonizer and colonized. While it seems to uphold such binaries, this text is critical of the brutal processes involved in colonialism. *Things Fall Apart* conveys the early colonial encounter from the perspective of prominent Ibo, Okwonko, and has been such an influential text in part because of the elegant diction of the Ibo people in the English-language text, directly contradicting colonial representations of colonized peoples as barbaric. While *Things Fall Apart* can be understood as a novel that counteracts problems with the representation of the colonized in *Heart of Darkness*, *Nervous Conditions* offers a further corrective by conveying the perspective of the young female protagonist undertaking missionary education in colonial Rhodesia; *Things Fall Apart* in comparison is a far more male-centred novel.

Chapter 7 brings together three pairs of texts, and in each case, a canonical British novel is rewritten from a postcolonial perspective to privilege a character silenced and disenfranchised in the original. The revisions also make the colonized location more visible, in order to rethink the imperial centre. Shakespeare's *The Tempest* is of fundamental importance to postcolonial literature, particularly from the Caribbean, as it directly represents the master–slave relationship on an island location. Césaire's rewriting is the most direct of many Caribbean literary responses to Shakespeare's play. *Wide Sargasso Sea* gives Brontë's silenced Bertha back her voice and her history, while Carey's *Jack Maggs* is an important novel to include because it reveals a latent imperialism in Dickens's attitude towards Australia which, for Carey, had an ongoing impact on the global reception of Australian literature. Chapter 8 examines novels of migration, from India to England, from Antigua to the United States, and from Sri Lanka to Canada. Novels conveying experiences of migration and diaspora are of key significance in representing the effects of colonialism in a contemporary, global context.

6 The Text in the Colony

The texts discussed in this chapter all convey the experience of life within an African colony. They are geographically and historically diverse: Conrad's *Heart of Darkness* depicts imperial trade in the late nineteenth-century Belgian-controlled Congo; Achebe's *Things Fall Apart* is set at the same historical period but takes place in Nigeria and relates the impact of colonial missionaries on an Ibo community; and Dangarembga's *Nervous Conditions* is set in colonial Rhodesia (now Zimbabwe) in the 1960s and concerns the missionary education of a group of adolescents. The novels include a death of central narrative importance, and all three share a preoccupation with texts: manuscripts, memoirs and novels.

Joseph Conrad, *Heart of Darkness*

As a short novel that directly addresses the ideologies and processes of colonization, *Heart of Darkness* conveys problematic binaries, while at the same time it is critical of the brutal processes behind colonialism. The main narrator Marlow is a young seaman who travels on an African river to find the ivory trader Kurtz, who is reputed to have exceptional talents for building relationships with native people to improve trade. Marlow locates Kurtz, who he realizes has become insane and actually controls the natives through fear: the rebellious natives are slaughtered and their heads displayed on pikes. The text implies either that Kurtz has gone mad because of the grotesque horror of Africa itself, its vast monstrosity too much for the civilized European to bear, or that madness is the inevitable result of the corruption and brutality of the colonial project. It is this pivot on which the text balances, and this question – of whether the text justifies colonialism by showing the primitive barbarity of Africa and the need to control and civilize it, or whether the text criticizes colonialism by exposing its basis in exploitation – is at the centre of postcolonial readings of the novel.

There is merit in Chinua Achebe's position that writers like Conrad present the African continent inadequately, as 'either a blank space or a monstrous presence', as Simon Gikandi has put it (1991, pp. 26–7). The landscape is rendered in imprecise but fearful images: the somehow 'formless' coast is bordered by 'dangerous surf' and the country is depicted as almost animate but grotesque: 'streams of death in life, whose banks were rotting into mud, whose waters, thickened into slime invaded the contorted mangroves, that seemed to writhe at us in the extremity of an impotent despair' (pp. 20–1). Marlow's description of the Africans evinces the same repulsion: they are described like animals, with 'bone, muscle, a wild vitality', and worse, their faces are 'grotesque masks' (p. 20). They are 'black shapes', 'nothing earthly', 'bundles' of bones (pp. 24–5). To an extent, though, their representation is based on Marlow's awareness that the colonial situation is responsible for their despair and ill-health.

The lack of an African voice in the text has been seen by Achebe and others as Conrad's failing. Edward Saïd points out instead that silence operates more broadly in the text. Saïd describes Marlow as anxious rather than racist, suggesting that Conrad's narrators demonstrate the discrepancy between orthodox imperialism and Conrad's own ambivalence towards empire, which is discernible in 'dislocations in the narrator's language' (1993, p. 32). Conrad was employed by the colonial British navy and worked on a steamship on a colonial project on the River Congo, yet he only arrived in Britain as an adult; he was Polish by birth and had experienced imperialism from the position of Poland's subordination to the Russian Empire. For Saïd, this authorial ambivalence is constantly at play in Marlow's narration and in the end, the reader has an 'acute sense that what he is presenting is not quite as it should be or appears to be' (1993, p. 33).

The short novel is punctuated by deaths, most notably – at least, from the perspective of the narrative trajectory – Kurtz's. Kurtz is the reason for Marlow's voyage to Africa in the first place, and his death forces Marlow to return to London and confront the ideology of empire from the place of its inception when he is instructed by the dying man to deliver letters to his fiancée. But there is another death in the novel that can be read as the real source of Marlow's ambivalence regarding his role in Africa and about the justifiability of colonialism; this death exemplifies Saïd's observation that the narration is not straightforward, that all is not as it appears to be.

Towards the middle of the voyage, the steamship is blocked in a narrow passageway on the river and attacked by natives.

The ship's helmsman, an African, is killed but his death is so unexpected because of the quietness of the attack and the fragility of the weapons: Marlow describes the arrows as 'sticks, little sticks', that looked as though 'they wouldn't kill a cat' (p. 65), yet the helmsman falls down at Marlow's feet, a thick spear stuck in his chest. His condition is not immediately apparent, and Marlow is alerted to his helmsman's injury because his feet 'felt so very warm and wet' (p. 66); they were covered with the helmsman's blood. Marlow's behaviour is odd: his first thought is for his feet and shoes, covered in blood – 'morbidly anxious' to change his shoes, he hurls them overboard, and when he is forced to admit that the helmsman is dead, he says in the same breath: 'And by the way, I suppose Mr Kurtz is dead as well by this time' (p. 67). Marlow's behaviour when the helmsman dies is not just callous: it is neurotic, and he transfers his feelings about the helmsman's death to his fears about the trip in general:

> By Jove! it's all over. We are too late; he has vanished – [...] I will never hear that chap speak after all, – and my sorrow had a startling extravagance of emotion, even such as I had noticed in the howling sorrow of these savages in the bush.   (pp. 67–8)

The transference of emotion from one death to a separate feared death (which is an unfounded fear – Marlow does meet Kurtz soon afterwards, as he is aware as he narrates this story) is revealed as Marlow's fundamental uncertainty about the legitimacy of his position in Africa: at this moment he expresses the fear that Achebe has accused him of, that the Africans – those 'savages' – might be human after all, that he might share their emotions. If they are equals, his role in Africa and the colonial endeavour is untenable. The impact of this realization is apparent in the narrative structure – Marlow's narrative breaks down and is interrupted by the external narrator who records long pauses of 'profound stillness' (p. 68) punctuated by a confused retracing of the events: 'Girl! What? Did I mention a girl?' (p. 69), he asks, then evaluates the trip and his tale, as well as his psychological state as 'Absurd! Absurd be – exploded! Absurd!' (p. 68), before revealing that he later meets Kurtz as expected. Marlow interrupts the chronology of his tale to dwell for an extended period on his meeting with Kurtz, on Kurtz's writings, and the voice that he had longed to hear, which leave an unsettling impression: the 'terrifying' post-script to Kurtz's documented plan for exploiting ivory and other resources from Africa reads, in contradiction

to his professed integration in the native community: 'Exterminate all
the brutes!' (p. 72). Marlow can only return to the episode of his helmsman's death pages later, after recounting his feelings about Kurtz, when
he suddenly interrupts his analysis with the admission that he missed his
late helmsman and their partnership. Undoubtedly, his grief and regret is
couched in the language of imperial paternity: the 'poor fool' had to be
looked after, had to have his 'deficiencies' (p. 73) carefully circumvented by
the fatherly, protecting colonizer, Marlow. Yet, he does respect the man's
dead body, pulling out the spear and throwing him overboard to spare him
the indignity of being eaten by the starving crew members, again an ambivalent position that elevates the individual native to a position of humanity
while degrading the majority to the status of cannibalism.

It is clear from this instance that Marlow's, and Conrad's, position on
colonialism is not straightforward: the text may present unpleasant late
nineteenth-century assumptions about the binary opposition of Europe
and Africa, European and African, but it does not do so simplistically:
the 'darkness' is not Africa's alone; it exists in the colonial offices in London,
in its streets and on the Thames. However, the ending of the novel is problematic: Marlow has been charged by Kurtz to deliver a set of papers to his
fiancée, a young woman in London. This is an arduous task for Marlow, who
has by this point come to understand that Kurtz is both corrupt and insane,
while Kurtz's fiancée still clings to an idealistic impression of the man.
Marlow is forced to confront his knowledge about Kurtz and colonial trade
in Africa, and also his ability or intention to act upon that knowledge, when
the woman asks to know Kurtz's dying words. Unable to tell her that Kurtz
had exclaimed 'the horror! the horror!', he lies: 'the last word he pronounced
was – your name' (p. 110). Marlow allows this lie, and with it the colonial
lie, to continue, and the 'darkness' that is colonialism remains ongoing,
'immense' (p. 111), at the narrative's close. By placing this power in Marlow's
hands, the text reveals its assumption that the colonizer is all-powerful, that
colonialism (or its brutalities) will only end at the colonizer's behest; this
reflects Edward Saïd's major problem with the text. Conrad's flaw, for Saïd,
is his inability to understand that 'the darkness' is in fact 'a non-European
world *resisting* imperialism so as one day to regain sovereignty and independence, and not, as Conrad reductively says, to re-establish the darkness'
(1993, p. 33). The danger perceived from the attack during which his helmsman was killed, while apparently slight, was actually deadly, and perhaps
it is this that Marlow cannot cope with; he realizes that the threat posed by
the colony is greater than anticipated but misinterprets the purpose of the
aggression while he refuses to countenance the fact that the colonized can

and will revolt in order to regain sovereignty, as Saïd describes. Kurtz's letters and papers remain the dominant representation of Africa, and Kurtz's death is the one remembered by the existence of those texts. This is not the case in Chinua Achebe's *Things Fall Apart*: the colonizer's document – a memoir – occupies the most marginal of positions at the end of the text, and its main function is to display its marked inaccuracy, representative of other colonial accounts of Africa. Achebe's novel works to challenge prior textual and linguistic representations of the African colony in English-language texts.

Chinua Achebe, *Things Fall Apart*

Chinua Achebe has famously resisted any positive reading of *Heart of Darkness*; he gave a lecture at the University of Massachusetts in 1975, titled 'An Image of Africa: Racism in Conrad's *Heart of Darkness*', where he argued that the novel could not be a great work of art as it dehumanized Africa, and made Eurocentric assumptions that the whole of the African continent could be reduced to the trigger for one European man's insanity. *Things Fall Apart* is as much a response to *Heart of Darkness* as it is to the novels Achebe was instructed to read at university, like Joyce Cary's *Mister Johnson* (1939), a novel that he has described as a misrepresentation of Africa. *Things Fall Apart* conveys the early colonial encounter from the perspective of prominent Ibo, Okwonko, and has been so influential in part because of the elegant diction of the Ibo people in the English-language text, directly contradicting colonial representations of colonized peoples as barbaric.

Achebe recognizes the need for African writers to alter the English language to suit their stories and ideological purpose. During the first narrated encounter between Okonkwo's Ibo community and the missionaries, language is used in order to convey the superior position of the Umuofia Ibo. The white missionary speaks through an Ibo translator from outside the community who uses a strange dialect and imprecise vocabulary rendering the missionary's words ridiculous: 'Instead of saying "myself" he always said "my buttocks"' (Achebe, 2006, p. 136). When the Ibo mock the translator's language and, with it, the white missionary's words, saying 'Your buttocks understand our language' (p. 137), they are placed in a dominant narrative position. This directly contrasts with encounters between colonizer and colonized in the colonial novel, where the 'natives' are ordinarily portrayed as lacking linguistic skills, speaking in broken English, in fragments and grunts. Language is a significant aspect of power: those who use language powerfully elicit respect from those around them and are intended to gain the reader's sympathy in the literary text. Conversely, comically imprecise command of language like the kind demonstrated by the missionary translator means that it is difficult for the intended audience to take his message seriously. Having been informed by the missionary that the Ibo gods are false and that the Christian God is the only true god, the Ibo are dubious: hearing that God has a son, they state that logically, he must also have a wife, meaning that there is a second god. Rejecting the missionary's mild protest, one of the men responds: "'Your buttocks said he had a son [...] So he must have a wife and all of them must have buttocks'" (pp. 138–9). The colonial missionaries are conveyed as out of their depth when their religion is ridiculed using a combination of logic (the Ibo have seen the power of their own gods that the missionaries dismiss as 'pieces of wood and stone'; if a god has a son he must have a wife and thus cannot be the only god) and linguistic superiority.

Though the missionaries' efforts damage Ibo society, they are portrayed as naïve and essentially well-meaning, while the colonial system that they represent is revealed as seriously ideologically unsound. The colonial commissioner is a figure with far more serious flaws: he instigates a violent regime to crush – in his own words, intended to effect a 'pacification' of – the Ibo. By the end of the novel the result of the colonial regime is Okonkwo's suicide, and his friend Obierika has the task of explaining this, as well as the customs regarding suicide, to the commissioner. Obierika says: "'That man was one of the greatest men in Umuofia. You drove him to kill himself; and now he will be buried like a dog...' He could not say any more. His voice trembled and choked his words' (p. 197). The fact that this angry accusation goes unchallenged demonstrates the high moral position held by Obierika and the other Ibo. The only response to Obierika's words comes from one of the messengers, who, after Obierika has ceased speaking, tells him to 'shut up', words intended to convey authority but which instead show groundless bravado as they are empty words, spoken 'quite unnecessarily' (p. 197). It is in this context that the commissioner takes charge of the narrative to close the novel, shifting the narrative voice from the Ibo and towards the colonizer in a move that could be seen as a surprising decision as narrative voice generally implies narrative authority. The engagement with colonial writing is brought sharply into focus in this final short section of the novel. The commissioner decides that 'the story of this man who had killed a messenger and hanged himself would make interesting reading' in his planned memoir. He reflects that 'One could almost write a whole chapter on him. Perhaps not a whole chapter but a reasonable paragraph, at any rate' (p. 197). It is clear to the reader that the commissioner's views are insupportable to the point of inhumanity, their cold objectivity ridiculous after Obierika's emotional yet controlled response to his friend's death. The passage also shows his flawed perception of events, conveyed by the brevity of the section narrated by the commissioner as much as by his ideas. Indeed, Elleke Boehmer has stated that the commissioner's position is a weak one, conveyed by his voice in the text which is given the status of a footnote (1995, p. 196). Footnotes, of course, can also have an authoritative status, even if they are marginal to the main text. The unsatisfying ending, with the suggestion that Okonkwo's story is one of many that will be, or have been, told by flawed narrators is a call to revolt and a claim for new representation, which does not defer to the colonizer.

Despite the strength of the novel's challenge to colonialism, *Things Fall Apart* remains an essentially masculine text. Biodun Jeyifo has noted the lack of critical exploration of the female characters, suggesting that the important relationships understood both in the world of the text and in scholarly readings of the text have been between Okonkwo and his father, and Okonkwo and his son Nwoye. For Jeyifo, the women in the novel are repeatedly subordinated to 'the spheres of male initiatives and control' (1993, p. 847). This is perhaps because the novel conveys the feminizing effect of colonialism: under the influence of the colonial missionaries, the men in Okonkwo's absence become 'unaccountably soft like women' (p. 173). Nevertheless, women in the novel are subject to ridicule – their stories are 'silly' (p. 71) in comparison to those told by men. The wedding ceremony at the centre of the novel represents, but does not critique, the patriarchal culture of the Ibo: the women are referred to by their association with their male relatives and are rarely named: they are 'Nwoye's mother', 'Obierika's wife', 'Okonkwo's daughter' or 'the bride' (pp. 104–5). The ceremony focuses on the bride's function as bearer of male children, the woman's value as a bride conveyed through the promises that 'she will bear you nine sons'; that she will 'bear us sons like you', like the champion warrior Okonkwo (p. 111). After the formalities of the ceremony have been completed the bride displays her body in dance and the attendees sing the latest song in the village, a song about the woman's coyness and her sexual availability:

> 'If I hold her hand
> She says, "Don't touch!"
> If I hold her foot
> She says, "Don't touch!"
> But when I hold her waist beads
> She pretends not to know.'   (p. 112)

Tsitsi Dangarembga, *Nervous Conditions*

In contrast with the silenced women in *Things Fall Apart*, Dangarembga's *Nervous Conditions* is a novel which privileges the female voice, exploring the colonial encounter from the perspective of Tambudzai. Adolescent Tambudzai is destabilized by an imposed colonial education yet unsatisfied with the alternative informal education from relatives who punctuate stories of the past with agricultural labour. Tambudzai challenges the injustice of her patriarchal community which assumes that only a male child could have the benefit of education, frustrated that her own education is infrequent and interrupted when the family cannot afford to send her to school. During these periods she works on the land and tolerates the slow delivery of history lessons from her grandmother: 'a stint in the field and a rest, the beginning of the story, a pause [...] Slowly, methodically, throughout the day the field would be cultivated, the episodes of my grandmother's own portion of history strung together' (pp. 17–8). Her brother Nhamo's death is the important death in this novel, but here death does not occur at the narrative climax: instead, Nhamo's death enables Tambu to take his place in the missionary school, and here she develops a close friendship with her cousin Nyasha. Unable to tolerate her colonial situation, Nyasha becomes very ill but avoids death, and this is important because it marks a resistance to colonialism that carries a message of hope, in contrast with Achebe's more desolate representation of resistance with Okonkwo's suicide and the wresting of control from the African at the end of the novel.

Rhodesia (renamed Zimbabwe at independence) was a British colony from 1890 until 1980. The colonial relationship changed in November 1965 when the Rhodesian government declared its independence by issuing the Unilateral Declaration of Independence (the UDI) in protest at Britain's sluggish efforts to enable the country to gain independence at a time when Britain was withdrawing from most colonies in Africa. Rhodesia's declaration was resisted, though, and until 1980 the country was placed under trade and other sanctions because Britain and the United Nations saw the UDI as illegal resistance. *Nervous Conditions* is set during the period of fraught colonial dependency immediately following the UDI and although the colonial context differs in many ways from the French Antillean colonies described by Frantz Fanon in *Black Skin, White Masks*, the texts have a common focus on colonial education. There is, too, an explicit reference to Fanon's *The Wretched of the Earth* in the epigraph to the novel, which locates the title of Dangarembga's novel in a quotation from

Jean-Paul Sartre's introduction to Fanon's work: 'The condition of the native is a nervous condition'.

Nhamo's mission education separates him from his family, a cultural separation which is accompanied by his use of the colonizer's language in the manner described by Fanon, who has described the Antillean's command of the French language as commensurate with his psychological distance from his community:

> He had forgotten how to speak Shona. A few words escaped haltingly, ungrammatically and strangely accented [...] Father was pleased with Nhamo's command of the English language. He said it was the first step in the family's emancipation. (pp. 52–3)

Nhamo has become the educated black subject that Fanon observes in *Black Skin, White Masks*, who, as a result of a colonial education experiences a psychological detachment from his race. This is welcomed by the colonized subject whose education has taught him to reject his 'primitive' race (1986, p. 16). In the Antilles, the programme of colonial education begins with the young black boy's introduction to comic books and adventure stories, which always feature white heroes vanquishing black or Indian (Native American) savages and 'bad men'. Through reading these stories, 'the little Negro, quite as easily as the little white boy, becomes an explorer, an adventurer, a missionary "who faces the danger of being eaten by the wicked Negroes"' (1986, p. 146). Yet, this missionary education always eventually works to impose the subjection of the black race, as Fanon has described: missionary education convinces the black man that he is white, and then the black man is told he has a dependency complex on the white man (1986, p. 216). Fanon explores this contradiction in the psychology of the subject in the colony and in the diaspora. In *Nervous Conditions*, it is Tambudzai's cousin Nyasha who experiences the most traumatic identity complex; Nyasha cannot reconcile her experiences in both Rhodesia and England with her knowledge that the colonial education she receives operates in the way that Fanon has described, to create a condition of colonial dependency.

Nyasha's perspective is difficult for Tambudzai, an intelligent but also a naïve observer, to understand. To her mind, Nyasha is 'Shocking and funny; disrespectful and irrepressible. [...] Nyasha had everything, should have been placid and content. My cousin was perplexing' (p. 96). She is, though, a figure who can be understood from a postcolonial perspective. In letters, she describes how her linguistic difference sets her apart from the other girls: 'They do not like my language, my English, because it is

authentic and my Shona, because it is not!' (p. 196). Cultural confusion
leads to an obsession with accuracy in her school work, and a simultane-
ous rejection of food: she eats when forced and then voluntarily vomits,
until she becomes skeletally thin. Eventually, Nyasha is able to see that her
colonial education has destroyed her: 'She rampaged, shredding her history books between her teeth ('Their history. Fucking liars. Their bloody
lies.')' (pp. 200–1). Her behaviour might be read as clarity of vision in
response to her colonial condition, but it is pathologized, and she is sent
away by a psychiatrist to 'recover' with the help of drugs.

Liz Gunner has read the depiction of Nyasha's 'colonial madness' as
a doubly subversive response to colonialism. On the one hand, the novel
challenges the canon in the form of the postcolonial woman's novel, while
at the same time the female-centred community depicted in the novel
(consisting of Tambudzai, her mother and sister and her grandmother, her
cousin Nyasha and her aunt, their servant Anna, and the girls' school that
she attends) makes reference to pre-colonial matrilineal Shona society
that is remembered through glimpses in Tambu's grandmother's stories. The
complex result of colonial education is conveyed through the narration of
a series of crises: Nhamo loses his sense of identity in his desire to become
different from his family through education; and Nyasha falls ill when she
attempts to resist the impact of colonialism and of her Westernized identity.
Tambu's quiet commentary gives the impression that by remaining aware of
the impact of the colonial missionary system in Africa she may be able to
avoid devastation and negotiate both 'familial patriarchy and the subtle mental dominance of the colonial system' (Gunner, 1994, p. 145). The rereading of
English literature in the African colony when the girls read *Lady Chatterley's
Lover* is another example of Dangarembga's challenge to the Western literary canon, and also an example of the kind of anticolonial and postcolonial rereading that is often carried out in textual translation or retelling. In
contrast to the missionary texts which exercise different levels of authority
over the colony in *Heart of Darkness* and *Things Fall Apart*, the postcolonial rereading and retelling of the sensational (once censored) English book
in *Nervous Conditions* is a textual act that can be redemptive. Nyasha and
Tambudzai survive and Tambudzai especially has learned, through her cousin's self-effacing subversive reading, to question her history and to think for
herself. This act of postcolonial retelling is the subject of the next chapter.

7 The Postcolonial Counter-Text

This chapter brings together a range of texts offering imperialist readings of 'native' or colonized figures, with their postcolonial rewritings.
The Tempest clearly portrays the master–servant/colonizer–colonized
relationship and depicts the colonial project. This chapter discusses ways
in which the play can be read by postcolonial theory, by comparing it
with Aimé Césaire's anticolonial rewriting, *A Tempest.* Jean Rhys's novel
re-imagines *Jane Eyre* with a postcolonial sensibility. A more recent postcolonial counter-text, Peter Carey's *Jack Maggs* offers a direct challenge
to the Australian criminal ancestry inherited from Magwitch in *Great
Expectations.*

William Shakespeare's *The Tempest* and Aimé Césaire's *A Tempest*

The retellings of *Othello* in the feminist *Desdemona: A Play about a Hand-
kerchief* (1977) and of *The Tempest* in Philip Osment's *This Island's Mine*
(1988) from a gay activist perspective raise questions about the assumptions in the original plays about authority and subordination. Postcolonial
adaptations of *The Tempest* also question power relationships within the
play, but the second motivation for retelling the play for postcolonial purposes is to reconsider Shakespeare's appropriation by colonial governments in colonized locations. Shakespeare's work was presented as a gift
to the colony. In colonial India, his plays were regularly performed for
audiences of elite Indians both to demonstrate the myth of English refine-
ment and superiority and to justify the colonial process as a civilising and
a benevolent mission, as Jyotsna Singh has argued (1989, p. 446). In this
way, for Singh, 'colonial administrators found an ally in English literature

to support them in maintaining control over the natives under the guise of a liberal education' (1989, p. 449). A first step towards reforming the literary and political landscape of India was inevitably the rethinking of the position of English literature in India, and this meant adapting or translating its figurehead: Shakespeare.

The Tempest has been of especial interest for anticolonial and postcolonial writers because of its characters and location. Lisa Hopkins has claimed that there is a clear historical relationship between the earliest attempts at British colonialism and the play, and in particular mentions the wreckage of a ship called The Sea Venture on the coast of Bermuda in 1609. Hopkins suggests that clear verbal echoes between William Strachey's account of this episode in 1610 and the play indicate that colonial travel to the Caribbean and this particular shipwreck were used by Shakespeare as a source for the play (2005, pp. 164–5). Caliban has the strongest claim to indigenous habitation on the island, having been born there when his mother Sycorax, a witch, was banished from her native Algiers. The only other inhabitants are spirits until Prospero, a member of European nobility, arrives and claims ownership of the island and dominance of Caliban, Ariel, and the other spirits based on his assumed cultural and intellectual superiority. Prospero takes the position of colonial master over Caliban, who becomes his slave, on an otherwise unpopulated tropical island reminiscent of the Caribbean.

George Lamming's The Pleasures of Exile (1960), which includes a lengthy discussion of the significance of the play in maintaining imperial thinking, is considered the first anticolonial or postcolonial retelling of the play. There have been retellings in poetry, including Edward Kamau Brathwaite's poem, 'Caliban' (in Islands, 1969) and Lemuel Johnson's volume of poems, The Highlife for Caliban (1973). Rob Nixon has discussed Fernandez Retamar's Cuba Hasta Fidel (1969) as a reflection on Cuba's decolonization which is influenced by The Tempest, and remarks that his later essay, 'Caliban: Notes towards a Discussion of Culture in Our America' (1971) both 'passionately chronicles the accumulative symbolic significance of Caliban and commemorates those whose deeds and utterances bodied forth the author's conception of the Calibanesque' (1987, p. 574). David Malouf's play Blood Relations (1988) resituated The Tempest in an Australian context, while John Murrell's play New World (1985) alludes to The Tempest to tell a story of race and migration in Canada. But Césaire's A Tempest (1969) is the most direct literary retelling, and it states its purpose explicitly: the title page notes that the play is based on Shakespeare's The Tempest and adapted for a 'black theatre'.

To reach the audience of its intended black theatre, the play must overturn Prospero's dominance in favour of Césaire's Caliban who is a black slave. This is achieved – there is no penitent Caliban like Shakespeare's, thanking Prospero for his pardon and promising to 'be wise hereafter, / And seek for grace' (5.1.294–5). In Césaire's adaptation, Prospero is left confused by Caliban's sudden empowerment, asking 'What in the hell is he up to?' before Caliban's song ends the play with the words: 'FREEDOM HI-DAY! FREEDOM HI-DAY!' (3.5). The method of resistance in Césaire's play is a call for black empowerment: when Caliban joins forces with Stephano and Trinculo, as he did in Shakespeare's version, he quickly becomes aware that the tyranny of Prospero is a different issue for him, and that if he wants to 'create the Revolution' he must win freedom 'all by myself' (3.4). With this statement, the play makes reference to anticolonials' insistence that the communist parties did not adequately represent black issues as a result of their insistence on humanism, or universalism, which eroded differences between working peoples. Caliban's right of freedom is elaborated in a long speech near the end of the play where he tells Prospero that the long years of ingratitude, insults and condescension that he has suffered are over, that Prospero's power is based on lies about his superiority, that the colonial 'mission' is a farce and an addiction.

A *Tempest* maintains the structure of the original play, scene for scene, almost exactly. The only differences are three omitted scenes in Césaire's play, one of which is the epilogue. In addition, an inserted scene allows Caliban (a 'black slave' in Césaire's text) and Ariel (a 'mulatto slave') to discuss their bound condition, and Ariel's hope for the future: 'we are brothers, brothers in suffering and slavery, but brothers in hope as well. We both want our freedom' (2.1). This is a pivotal scene for analysing resistance; while Ariel occupies the role of the 'good nigger', the obedient slave that Césaire railed against in 'A Return to My Native Land', Caliban fights for violent resistance. As Rob Nixon has described:

> from Caliban's perspective Ariel is a colonial collaborator, a political and cultural sellout who, aspiring both to rid himself nonviolently of Prospero and to emulate his values, is reduced to negotiating for liberty from a position of powerlessness. (1987, p. 573)

Caliban's comment on language (that his only profit was an ability to curse) is frequently cited in postcolonial responses to the Prospero–Caliban relationship as evidence that the colonial project did not, as it claimed, function primarily from benevolent motives: learning Prospero's language was not enlightening for Caliban. However, Shakespeare's play insists that Caliban had no language before Prospero arrived, maintaining colonialist assumptions that the colonized is inherently inferior. One important amendment made by Césaire is Caliban's use of his native language: 'Mumbling your native language again! I've already told you, I don't like it!' (1.2), Prospero complains.

The play is directly polemical in nature and this method was appropriate for both theatre performance and Césaire's context of resistance. Jean Rhys's novel *Wide Sargasso Sea* (1966) is a more indirect retelling of Charlotte Brontë's *Jane Eyre*, which tells the story of Brontë's Bertha, the madwoman in the attic who was an archetypal figure in Victorian literature, but whose portrayal was complicated because she was a migrant from the Caribbean, tainted by the assumption that she had 'bad' (in other words, racially mixed) blood.

Charlotte Brontë's *Jane Eyre* and Jean Rhys's *Wide Sargasso Sea*

Gayatri Spivak insists that a commitment to postcolonial thinking involves rereading the nineteenth-century novel. This is especially the case when considering nineteenth-century novels written by women, which might otherwise be celebrated from a feminist perspective, because of the tendency Spivak observes in these women writers from the dominant culture to create an 'inchoate "other" (often female)' (1999, p. 113) to establish once again the Western/Other binary. Spivak writes that in order to resist the received ideas arising from such representations, it should be impossible to read nineteenth-century British literature without remembering that imperialism was at work in those texts representing England and especially England's social mission. It is with this in mind that Spivak rereads *Jane Eyre*, paying particular attention to the figure of Bertha Mason, Rochester's insane, West Indian wife, who is secluded in the marginal space of an attic room, and the marginal textual space of rumour, silence, darkness and the indistinguishable grunts of bestial existence. Spivak's approach to the novels is a particularly persuasive and illuminating one.

Jane and Rochester's life is first disturbed by the spectre of Bertha Mason when Bertha's brother arrives at the house from the West Indies. At this point in the text neither Jane nor the reader is aware that Rochester has already been married to a Jamaican woman and that she is hidden in an attic room. The arrival of Bertha's brother is presented in the text as Rochester's comeuppance, his punishment for frivolous trickery in the costume of a fortune-teller and for the liberty he has taken with Jane in assuming to be able to dictate her future, advising her in his gypsy costume to pursue marriage. His position of assumed power and knowledge is shaken, and he is rendered senseless, repeating 'Mason! – the West Indies!' three times like the words to a dangerous incantation, before staggering, requiring Jane's support to collapse into a chair. Rochester's presentation as the victim in this situation belies his treatment of his wife, Bertha.

Later that night, there is a much more violent event: Bertha attacks her brother Robert Mason viciously and Jane is awoken by her 'cry', which is 'savage' and 'sharp' (p. 205). For Spivak, it is this portrayal of Bertha as animal that renders her powerless in *Jane Eyre*: 'Bronte renders the human/animal frontier as acceptably indeterminate, so that a good deal greater than the letter of the law can be broached' (1999, p. 121). While locked in a room tending Mason but forbidden from speaking to him, Jane hears 'a snarling, snatching sound, almost like a dog quarrelling' (p. 208). At this point, Jane is forced to ask, 'Why *did* Mr Rochester enforce this concealment?' (p. 210). Though Jane assumes a former servant (Grace Poole) is the one concealed, her question is still an important one. Brontë's answer is that Rochester displays a certain moral frailty, having been tricked into marrying a woman with 'bad blood', but that he is not so evil that he cannot be saved, at Bertha's expense, of course, and after having suffered burns, blindness, and disempowerment. A postcolonial reading must answer Jane's question differently: not only is the portrayal of the colonized other highly problematic, but in addition, the episode recounts nineteenth-century England being revisited by the colonial monster it had created.

Spivak suggests that the most powerful act of revision for Bertha in *Wide Sargasso Sea* is Rhys's insistence that 'the woman from the colonies is not sacrificed as an insane animal for her sister's consolation' (1999, p. 127). A feminism that requires the sacrifice of the foreign other woman is not good enough for Rhys. Bertha's insanity and her inhumanity in the episode where in *Jane Eyre* she is heard snarling like a dog is, Spivak points out, expelled by Rhys's careful rewriting of the scene, in which Grace Poole points out that Antoinette (the rewritten Bertha) reacted violently to her brother's insistence that he could not interfere 'legally' between the couple. Antoinette is driven to her violent act in Rhys's retelling by her dependent status; she is not simply a wild creature who attacks without motive. Antoinette's violence is legitimized by the narrative shift in Rhys's text from the centre to the margin: the woman from the colonies generally controls the perspective from which the story is conveyed. The text is modernist in style, combining long stretches of conversation, letters, and character-narration that sometimes slips into what is often termed a stream-of-consciousness style, where the character-narrator's thoughts drift and associations and memories interrupt the focused narration of the story. The narrative perspective shifts, too: though Antoinette narrates the first and the third parts of the novel, long sections of the second part are narrated by the rewritten Rochester figure. As Spivak has pointed out, Rochester's control of the narrative has been seen as problematic for some postcolonial commentators, who insist that Antoinette's voice should dominate if there is an intention to equalize the presentation of the woman from the colonies. However, there are a few ways in which the text moderates Rochester's voice: the Rochester figure is never named in the text and instead is simply referred to as 'the man'; for Spivak this important act denies Rochester the Oedipal Name of the Father or patronymic, thus leaving him vulnerable when 'feminism and a critique of imperialism come together' (1999, p. 128). Secondly, Rochester's – or, the man's – narrative is consistently interrupted, mostly by Christophine, Antoinette's black maid, who alone is able to directly challenge Rochester. Christophine's voice is a 'judge's voice' (p. 98), not the kind that can be ignored. Christophine neither fears nor reveres Rochester as he expects, but tells him '"you are not the best, not the worst. You are – " she shrugged' (p. 101). Her uncertain description of Rochester reveals how little she values him: her authoritative voice resounds in a long stretch of text given over to telling Rochester how much damage he has caused Antoinette. Responding to further critiques of Rhys's text that Christophine's story is allowed to slip away from the narrative rather than being given fuller representation, Spivak considers her story a direct parallel in structural terms to a similar tangential one in *Jane Eyre*, that of St John Rivers, Jane's cousin who sacrifices his life in order to take the imperial mission to India. It is telling that the white, male imperial missionary's story is replaced in Rhys's text by the story of a black servant, a former slave (Spivak, 1999, p. 129). Christophine's voice and her position are strong, and reveal their strength in her ongoing presence beyond the bounds of the narrative as much as in her confident upbraiding of Rochester. Rhys's text provides a motivation for Antoinette setting fire to the house in *Jane Eyre* instead of retaining Brontë's reductive portrayal of the foreign female other. An extension to this is Rhys's implicit reference to the textuality of Brontë's novel: Spivak interprets Antoinette's discomfort and confusion in England in a 'cardboard house' as a reference to her restriction as imposed by Brontë's text: a book between cardboard covers. Rhys responds to the canonical status of the original text and its reception, rereading the text with a critical glance towards imperialism but also engaging with the textuality of the retelling.

In keeping with the text's intention to call into question the motivations of Brontë's characters and to represent those who were unfairly represented in the earlier text, Rhys also allows Grace Poole a voice in the final part of *Wide Sargasso Sea*. This final section of the novel is located in Thornfield, and contains the closest parallel with *Jane Eyre*. The gaze is reversed, though; Jane's gradual awareness of something hidden within Grace Poole's quarters in *Jane Eyre* is paralleled by Antoinette's gradual awareness of something happening outside her living space in *Wide Sargasso Sea*. The episode narrated from Antoinette's perspective contains her description of her accommodation: the bare room containing just semblances of life and vitality: 'the table in the middle and two black chairs carved with fruit and flowers', a tapestry, the fire, the single window high up, out of which she cannot see. Antoinette's sense of identity is distorted: she says, 'I don't know what I am like now' comparing the lack of a mirror with the loss of her real name when she was renamed Bertha and 'saw Antoinette drifting out of the window with her scents, her pretty clothes and her looking-glass' (p. 117); the loss of the mirror also symbolizes the inability to look, which she takes back when she sees 'the ghost', 'the woman with streaming hair' (p. 123) – this woman is Bertha in the looking glass, 'surrounded by a gilt frame' but it is also Jane, creating the parallel moment where the two women meet in the original text. Seeing herself in the mirror – though she only recognizes the ghost and the rumour that she had become in Brontë's novel – brings back her ability to see, and she replaces the marginalized Caribbean in the story of an English romance enabled by imperial wealth:

> I saw the grandfather clock and Aunt Cora's patchwork, all colours, I saw the orchids and the stephanotis and the jasmine and the tree of life in flames. I saw the chandelier and the red carpet downstairs and the bamboos and the tree ferns, the gold ferns and the silver, and the soft green velvet of the moss on the garden wall. (p. 124)

Caribbean plants – the orchids, the jasmine and the bamboo – dominate her vision and undermine the potency of colonial intervention, which is symbolized by the grandfather clock, the garden wall and the patchwork quilt.

Charles Dickens's *Great Expectations* and Peter Carey's *Jack Maggs*

It might be less apparent that Charles Dickens's nineteenth-century novel *Great Expectations* has resonance in postcolonial thinking. *Great*

Expectations is a novel about Pip, a poor English boy who gains wealth and status, told in the bildungsroman tradition. It is only when Pip finds out that the source of his wealth is the patronage of Magwitch, a convict who earned money having completed his sentence in a penal colony in Australia, that the novel's concern with Britain's colonies is revealed. Peter Carey's 1997 novel *Jack Maggs* rewrites Magwitch as Jack Maggs and retells his return to London to seek the boy he has supported financially in secret, while shifting the focus of the narrative so that the psychological development of the returned convict is the focus of the story, and Pip is marginalized in the figure of Henry Phipps, Maggs's violent and ungrateful heir. The purpose of Carey's retelling is to respond to Dickens's portrayal of Australia and the Australian, a representation that Carey has described as unfair. Carey has specifically stated that *Great Expectations* is 'a way in which the English have colonized our ways of seeing ourselves' (in Woodcock, 2003, p. 122). In revising this unfair representation, the text conveys the violence in London, the colonial fatherland, that has rejected its colonial 'offspring'.

Australia became a British colony following James Cook's expedition, and was formally claimed as a British imperial territory in the 1780s. Areas of New South Wales were used for a long time as penal colonies, and this use of Australia was a main purpose of claiming the land: following the American War of Independence Britain no longer had a place to send convicts. Edward Saïd has talked about *Great Expectations* in *Culture and Imperialism*, saying that the returned convict Magwitch can be seen as a metaphor for the relationship between England and Australia as its colonial offspring. If this is the case, though, the relationship is a highly problematic one: Australia and its British convicts are imagined as irredeemable, as the colonial offspring is thoroughly rejected by its parent.

The relationship of parent and child is a complex one in both *Great Expectations* and *Jack Maggs*. Given that he provides Pip with the means to feed and clothe and house himself, Magwitch sees himself as a kind of parent, telling Pip 'I'm your second father' (p. 315). However, in the end Pip becomes the more parental figure of the two and ends up housing and feeding the infantilized Magwitch and planning for his safe return 'home' to Australia, eventually looking after the dying Magwitch in prison. This relationship reveals an imperialistic assumption that the civilized, sensible England fathers the unruly, dangerous and weak child Australia. Jack Maggs's return to England is likewise initiated by his strong attachment to the memory of Henry Phipps, the rewritten Pip figure. Unlike Pip, Phipps continues to reject Maggs utterly, attempting to kill him rather than admitting that the source of his prosperity is the Australian convict. Maggs is a more autonomous character than Magwitch, though. Magwitch was, from the start, demonized: cannibalistic, threatening to eat Pip's fat cheeks, and animalistic, 'very like a dog' (p. 19). His misshapen, 'shuddering' body is representative of his fragile status in English society: he limps away from his first meeting with Pip, 'clasping himself, as if to hold himself together' (p. 7). Magwitch is dressed in tattered, dirty rags and broken shoes, and marked out as an escaped convict by the 'great iron on his leg' (p. 4). Maggs wears a red waistcoat and carries a silver-tipped cane, and his occupation is difficult for observers in the city street to discern: 'one privately imagined him a book-maker, another a gentleman-farmer and a third, seeing the excellent quality of his waistcoat, imagined him an upper servant' (p. 1). While Magwitch is rough, loud and brutal, shouting threats with 'a terrible noise' (p. 5); Maggs makes a confident yet silent return to London, and it is a very public return: he arrives on a crowded horse and cart at six o'clock on a Saturday evening, in sharp contrast to Magwitch, who had to hide in the shadows on a stormy evening and gain anonymous passage into Pip's home before revealing his identity.

Although Dickens's representation of Australia seems a thoroughly negative one, Edward Saïd notes an opportunity for redemption in *Great Expectations*: though Magwitch remains weak and undisciplined, Pip acknowledges that his life has been dependent on Magwitch and he vows to live less selfishly. While this goes some way towards repairing the earlier representation of Australia as a despised colonial dependent, the novel reinstates its imperial bias in the method of Pip's redemption: at the end of the narrative, Pip sets off to work as an imperial trader, a strategy that reinstates Britain's imperial outlook (Saïd, 1993, p. xvii). Pip's occupation is, like St John Rivers's missionary work in India in *Jane Eyre*, seen as redemptive because it is represented as a sacrifice: the centre gives a little of itself and that little is intended to be spread a long way in the underdeveloped colony.

Peter Carey responds to the broader colonial assumptions in Dickens's writing as well as to the specific representation of colonized Australia because the novel is more than a reimagining of Magwitch's life in Maggs's narration. It is also a retelling of Victorian London and of the notion of proper and improper parenthood, which extends to the literary parenthood attempted by Tobias Oates, a fictionalization of Charles Dickens who is a key aspect of Carey's retelling. Tobias Oates is a writer who also specializes in mesmerism and magnetism, Victorian pseudo-scientific methods of curing illnesses and psychological problems. Oates sees his opportunity to capture Maggs's tale and to retell it when he witnesses Maggs's *tic doloureux*, a facial twitch so painful that he passes out while serving dinner, working as a butler. Claiming to be able to cure Maggs, he hypnotizes him and creates The Phantom, a threatening imaginary figure in Maggs's psyche who he claims is causing the painful tic. While Maggs is in a semi-conscious, hypnotized state, Oates forces him to describe his surroundings, which he recognizes as Australia from the colourful plants and birds and the searing heat, and to undress – Oates's arrogant suspicion that Maggs is a convict and can therefore be controlled is confirmed when he sees the deep scars on his body caused by corporal punishment.

The paternal figure is not the only one under scrutiny in Carey's text. Ma Britten – Maggs' adopted mother – is so named because she represents the colonial motherland, Mother Britain. Ma Britten is a thief and an abortionist, who provides pills to be dissolved in tea and 'belly-ache sausages' containing drugs that will abort a growing foetus. By portraying the figure who represents Britain as colonial motherland as an abortionist and an uncaring maternal figure, Carey is suggesting that Britain had neglected its parental responsibility to Australia, or that it had no ability to carry out such duties in the first place. Ma Britten's provision of abortion drugs reveals the dirt, the danger, and the deception lurking in the back streets of imperial London, and this, as Bruce Woodcock suggests, 'exposes the violence beneath the colonial illusion, suggesting that the darkness originates not in the colonies but in the heart of imperialist London itself' (2003, p. 126).

There is a shifting narrative perspective in *Jack Maggs*, a strategy that was also a feature of *Wide Sargasso Sea*: the retelling does not only defer control of the narrative to Maggs in a straightforward reversal, but, similarly to *Wide Sargasso Sea*, the story is given over to multiple voices and sources. The inclusion of letters and diary entries as well as Oates's writing combine with multiple narrative perspectives so that the point of view is constantly shifting and unstable. The style of the novel is key to its ability to produce a postcolonial retelling. Bruce Woodcock notes that Maggs uses the traditions of nineteenth-century fiction to tell his stories, that the novel begins with the air of mystery common to Victorian melodrama, and that the text employs the genre of Australian convict literature (2003, pp. 119, 121, 132). Woodcock insists that instead of simply reproducing the literary genres which have served a colonial purpose previously, in this text Carey is revising those genres to do more than simply reverse colonial binaries and thereby produce a postcolonial retelling; in its structure, it produces an interruptive reading in Spivak's terms, or a contrapuntal one in Saïd's. Multiple narrative voices convey the story in different forms in a manner that resembles Saïd's contrapuntal strategy, while the fact that one of those voices belongs to Tobias Oates, the fictionalized Dickens, permits the text to approach Spivak's notion of an interruptive reading, which is helped by the inclusion of chapters where focalization switches to the servant girl Mercy Larkin, to Tobias's wife Mary, and to her sister, Tobias's lover Lizzie.

8 The Diaspora Text

This chapter examines novels of migration to England, the United States, and Canada. Both *The Satanic Verses* and *My Brother* force an apparently integrated migrant to reconsider their stable position in an adopted location in response to a sick relative at home. *Funny Boy* is a memory of Sri Lankan childhood and adolescence, narrated from the diaspora in Canada. All three texts explore the condition of the postcolonial migrant who inhabits Bhabha's hybrid third space, somewhere between both locations: origin and destination, neither of which offers a satisfactory definition of home. In all three texts, there is a level of celebration in attaining the diaspora. This is sometimes because of political turbulence at home (depicted in *Funny Boy*), other times because of received ideas about the superiority of the imperial centre (Saladin's view in *The Satanic Verses*), or, as Kincaid's text shows, because home, a location formerly administered as a slave plantation and subsequently neglected, never really felt like home.

Shyam Selvadurai, *Funny Boy*

Arjie is the young protagonist and narrator of *Funny Boy* who in episodes presented chronologically, gradually becomes aware of both his sexuality and the national situation. The narrative takes place in Sri Lanka in the 1970s and 1980s, during the years leading up to the communalist riots of 1983. An attack on the Sri Lankan army on 23 July 1983 is recorded as the beginning of the civil war which was ongoing until May 2009 when the government declared their defeat of the separatist Tamil Tigers. In a politically turbulent Sri Lanka, Arjie is reminded that to be gay would be unacceptable to his father, who expects him to take a traditional middle-class masculine role for which his exclusive school is intended as preparation. The novel ends with a riot journal which culminates in the family's migration to Canada, a diaspora location that remains peripheral.

Sri Lanka gained independence from Britain in 1948 and the independence movement was founded on nationalist statements which had the effect of creating divisions between the Sinhalese and Tamil groups. This was marked by a linguistic distinction when the Official Language Act was passed in 1956; in making Sinhala the sole official language of Sri Lanka, Tamils were effectively excluded in what has been seen as a government-sponsored disenfranchisement. Jonathan Spencer has described how in the mid-1970s the hostility between the two groups shifted emphasis, with new demands for a separate Tamil state in the north-east of Sri Lanka. This became the aim of the Tamil United Liberation Front, the main Tamil political party, and of the unaffiliated radical, armed groups. The most well known among these was the Liberation Tigers (popularly referred to as the Tamil Tigers), the group that Jegan, who lives at Arjie's home and works for Arjie's father, is accused of being involved with. The Sinhala-dominated government response was to fight back with equally aggressive measures.

As Jonathan Spencer points out, it is commonly maintained by the Sinhala in politics, the media, and education, that Buddha entrusted Sri Lanka to the Sinhala people, yet equally certain historical origins on the island are claimed in Tamil histories (1990, p. 3). A fundamental distinction between the two groups forges a sense of inevitability, implying that the violent division can never end. It is also flawed, though, according to Elizabeth Nissan and R.L. Stirrat, who suggest that both sides' representation of Sri Lankan history is based on the systematic destruction of archaeological and historical evidence of the far more fluid boundaries between the two groups. They point out that Anuradhapura and Polonnaruwa, considered major historical centres of Sinhala-Buddhist civilization, were once populated by Tamil speakers. Similarly Jaffna, a Tamil heartland, has place names which are Sinhala in origin. There are even Sinhala groups in the region who use Tamil as their domestic language (1990, p. 23). The novel shows this interrelationship: people live, work and are educated together, and though Arjie is Tamil he does not speak the language: his father insists he must speak Sinhalese to succeed in the future. Yet, Arjie is questioned on his legitimacy to enter a Sinhala class by the other boys, and his older brother Diggy recognizes his marginal (and thus inferior) status in the Sinhala-dominant school. The school is representative of the wider culture, and Arjie's father is forced to exercise similar practices: knowing that his employees would not take direct orders from a Tamil, Arjie's father insists that Jegan's instructions go through a Sinhala manager. The novel reflects the difficulty of maintaining a balanced society in the face of prominent popular and political histories which repeatedly insist on a clear-cut division between ethnic groups.

For Arjie there are further social regulations that must be broken before he can experience personal freedom. Arjie has vaguely understood homosexuality as something that marks him apart in his family as embarrassing, 'a funny one' (p. 14), a 'pansy', a 'faggot', a 'sissy' (p. 11). *Funny Boy* relates Arjie's gradual sexual empowerment, but the context of postcolonial migration complicates the representation of gay identity, as Pramod Nayar has pointed out regarding queer theory:

> Race and sexual identities intersect. Being a white lesbian or gay is remarkably different, many writers argue, from being an Asian queer in an American metropolis. (2008, p. 162)

Nayar suggests that there is sometimes a colour bar to queer identity, and that a dual discrimination is a theme in much postcolonial queer writing, making reference to Audre Lorde who has identified multiple reasons for placing her in a 'deviant category'. In particular, Nayar points out that this has the effect of placing the family at the focus of much postcolonial queer literature: the family is a heterosexual symbol for the state and the maintenance of correct social order. Thus, to be queer is also to opt out of the state. Arjie's subversive act of misreading poetry can be understood as a 'queer' reaction to the family and the state.

Arjie's sadistic headmaster, Black Tie, expects him to perform Henry Newbolt's idealistic and nostalgic poems proclaiming loyalty and obedience at a prize-giving ceremony. In the context of postcolonial Sri Lanka, the poems have special significance: just a generation or two earlier, they operated to influence the young to honour not just their teachers' rule but also colonial rule. When he is punished by caning for making mistakes, the inappropriateness of the poems for Arjie's reality is crystallized and he decides to recite them incorrectly. In the crowded hall, he 'mangled those poems, reducing them to disjointed nonsense' (p. 281). His decision is emblematic of postcolonial resistance: Newbolt's poetry exemplifies imperial order, and its use in decolonized Sri Lanka in the 1980s speaks of the continued influence of British colonial attitudes and the school's intention to produce a generation of young men obedient to the values of empire. The novel demonstrates the ability of postcolonial literature to fragment the textual history on which colonialism was based. Far from defiling a 'thing of beauty' (p. 287) as Black Tie suggests, Arjie reveals structures and opens them up to question. Black Tie had been relying on the maintenance of the order of lines in those poems to sustain his own position; his speech, intended to secure his role as headteacher, collapses when its basis – imperial poetry – is fragmented. Arjie acted from personal motivations, too, rebelling against Black Tie in order to support Shehan: personal, sexual identity and the national situation combine to convey the physical impact of postcolonial violence on the body.

Textually, the diaspora location of Canada is contained in an epilogue, so migration remains at the narrative margin. This final chapter is a series of diary entries recounting Arjie's experiences, during which his grandparents are burned to death in their car, and family homes are burned down. The disjoined structure, in contrast with the chronological narrative of the previous chapters, is a reflection of Arjie's disengagement from Sri Lanka. Until this point, the events in Sri Lanka's political history have formed a narrative parallel to Arjie's personal development; here there is a narrative fragmentation that reflects the trauma that both his impending migration and the proximity and extent of the violence create. It is notable too, though, that Arjie attains a certain amount of self-knowledge before he leaves Sri Lanka, and so the novel is no longer a vehicle for his analysis of his developing sexual identity. Earlier chapters evoke the bildungsroman genre which requires that the developing protagonist bends to fit into society. For Arjie, this is impossible: society is, for him, a place of violent division where the love he felt for Shehan is demonized. The fragmented structure of the text reflects a wilful disengagement with the conventions of society. Yet, at the same time, it points to a fundamental loss of coherence in the individual, caused by enforced separation from Shehan, and from Sri Lanka.

Salman Rushdie, *The Satanic Verses*

The Satanic Verses (1988) is the migration story of Gibreel Farishta, a Bollywood actor who travels to London to create a new identity after losing his faith, and Saladin Chamcha. Saladin moved from India to the UK as a child, and has developed what he proudly regards as a thoroughly English identity. To become this 'goodandproper Englishman' (p. 43), complete with upper-middle-class English wife and a job as a voice-over actor on children's TV, Saladin rejects his Indian identity.

Saladin's transformation was not gradual and organic; it was violently self-enforced: he anglicizes his name from Salahuddin Chamchawala to

Saladin Chamcha, and develops a distaste for Indian food, calling it 'filthy foreign food' (p. 258). Saladin adopts what he perceives as English customs and desires comprising 'tepid, used [bath-]water full of mud and soap'; 'summer pudding, hockey-sticks, thatched houses', 'Yorkshire pudding and hearts of oak', 'ye olde dream-England' (pp. 43, 180). Having become 'an Indian translated into English-medium' (p. 58), Saladin cannot tolerate any reminder that he was once un-British. His fragile identity is revealed when, on waking suddenly from dozing on an aeroplane to London, he 'found his speech unaccountably metamorphosed into the Bombay lilt he had so diligently (and so long ago!) unmade' (p. 34). Gibreel witnesses what Saladin calls 'his traitor voice' (p. 34) and this begins their pairing in the text: both men survive the terrorist bomb which blows up their aeroplane, falling hundreds of feet through the air. The practical impossibility of their survival both permits the men (believed dead) to enter London on new terms instead of by reclaiming their former identities, and also provides a vehicle for the magical realist elements of the text and explains Gibreel's visions, dreams, or dual identity (any and all of those terms define his experiences as the Angel Gibreel). The most affecting element of the two men's re-entry into London is their role reversal. As well as undergoing physical mutations, the men switch status: while Gibreel happens upon an elderly lady and adopts the place of her dead husband, taking on a properly English role, Saladin is considered 'foreign' and arrested by the police.

For Homi Bhabha, Gibreel's experience of England masquerading as the English colonial is an important narrative moment of hybridity. Gibreel is held in the elderly widow Rosa Diamond's rapture: she tells him he is the double of a man she once loved, Martín de la Cruz, a man who had the passion that her husband Henry Diamond lacked. Rosa cooks for Gibreel, and he wears her dead husband's clothes, his 'maroon smoking jacket and jodhpurs' (p. 141). Bhabha explains that this event brings together a migrant present (Gibreel's) with a nostalgic past (Rosa's memories about the time she spent in Argentina with her colonialist husband) and this past becomes a disruptive force once it includes Gibreel. It displaces the present, which is opened up to admit other histories and other narrative perspectives:

> Gibreel, the migrant hybrid in masquerade, as Sir Henry Diamond, mimics the collaborative colonial ideologies of patriotism and patriarchy, depriving those narratives of their imperial authority. (Bhabha, 2004, p. 240)

Gibreel's part in the narrative, as hearer, is the disruptive presence in an old English colonial tale that Bhabha locates as part of the linear history of England that begins with William the Conqueror and the Battle of Hastings. When the migrant Gibreel takes the place of the proper English gentry, historical certainties are called into question. What results is an 'ambivalent, ragbag narrative' in place of the historically linear and conventional one. But it is precisely this 'narrative sorcery' that allows Gibreel to enter contemporary England. Gibreel is, Bhabha says, 'the history that happened elsewhere, overseas', the 'problem with the English' that Whisky Sisodia has identified. Gibreel's postcolonial, migrant presence insists that the metropolitan centre must be perceived in relation to its postcolonial, subaltern facet: the nation exists within its boundaries and beyond them, and whatever was assumed 'other' exists within that nation, too, disturbing the notion of wholeness or otherness and revealing a fundamental hybridity (Bhabha, 2004, p. 241).

Rushdie observed that 'the act of migration was to turn people somehow into things, into people who had been translated, who had, so to speak, entered the condition of metaphor' (Reder, 2000, p. 77). This process may have the undesired effect of turning migrants into metaphors in the gaze of their host location, or turning people into 'things' like the manticores and glass-skinned women housed in the sanatorium in London and like Saladin Chamcha who mutates into 'a fully developed devil, a horned goat-man' (p. 251). The metaphorical transformation has the result of mutation, and in response to this mutation, both Saladin and Gibreel experience a kind of madness. Saladin's is an obsessive madness; he becomes fixated on Gibreel, his opposite. Using the ventriloquist voice that he had cherished until it was revealed as a mask that he had to wear to gain acceptance into English society, he taunts Gibreel, indulging in a prolonged series of malicious phone calls in a variety of voices. Gibreel, though, experiences an alternative identity as the Angel Gibreel ⁻(or Gabriel) while he is asleep. In his dreaming state, he encounters Mahound, a prophet figure, and the ghost of Rekha Merchant, his former lover who killed herself and her children by jumping from the apartment block where they both lived.

Gibreel struggles against his angelic destiny and migrant status, creating a heat wave in London, to impose a tropicalization that allows the colonized to impose his structure on the former colonizer in a reversal of the colonial desire to impose a familiar lifestyle on the colony. London, under Gibreel's tropical gaze, is revealed as suddenly smaller, and papery: Gibreel's agent has organized a comeback performance which will take place in a miniature, Dickensian London. The 'counterfeit streets' (p. 422) are described in appropriately theatrical language interspersed with song, 'musical Podsnappery', to echo 'the madness of the street' (p. 424). In language resembling stage direction, the migrants act out their conflict in the safe space of their pretend London, a city as false as Gibreel's awareness of the bigger one ('Properlondon') outside it. Eventually the tragedy is set in India, when Saladin returns to visit his dying father and Gibreel commits suicide, each confronting their hybrid status in separate ways. Saladin's survival marks his eventual acceptance of his Indian origin.

The novel is well known because of factors other than its representation of the experience of diaspora, though: Salman Rushdie was subjected to a fatwa imposed by the Ayatollah Khomeini on 14 February 1989, based on accusations that the novel was offensive to Islam and to the Prophet Muhammad. Much work has been done to illuminate the events surrounding the fatwa, including Appignanesi and Maitland's edited collection of articles and essays, *The Rushdie File*. The fatwa became a focus for critical interrogation at the expense of the important things that Rushdie was doing in his texts. Laura Chrisman suggests that, similarly, 'the Rushdie Affair [...] risks obscuring other important dynamics of 1980s Englishness' (2003, p. 9). The novel has been criticized by some postcolonial scholars for other reasons entirely; as one text among a number of postmodern narratives having been written by postcolonial diaspora authors involving the diaspora location, it has been accused of presenting an Indian or a Third World package for consumption in and by the West. Aijaz Ahmad has also criticized the use of Islam from a postcolonial perspective (rather than a censorious one), considering the novel as part of a long tradition of anti-Islamic sentiment in the West. Ahmad is resistant to the idea that Westernized, privileged migrants based in the West are considered authentic representatives of the Third World, and claims that such texts gain international renown and become the focus for academic interest at the expense of texts that he considers more genuine examples of postcolonial literature, such as texts written in native languages (Ahmad in Moore-Gilbert 1997, 19). Here, postcolonial texts are subject to accusations of universalism and of promoting a totalizing view. These critiques fail to acknowledge that the texts intend to convey the specific location and the particular view of the migrant intellectual working in the diaspora. Such commentators would probably be less hostile towards a work like Jamaica Kincaid's *My Brother*. Undoubtedly, Kincaid also occupies the position of migrant intellectual, but due to the autobiographical nature of *My Brother*, Kincaid actively negotiates her role and her right to represent poverty and illness in postcolonial Antigua.

Jamaica Kincaid, *My Brother*

Jamaica Kincaid was born in Antigua, but left the Caribbean for America as a teenager. *My Brother* is a memoir recounting Kincaid's trips to Antigua to visit her brother, Devon Drew, after learning that he was dying from AIDS. The author contemplates both her past in Antigua and her relationship with her mother, stepfather and brothers, and her life in America.

Antigua was a British colony with vast sugar plantations which were worked by slave labour until the 1830s. British colonies including Antigua were intended as ongoing, sustainable projects, as Edward Saïd has pointed out in 'Jane Austen and Empire' (1990). Saïd's essay rereads Austen's *Mansfield Park* with an awareness that the source of the gentry's wealth is the Antiguan sugar plantation. Because of the effort to achieve sustainability, the British attempted to establish functioning social systems in colonies like Antigua, rather than simply exploiting the land on a short-term basis. Writing approximately 200 years later, Jamaica Kincaid's work marks the ongoing impact of the colonial social system in a decolonized Antigua.

Kincaid's earlier works have received more critical attention for their response to British colonialism in Antigua. *Annie John* (1985), a novel, deals with the relationship between a mother and daughter, both named Annie John, and the fluid boundary between the two figures: the women are so close that they cannot easily separate their identities. The uncomfortable mother–daughter relationship is also conveyed in a later work, impossibly titled *An Autobiography of My Mother* (1996), which is concerned with the narrator's repeated insistence that her mother dies at the moment she was born, and conveys her inability to come to terms with her motherless status, leading her to repeatedly abort her unborn children, and to gaze at her own motherly/unmotherly body, touching it, smelling it, and hurting it. Both of these novels are situated in postcolonial Antigua and imply the impossibility of motherhood in an impossible motherland, one that has a history of slavery which brings with it a disconnection from origins, and is itself a supposed daughter-nation of a neglectful colonial motherland (Britain). Laura Niesen de Abruna has suggested that *Annie John* demonstrates only a cautious critique of the impact of imperialism: it is significant that whites in the novel own the banks and offices and segregate the beaches, keeping the choicest for their own use (1991, pp. 274–5). However, with *A Small Place* (1988), a collection of essays, Kincaid wrote much more directly about the impact of colonial education, government, and colonial consciousness on Antiguan life.

My Brother differs from all three of these earlier texts because it is above all an examination of the diaspora status of the narrator, while the postcolonial condition of the Antiguan inhabitant is a secondary theme. Though Kincaid visits Antigua and revisits her experiences there, she does so from the distance of the migrant; she has to accept her memories but also what she has forgotten and the things she now takes for granted. Unlike *Funny Boy* where the diaspora location of Canada remains distant, the presence of America is an important part of this text. At her home in Vermont she can concentrate on 'the well-being' of her children, her husband, and herself (p. 7). Well-being is a luxurious condition that can be enjoyed only after securing health, sustenance, and shelter. Her own wealth and privilege is something that she has to negotiate when faced with her brother's illness and the inadequacy of Antiguan health provision. There is a sense of bitterness in her description of her 'now privileged North American way' (p. 125), in her awareness that she embodies privilege and can transfer a few months of that privilege to her brother's body when she brings him the medicine that he needs from 'the prosperous North' (p. 164).

Kincaid's brother is sent to die in a hospital used only for those who cannot afford anything else. Kincaid is able to access AZT to improve her brother's condition, medicine unavailable in Antigua, through a doctor friend who is willing to write the prescription for her. Even painkillers are scarce in the hospital, and he is on one occasion given a nurse's own painkillers when nothing else is available, a situation that compels the writer to applaud the expensive American system when the alternative to expensive medicines is none at all, or a policy of 'bring your own' (p. 34). Of course, the American system is not only expensive, but stratified according to wealth, an aspect that Kincaid neglects to mention, and an inequality which is from 2010 being addressed to some extent by Barack Obama. Nevertheless, the Antiguan hospital is completely substandard:

> The walls of the room were dirty, the slats of the louvered windows were dirty, the blades of the ceiling fan were dirty, and when it was turned on, sometimes pieces of dust would become dislodged.   (p. 22)

Kincaid's narrative of her brother's illness and hospital treatment is bound up with colonialism. On her first visit to the hospital she sits in the hospital garden and looks out on to a 'deliberate planting' (p. 10) of willow trees, which she assumes were planted in Antigua's colonial period when the colonial government administered the hospital. This is the critical diaspora gaze of the conscious postcolonial migrant, and the description of the landscape is an intellectual one which intentionally locates both the inevitability of her brother's illness and the ineffectuality of his treatment within the imprisoning barrier of trees which marks the constructed colonial landscape. Kincaid's gaze is directly opposed with her brother's, who, as an inhabitant of the island and a victim of its social problems cannot take a critical view of colonialism: instead, he develops a love of English literature, as his sister recounts with a tone of some despair: his love of John Milton was, she explains, a love not so much for Milton as for 'all the people who came after and were influenced by John Milton' who were 'servants in the British colonial enterprise' (p. 176). Kincaid knows that her brother was of her opinion that the history of the West Indies was 'primarily an account of theft and murder', yet her brother was compelled to read it: 'he liked the endings, the outcomes; he liked the people who won, even though he was among the things that had been won' (p. 95). Kincaid is grateful that she escaped her brother's fate due to her own powers of discernment that allowed her to question the literature that supported and maintained empire, by rewriting the books that she had once read from the library and her school, 'writing them again and again' (p. 198), in a postcolonial counter-narrative.

Kincaid confronts her uncomfortable relationship with her mother and brother through the narrative repetition of an unhappy memory involving all three of them, a moment that the adult writer Jamaica Kincaid understands as a catalyst for her writing career. When she was fifteen years old and her brother Devon a two-year-old infant, she was kept away from school to babysit and instead of carrying out the list of tasks provided by her mother, she read a book all day, forgetting to change her brother's nappy. As a punishment, her mother burned all of her books. This event is presented as a repressed memory that, once recalled, haunts the adult writer when she is again placed in the position of responsibility between her dying brother and her authoritarian mother. Her role is once again to provide the care that her mother can not: while her mother feeds Devon the food that she has prepared, washes him, and visits him at the hospital three times a day, Jamaica brings drugs from America to counteract his symptoms and prolong his life. This is something that she finds essential yet difficult because of her sense of disconnection from this man who she last knew when he was a baby, and because she is aware that he has lived a reckless life while she has worked hard to build a family, a home and a career. His recklessness convinces him that he has 'recovered' and he begins having unprotected sex with a young woman without telling her that he is an AIDS patient. Kincaid's attempt to rebuild the books lost to fire, to bring those books not exactly back to life, but back to *her* life (p. 198) is presented as a survival mechanism, something that Kincaid began 'out of desperation' (p. 195), but also, after colonialism, as a method of taking back control, of questioning the familial ties that reflect the state of Antigua as a former colony.

Part IV

Postcolonial Futures

9 Afterword: Postcolonial Futures

> Since the events of 11 September 2001, the so-called global war on terror, and the US invasion of Afghanistan and Iraq, it is harder than ever to see our world as simply 'postcolonial'.
>
> Ania Loomba, *Colonialism/Postcolonialism*

Ania Loomba's statement challenges postcolonial theory to address new manifestations of international intervention including terrorism and practices of neocolonialism and globalization. The self-reflexivity evident in Loomba's comment demonstrates the trend within postcolonial studies to regularly reassess the field's direction. Recent discussions include those in a volume co-edited by Loomba in 2005, titled *Postcolonial Studies and Beyond*, as well as Bill Ashcroft's *On Post-Colonial Futures* (2001), and Graham Huggan's edited volume, *Interdisciplinary Measures: Literature and the Future of Postcolonial Studies* (2008), which foregrounds the interdisciplinarity inherent even in postcolonial literary studies, a focus implicit in the areas covered in this final chapter. This chapter considers the impact of globalization on conjunctions between postcolonial literary studies and ecocriticism, representations of the local, sexuality, publishing and digital technology. Chapters 3, 4 and 5 of this book considered theories relating to national and cultural identity, migration and diaspora. These ways of thinking about individuals, histories and locations are affected by twenty-first-century global travel, trade and economic migration as well as the Internet. Individuals are more able nowadays to be mobile and global, either in physical terms or by being in contact with global networks online. Businesses and academic institutions cultivate their global connections, and while India and China emerge as new global financial and manufacturing centres, the balance of world power, economics and also culture may be due to shift once more. The English language is a prominent factor in this: the language has, for centuries, developed and changed. New global standards have emerged, and in an age of global media and digital communication, a global form of dialect levelling means that Britain is no longer seen as exerting such a strong force as the centre of the English language over literary and linguistic 'peripheries'. Even teaching methods in school curricula use modern adaptations, and teachers are less likely to reflect on the glory of canonical texts uncritically. The future of postcolonial analysis involves engaging with the many complex interactions between the local and the global, in terms of places, bodies, and ways of thinking.

Postcolonial ecocriticism

Greg Garrard's *Ecocriticism* (2004) is a defining theoretical work on a relatively young field of scholarly interest relating to the environment and the landscape. Ecocritical approaches to literature focus on pollution, destruction and exploitation of natural spaces. Modern environmental writing tends to discuss industrial waste and natural disasters, while nineteenth-century literature lamented nature's destruction in the name of industrial progress. Rachel Carson's *Silent Spring* (1962) offers the first sustained response to the environmental effects of modern industrial processes. Carson's work is part novel, part environmentalist critique, and it describes a rural idyll blighted by the creeping death of pollution as a side effect of the use of newly developed pesticides.

Arundhati Roy's Booker Prize winning novel, *The God of Small Things* (1997), conveys ecocritical concerns in a postcolonial context. The novel is dominated by the environment rather than the events or the characters themselves. This is apparent in the novel's structure: many chapters begin with descriptions of the natural world, the shrinking river in the drought where 'black crows gorge on bright mangoes in still, dustgreen trees' (p. 1); of nature captured and contained like the dead butterflies turning to dust in glass cases (p. 155), of managed nature on rubber tree plantations, but also the impact of nature on the built environment including domestic interiors and temples. Roy's concern in her later non-fiction is the river, and the river dominates this novel, at times rendering its human protagonists powerless. The children can only passively observe when their cousin Sophie Mol is drowned: the event is registered only with a sad 'silence', 'no storm music', 'no whirlpool', 'just a quiet handing over ceremony' (p. 293). Otherwise, the river empowers: it is the site both of Ammu's sexual reawakening when she makes love to Velutha, and of the twins' lovemaking, both relationships being socially unacceptable, the first because it is undertaken across caste boundaries (Velutha being a Paravan ('untouchable') and the second as it is incestuous. Ultimately, the position reinforced throughout the novel is that human life is fundamentally bound up with the natural environment. The novel is set in Ayemenem, a village in Kerala on the West coast of India, geographically distant from the usual industrial settings of postcolonial Indian novels, which are more frequently located in cities like Bombay/Mumbai (approximately 1000 miles away) and Calcutta (almost twice that distance). The region has a history in the colonial spice trade, and the colonial presence in the novel lingers as Ammu recalls her marriage to a violent, alcoholic tea plantation manager. Both the power of the natural environment and Ammu's sexual freedom are symbolic of the throwing off of imperial domination.

Postcolonial and ecocritical perspectives have much in common: both pursue political commitments, and postcolonial literature and theory examines and remaps the representation of the physical environment in both literary and non-literary texts, such as anthropological accounts and travel writing. Postcolonial rereading reveals that the colonized landscape is conceived by the colonial metaphor as a female body – virgin territory to be appropriated, conquered and fertilized by the masculine colonial power. Ecocritical analysis extends those concerns by revealing present-day 'neocolonial environmental scientification' (Garrard, 2004, p. 168), an enforced global environmentalism that replicates colonial paternalism, environmentalizing the globe because the local population 'can't'. Graham Huggan and Helen Tiffin take the position that Northern environmentalisms (Northern being used to identify sections of the world that might also be termed, with differing nuances, Western or First World) are 'always potentially vainglorious and hypocritical' while Southern (or Third World) environmentalisms are 'often genuinely heroic and authentic' (2009, p. 2).

Arundhati Roy's environmental activism is closer to the heroic and authentic than the vainglorious and hypocritical, with its thoroughly local commitment. In *The Cost of Living* (1999), Roy describes government plans to deliberately flood the Narmada valley in order to create a series of dams along the river, the most damaging being the construction of the Sardar Sarovar megadam. This was part of a vast dam-building project which had in the 50 years since independence flooded the homes and communities of millions of people without formal provision for rehabilitating the displaced populations and, as Roy suggests, without producing official records about numbers of people affected. The purpose of the massive-scale dam-building project is to alleviate the periods of drought and flood that occur in many areas of India. One of Roy's issues is with the claim that, as the title of her essay states, the government's motivation is 'The Greater Common Good'. She is dubious about the dams' effectiveness, but she also suggests that the word 'Common' is out of place, because the dams actually serve the few: 'only those who can afford it will get it'; for others, the dams will not help: 'will the water *ever* reach them?' (1999, pp. 92–3).

With the publication of Graham Huggan and Helen Tiffin's *Postcolonial Ecocriticism* (2009), connections between the two fields were brought to the forefront of postcolonial studies. The book examines relationships between humans, animals and the environment in postcolonial literature (postcolonial defined as from the period of colonization onwards – the book includes examinations of *Robinson Crusoe* and *Heart of Darkness* as well as recent literature from the period following decolonization in South Asia and the Caribbean). The authors insist on a rethinking of the hierarchical relationships between people, animals and the land. Bringing together postcolonialism and ecocriticism is not as straightforward as it might appear, Huggan and Tiffin suggest, recalling that postcolonial studies is divided between what they term broadly Marxist and post-structuralist positions, and that ecocriticism is equally divided in focus between environmental concerns and animal rights (2009, p. 2). To avoid simplifying the concerns and methodologies of both fields, Huggan and Tiffin focus on colonialism as the object of postcolonial studies, and combine this focus with similarly imperialist tendencies in environmental practices of colonizing and colonized societies (2009, p. 3). An emphasis on landscape inevitably involves dialogue between global and local voices, another ongoing concern within recent postcolonial thinking.

Global and local voices

In an article on world history and historians, Ashis Nandy claims that 'historical consciousness now owns the globe' (1995, p. 46), but insists that this is not compulsory: history can be opposed with other ways of understanding places, people and times. Ahistoricism has been perceived as local deficiency:

> Enlightenment sensitivities, whether in the West or outside, presume a perfect equivalence between history and the construction of the past; they presume that there is no past independent of history. If there is such a past, it is waiting to be remade into history.   (Nandy 1995, p. 53)

Nandy suggests that other ways of organising the past including myth should be understood as a separate means of perception, and any deficiency should be perceived where it is most deserving: in the discipline itself, and its inability to question its own remit. Nandy claims that as yet, nobody has sufficiently questioned the dominance of the historical mode, either within historical scholarship or in the discourse of local disputes. The Ayodhya mosque is one instance of a local dispute where both sides justified their actions entirely by relying on history. The dispute arose when Hindu protestors claimed the existing mosque stood on the ground of a former temple which had been destroyed by Muslims. Both sides used the same historical mode to make their claims, offering contradictory (but historical) evidence of the pre-existence or otherwise of a temple on the site. Nandy asks why neither side took a different approach: the Muslims could, he suggests, have broken the deadlock of historical reasoning:

> No Muslim in India has claimed till now that the Muslims broke temples *and* are proud of that past as a measure of their piety. Nor has any Muslim affirmed the right to break temples or even retain mosques built on demolished temples.   (1995, p. 63)

Such arguments would demonstrate that historical existence does not take precedence. Instead, relying utterly on the power of history to affirm their right to the plot of land, both sides want to 'capture and correct' history (Nandy, 1995, p. 64). If it is difficult to admit the ahistorical mode, this difficulty reveals the dominance of the historical. History – with its ultimate control over ways of thinking – is revealed as a form of colonization itself, its 'complete hegemony' showing that 'alternative concepts related to the domains [of the past] are literally banished from human consciousness' (Nandy, 1995, p. 54).

Throughout the piece, Nandy's position that history has been unable to question the historical mode of organising knowledge engages with the local and the global: the historical is positioned as a global, universal force which stifles the voice of the local. As a body of work, postcolonialism is nowadays self-consciously resistant to universalizing discourses and does not deserve the charge sometimes levelled against it that it offers a simplistic reversal of former colonial binaries, or that it is a form of 'political correctness'. Recent work has made this explicit with a focus on comparing the local and the global. Bill Ashcroft, for example, posited the existence of 'alternative modernities' at a plenary address given at the inaugural conference of the Postcolonial Studies Association in 2009 in Waterford. He defines modernity as an idea of development taking an antagonistic position towards the past, to purport the superiority of the present through the use of technologies. Ashcroft asked how postcolonial theory is positioned to address a global future, and referred to a range of ways in which the field has already made firm connections with issues of globalization, by considering diaspora, cosmopolitanism, and cultural and ethnic mobility. In addition, though, Ashcroft suggests that postcolonialism reveals a proliferation of modernity and asks why there are so many diverse modernities. Formerly, modernity relegated the local to the past, but in postcolonial contexts, new, alternative modernities are instigated by the local. Implicit in this is the priority of the local over the global, or the multiple and specific over the unitary and universal. These multiple, alternative modernities are not peripheral, Ashcroft insists: they dominate imported culture by radically transforming and localizing it. The Ambassador car in India is one example, a vehicle that seems to represent conservatism because it was the first car to be manufactured in India and has traditionally been associated with the country's dignitaries and prime ministers. Ashcroft points out that it is nevertheless suitable to local conditions and easily and cheaply maintained. This has made it an attractive vehicle for taxi drivers: painted yellow, like the New York City yellow cab, it has come to represent modernity, and an alternative modernity, because its use involves transformation. Nevertheless, Ashcroft's view is seen by some as idealistic. At the conference he was asked to justify the celebration of capitalism (the cause of globalization) implied by his discussion. Ashcroft suggests that alternative modernities do not need to operate within capitalism, and to return to Ashis Nandy's proposition, he situates the engagement with the past employed by such alternative modernities in memory, and not in history: memory, he suggests, lies outside of history, meaning that rather than simply writing marginalized histories back into the dominant narrative, the alternative modernities visible in the local offer alternative and additional ways of perceiving the past which are based on memory and transformation. It follows from this that the memory of the British precursor to the Indian Ambassador car is different from the history of British colonial occupation of India; thus the creative transformation of that vehicle for use by city taxi drivers in Kolkata is not a nostalgic tribute to British presence in India and nor is it simply a direct reversal of imperialism – it is a genuine alternative. Postcolonial modernities employing technology creatively to break with the past are found in literature as well as popular culture. Most notably, new publishing opportunities for regional writers are to be found online.

Digital postcolonialism

An emerging focus for attention in postcolonial scholarship is the digital – both the impact of digital technology on living and working practices and conditions, and digital publishing. Literary texts have led the way in critical examinations of the digital world: Aravind Adiga's epistolary narrative in *The White Tiger* (2008) is conducted via email in the novel. This recent example has a precursor in Amitav Ghosh's *The Calcutta Chromosome* (1995). In this novel, Asian and Middle-Eastern migrants remain marginal even while they are located in New York, a global commercial centre. *The Calcutta Chromosome* was described by Christopher Shinn as a warning about the hidden dangers of new technologies, where immigrants live and die quietly, 'hidden and marginalized by a world of transitory existence' (2008, p. 145). The promise of global connectedness implicit in Internet technology is replaced in this damning fictional account by increased marginalization. Postcolonial theorists generally take a more ambivalent approach. The possibilities for challenging dominant ideologies implied by collaborative technologies and independent online publishing concur with postcolonial commitments to challenge the centre from the margins. Rey Chow wrote with a genuine sense of the possibilities offered by the Internet:

> Hypertext [...] arranges knowledge as a network and thus makes irrelevant classical hierarchical constraints [... and] is regarded by some as the ultimate freeing of learning. Hypertext's endless, multiple entry capabilities demystify once and for all the barriers that writers and readers have collaborated in establishing.   (1993, pp. 170–1)

This ideal remains: online text can be mediated and negotiated and contributed to by readers. The literary text becomes a negotiable site; without a fixed location or route through the text, users can read according to their own purpose. There may not be two identical readings (never mind interpretations), because technotexts and hypertexts 'can change for each reader and with each reading [...] readers of a hyperfiction [...] can only assume that they have travelled in the same textual network' (Bolter, 2001, p. 11). Digital reading practices defer authority to a reader or to multiple readers and in general terms have a tendency to question the authority of a text and its author. Clearly this has direct parallels with postcolonial endeavours.

Celebration of the digital age is undercut by an awareness that such technology remains obscure in some areas. Only in 2009 a new high-speed

Internet cable was installed which connected South Africa, Tanzania, Kenya, Uganda and Mozambique to Europe and Asia, but everywhere, access to technology is congruent with wealth. Postcolonial studies also warns about an over-reliance on the kind of global, cosmopolitan existence enabled by the internet. Efforts to curb neocolonialism via globalization in trade and public policy may be undermined by cultural influences of the global media which permeate the Internet in advertising and in access to online global news, music, television, radio and film. Mamadou Diouf (2003) has warned that though it offers creative potential, the Internet, composed of multiple influences, can impose a fragmentary sensibility.

Attempts to control the influence of the global media via the Internet have recently been curtailed when Google refused to offer a tailored search engine for China in March 2010. The dispute between China and Google has received various responses: Google claims to be acting in the interests of free speech by refusing to block searches to certain terms as requested by China; Chinese IT specialists and journalists suggest that Google has broken its contract and should operate according to the country's laws: instead, Google searches are redirected to the unrestricted Hong Kong Google. Judging a specific case like China's is not the main issue: what is clear from this case is that the Internet enables unrestricted access to global media, ideologies and information, and many acknowledge that this may have an impact on Internet users' identities and conceptions of national belonging.

Paul O'Brien has suggested that digital transnationalism is particularly pertinent to the Irish situation. He suggests that the Internet can forge connections between individuals of antagonistic nationalities and produce global connectivity while erasing distances of space and time. He explains that Ireland became a leading translator of computer materials and software exporter, an economic and cultural transformation, which is accompanied by a sense of cultural dislocation. Virtual life means that if the individual may be freed from the nation, there is a risk that the Internet can 'undermine national cultures' (2007, p. 9). The Internet does provide an outlet for local languages and cultures: O'Brien cites the ability to use the Irish language on Google and to locate Irish traditional script fonts. In addition the Internet means that both ancient and modern Irish literary texts can be made internationally accessible. Yet at the same time, the English-dominant Internet can hasten global use of the English language. Similarly, Mark Poster's term 'virtual ethnicity' can undermine national-based ethnicities and cultures (cited in O'Brien, 2007, p. 11). Identity as constructed through the Internet may even offer an alternative position from those binaries of particularism and universalism or local and cos-mopolitan cultures that postcolonial theories are currently negotiating (Poster, cited in O'Brien, 2007, p. 11). O'Brien explains that in the Irish con-text, this emancipates Ireland from its relationship with Britain which has dominated the way that Ireland has been read: as colonized, or formerly colonized. Postcolonial queer identities can also neglect the local in favour of the global or transnational.

Postcolonial queer

In an edited collection of photographs from exhibitions of artistic works by African, Asian and Caribbean artists in Britain, Kobena Mercer writes about the representation of the black nude. She suggests that there is a 'potent contradiction' implied by the visibility of the black nude. Empowering because it challenges ideas that beauty can only be found in whiteness, at the same time the blackness of the Other body maintains the binary where blackness is bodily and whiteness involves the life of the mind (1997, pp. 53–4). However, the very contradictoriness of the black nude means that notions of the exotic and the aesthetic are called into question in the manner of queer and gender theory. Mercer suggests that the prominence of black lesbian and gay artists in British art exempli-fies the hybrid queer subject as transnational, with reference to Gloria Anzaldua's concept of gay transnationalism. This transnational queer is not the only way that the postcolonial queer has been represented, and though Mercer's examples refer to a sense of emancipation and visibility for an unfixed, 'queer' sexuality, there is a distinction to be made between gay activism which tends to privilege emancipation, and queer theory which rejects the sense of a fixed gay identity.

As discussed in Chapter 2, both anti-gay and gay activist positions in Hong Kong imply a clear relationship between homosexuality and colonialism, whether it is the instance of homosexuality or the criminalization of homo-sexuality which is cited as having a colonial origin. This assumed influence is present elsewhere in Asia in recent studies of gay activism. Chong Kee Tan has read the contrast between postcolonial gay and queer interests as hybridization, which differs from the kind of hybridity referred to by both Mercer and Bhabha in relation to the postcolonial diaspora. Chong Kee Tan notes that emerging gay activist organizations in Taiwan were heavily influ-enced by America: Gay Chat, the first homosexual student organization, which began in 1992 at the National Taiwan University, was promoted with reference to the Stonewall riots in America in 1969 as a founding event. The Stonewall riots took place in response to a police raid of the Stonewall Inn, a gay bar in Greenwich Village in New York City. These riots were the first instance of the gay and lesbian community fighting back collectively against a repressive government. Organized street protests and new newspapers, including *Gay, Come Out!* and *Gay Power* made the gay liberation movement far more prominent. This incident was so renowned that more than twenty years later, as Chong has pointed out, it was seen as more important than local events such as discussions with the university in establishing Gay Chat. Such strong American influence has been considered evidence of a kind of Western colonization of gay identity, a view that Chong disputes with the notion of hybridization.

Queer identities are often seen as differently hybrid, as being transnational because there may be more similarities and shared concerns between gay and lesbian individuals from various places than between a gay man in Sri Lanka and a heterosexual man in Sri Lanka, for example. Chong Kee Tan has talked about hybridization rather than hybridity, explicitly differentiating from Homi Bhabha's term. Chong suggests that Bhabha's understanding of hybridity tends to refer to a process of intercultural interaction which is catalysed by migration and therefore characterized by linguistic differences and the development of new languages, such as creoles, or new Standard Englishes and non-standard Englishes. Within Taiwan, such a linguistic conflict does not arise between Taiwanese people, and there are shared cultural, racial and historical characteristics. But there are still features of gay and lesbian identity which demonstrate a hybridization, and for Chong Kee Tan, this indicates the limitation of postcolonial theory for theorizing sexuality (2001, p. 124). Chong acknowledges a mimicry of American models of gay and lesbian identity, but this is something that he suggests has fallen out of use to make way for 'hybrid positions' which remain unstable (p. 132) – these are constructed from a negotiation between gay conservatism and queer radicalism. Gay conservatism involves an expression of sameness with other tax-paying and law-abiding citizens with the same basic concerns of family, work and community, whereas queer radicalism does not recognize stable categories of sexuality or identity but instead celebrates difference. Across these two groups are shared influences from foreign conceptions of sexuality, but these do not simply reflect American and/or Western European models of (homo)sexuality, but, as Chong insists, are also influenced by Hong Kong, Japan and China, culminating in the notion that there cannot be a 'pristine Taiwanese homosexuality'; there emerges instead a hybrid sexual identity constructed from local and global influences – a specific model of hybridized sexuality.

Postcolonial prize books and bestsellers

The multiple influences acting upon sexual identity are indicative of the global economy, which manifests in a global literary economy comprising international literary prizes and bestsellers. For Graham Huggan, the literary prize is a corporate sponsorship of the arts, operating as part of 'a global cultural economy controlled by huge multinational companies' (2001, p. 105). Increasingly, postcolonial writers are the beneficiaries of such global corporate sponsorship, a phenomenon which could indicate the powerful global presence of postcolonial literature, or, alternatively, a new form of global neocolonialist control of the literary text. Graham Huggan's 'Prizing otherness: A short history of the Booker' engages with The Booker Prize which is awarded to writers from the Commonwealth, and as such includes numerous texts with postcolonial themes. The Booker Prize (now renamed the Man Booker) has been awarded in recent years to Aravind Adiga for *The White Tiger* (2008), Kiran Desai for *The Inheritance of Loss* (2006), J.M. Coetzee for *Disgrace* (1999) and Arundhati Roy for *The God of Small Things* (1997), as well as to V.S. Naipaul, Salman Rushdie, and Ben Okri in earlier years. Other indicators of popularity or acclaim are also dominated by writing of interest to postcolonial studies, such as the Pulitzer Prize which was won by Jhumpa Lahiri in 2000 for *The Interpreter of Maladies*, and the Nobel Prize for Literature which has been awarded to Nadine Gordimer (1991), Derek Walcott (1992), Toni Morrison (1993), V.S. Naipaul (2001), J.M. Coetzee (2003) and Doris Lessing (2007).

In other popular literary contexts, Oprah's Book Club explicitly aimed to promote books by women, by new authors, and by writers of non-European heritage. Meeting some or all of these criteria were books by Toni Morrison, Maya Angelou, Rohinton Mistry and Gabriel Garcia Marquez read by the club from 1996 onwards. The Richard & Judy Book Club, the closest British counterpart to Oprah's club, also featured a number of texts of interest to postcolonial scholars, including Anchee Min's *Empress Orchid*, Chimamanda Ngozi Adichie's *Half of a Yellow Sun*, Khaled Hosseini's *A Thousand Splendid Suns* and *The Pirate's Daughter* by Margaret Cezair-Thompson. Novels with postcolonial themes regularly top bestseller lists, and as a result an emerging direction for postcolonial literary studies is an engagement with literary taste, marketing, and the publishing industry.

For Huggan, literary awards have emerged as a result of globalization, and rather than fostering postcolonial literature, they have created a market for the commercial, postcolonial exotic (2001, p. 106). The Booker Prize has a dubious history, with origins in the nineteenth-century Booker-McConnell company which distributed sugar from colonial Guyana. Even aside from its colonial past, Huggan asserts that the Booker Prize operates within 'an Anglocentric discourse of benevolent paternalism' (2001, p. 111). For Huggan, it represents a 'fetishisation of cultural otherness' with an assimilationist tactic. Though many of the prizewinners are from the Commonwealth, the judges are generally British. Inevitably, British patronage of Commonwealth writing can recreate colonial relationships in the form of literary sponsorship: as Huggan describes, the revisionist approach to colonial history in a number of the selected books (Ruth Prawer Jhabvala's *Heat and Dust*, JG Ballard's *The Siege of Krishnapur* and Paul Scott's *Staying On*) is complicit with Orientalist thinking rather than transformative. The complicit colonial attitude noticed in these historical novels is promoted by the Booker Prize which circulates reconstituted colonialist mythology when it awards the prize to novels which mimic colonial ideologies (2001, p. 115). Huggan concludes with a reminder that 'the attempt to reward literary excellence, however generous or well-intentioned, may well contain an unannounced ideological agenda – a hidden politics – all of its own' (2001, p. 119). The award of a literary prize, then, can be read as neocolonial patronage in the context of a global capitalist economy.

A further area for consideration is the emergence of popular postcolonial novels, noticed in style or accessibility (which might be the case for Monica Ali's bestselling *Brick Lane*, with its narrative of belonging and its happy ending) or generic conventions. Gina Wisker has written about the Postcolonial Gothic, suggesting that Maxine Hong Kingston's combination of the magical, mythical and historical in contemporary literature about migration explored in *The Woman Warrior* (1976) could occupy the generic space of the postcolonial gothic. An anthology of short stories edited by Hopkinson and Mehan published in 2004 marks a formal coming together of the popular science fiction genre and writers from a postcolonial background. Graeme Harper's *Comedy, Fantasy and Colonialism* (2002) insists that the colonial condition with its imposition of competing and contradictory cultures, economies and laws, is paradoxical. He suggests the colonial context offers too much of a 'challenge to the literal' (2002, p. 1) to be represented by literary realism, which is why fantasy and comedy are the genres so often used in postcolonial literature. The postcolonial crime novel has been analysed in a volume of essays edited by Christine Matzke and Susanne Muehleisen who observe that traditional American and British settings are no longer the only contexts for crime stories, which increasingly have transcultural locations, including Australia, African countries, and India. The editors insist that post-colonial crime novels can reshape the whole generic narrative strategy: the social order is questioned through alternative notions of justice rather than being restored, and the postcolonial crime story concludes that:

> Power and authority can be investigated through the magnifying glass of other knowledges, against the local or global mainstream, past and present, or against potential projections of a dominant group and a (neo-)imperial West. (2006, 5)

Postcolonial criticism is beginning to reflect postcolonial literature beyond the more common literary genres of realism and magical realism, as well as through new publishing outlets and online sources for distributing literature. In response to changing global concerns, postcolonial theory encounters new ethical questions. Theorists have modified predominantly national, racial and ethnic concerns to include representations of global economy and class, language and translation, bodily difference (including disability, as discussed in recent work by Clare Barker and Stuart Murray), sexuality and gender, and representations of human interaction with the natural environment. All of these subjects share an awareness that globalization and neocolonialism, propelled by global trade and by the internet, represent an extended focus for postcolonial attention. Far from postcolonial studies coming to an end in the twenty-first century, the field is growing in importance in an era of globalization. Postcolonial theory is well placed to address the changing world: the field brings together multiple voices and resists a dominant perspective; it has a political commitment to justice and equality, recognizing all facets of injustice; and scholars and students in the field keep a critical eye on the global and the local at a time when economies are changing, failing, and being renegotiated. Postcolonial theory is well placed to analyse the events that are often taken for granted by the media, such as the renationalization of banks, the knock-on effect of decisions made in global financial institutions, and new global trade relationships.

The beginning of colonial thought might be located in explorers' travel narratives and the establishment of trading companies. The modern equivalent of these tales and trades includes the increasing global access to collaboratively updated online writing, and global trade that props up

the capitalist economy. Again, the local and the global, or the particular
and the universal, come into conflict. As Ngugi wa Thiong'o, Bill Ashcroft
and many others have intimated in different contexts, the future of postcolonial studies may involve finding ways to erode the distinctions between
the rigidly held positions of local and global, particular and universal, in
order to illuminate the ongoing impact of past and present cultural conflict and contact.

Annotated Bibliography

This selection is intended to act as a guide to further reading and to provide an indication of the breadth of postcolonial theories. It includes selected works exploring some areas of postcolonial studies that there was no scope to address in the preceding chapters. In addition to the texts listed here, readers may be keen to consider postcolonial work on South Africa, Latin America, or the Asia Pacific region.

Anderson, Clare (2004) *Legible Bodies: Race, Criminality and Colonialism in South Asia* (Oxford: Berg).

Anderson's historical analysis explores the control of the colonized body in South Asia, considering prisoners' bodies and practices of tattooing, photographing and containing, to analyse the cultural impact on the convict from a historical perspective.

Anzaldúa, Gloria (2007 [1987]) *Borderlands/La Frontera* (San Francisco: Aunt Lute Books).

Chicano/a literature and theory explores the Mexican–US border populations, territories and citizens, and Mexican diaspora communities in the US. The relationship between Mexico and the US is not strictly a postcolonial one, yet Anzaldúa explores borders of sexuality and geography making this an important response to border identity and unequal national power relations.

Bartolovich, Crystal and Lazarus, Neil (eds) (2002) *Marxism, Modernity and Postcolonial Studies* (Cambridge: Cambridge University Press).

The editors notice the somewhat combative relationship between two fields: postcolonialism has been called neoimperialist by Marxists because of its tendency to enter (intellectually, at least) territories and represent them from a privileged academic distance, while Marxist theory has been dismissed by postcolonial theorists as Eurocentric and essentializing. The editors collect essays representing the potential of a collaborative Marxist and postcolonial approach to consider common areas (such as subalternity, imperialism, race and nationalism) with new insight and vigour. This book offers a useful foundation for considering the turn towards production and globalization within postcolonial studies.

Bassnett, Susan, and Trivedi, Harish (eds) (1999) *Post-Colonial Translation: Theory and Practice* (London: Routledge).

Translation has always been thoroughly bound up with colonial and postcolonial encounters. The essays in this book examine specific postcolonial engagements with translation, while the editors' introduction provides a fascinating account of the development of translation in postcolonial contexts, including missionary interventions.

Ezra, Elizabeth and Rowden, Terry (eds) (2006) *Transnational Cinema: The Film Reader* (Abingdon: Routledge).

An accessible collection of essays on transnational film, this book includes essays by Homi Bhabha, Ella Shohat and others on film particularly appropriate for postcolonial analysis, including new Indian film, the idea of authenticity in African film, and Hong Kong cinema as a Chinese diaspora art form.

Chaturvedi, Vinayak (ed) (2000) *Mapping Subaltern Studies and the Postcolonial* (London: Verso).

This book presents an overview of subaltern historiography, tracing the Subaltern Studies project from its beginning in the late 1970s headed by Ranajit Guha, to the present day. The essays collected here consider developments in both the political objectives and the geographical scope of the field, while the emphasis remains on South Asia.

Forsdick, Charles and Murphy, David (eds) (2003) *Francophone Postcolonial Studies: A Critical Introduction* (Oxford: Oxford University Press).

There is a tendency to regard Francophone (French-speaking) and Anglophone (English-speaking) postcolonial contexts and studies separately. However, there are multiple points of connection, as is demonstrated by the importance of Frantz Fanon, Aimé Césaire, and others, who wrote in French, for Anglophone postcolonial studies. This collection of essays seeks to make connections between the two strands, while offering a thorough introduction to Francophone postcolonial texts and contexts.

Gandhi, Leela (1998) *Postcolonial Theory: A Critical Introduction* (New York: Columbia University Press).

Gandhi considers postcolonial theory in the context of wider intellectual and philosophical debates. Gandhi considers the interdependences of postcolonial thinking and Marxist, poststructuralist, postmodern and feminist critical approaches, and situates postcolonial theory within the history of philosophy. This book offers a strong historical analysis rather than a literary bias, and key literary texts (including *The Tempest* and *Midnight's Children*) are discussed in relation to their impact in the development of postcolonial thought.

Gilbert, Helen and Tompkins, Joanne (1996) *Post-Colonial Drama: Theory, Practice, Politics* (London: Routledge).

As well as considering in detail the impact of European drama in colonial education and performance, this book considers how drama has developed in reaction to colonization, exploring performance in carnival and ritual, the body in performance and the performance space. The authors discuss African, Australian, Canadian, Caribbean and Indian theatre and this is a recommended resource for detailed consideration of postcolonial counter-discourse in performance.

Huggan, Graham (2001) *The Postcolonial Exotic: Marketing the Margins* (London: Routledge).

Postcolonial theory places literary texts firmly within their material context. Huggan's book is among the first to do this in terms of the book publishing and marketing industry. He considers the way that postcolonial literature has been produced, promoted and consumed in the neocolonial context of globalization.

Kiberd, Declan (1996) *Inventing Ireland: The Literature of the Modern Nation* (London: Vintage).

One area that I did not have space to address in detail is the postcolonial condition of Ireland. Kiberd's book offers a thorough analysis of Ireland's colonial and postcolonial history as well as its recent relationship with the British, and the relationship between Ireland and the rest of the world through migration and the Irish diaspora. This book is particularly valuable for students of literature because it discusses key literary texts as well as literary movements at length, alongside the historical circumstances that influenced those texts.

McLeod, John (2004) *Postcolonial London: Rewriting the Metropolis* (Abingdon: Routledge).

As well as very recent, bestselling postcolonial literature about London (including Monica Ali's *Brick Lane* and Zadie Smith's *White Teeth*), there is a tradition of rewriting London from the perspective of the postcolonial migrant. This book addresses a number of writers doing just that, including Buchi Emecheta, Sam Selvon, Bernadine Evaristo and Joan Riley.

Mernissi, Fatima (2001) *Scheherazade Goes West: Different Cultures, Different Harems* (New York: Washington Square Press).

This is Mernissi's second book, which takes as its starting point her book tour following the publication of her autobiographical *Dreams of Trespass: Tales of a Harem Girlhood*, contemplating the reception that she and the book had in Europe. Western journalists' responses to the harem contradicted with her experiences of that space. *Scheherazade Goes West* is an analysis of the Eastern woman in the Western imaginary, and it includes responses to and retellings of *The Arabian Nights* stories, discussions of the Muslim woman, the veil, the harem and the home, and their representations in art, the media, theory and literature.

Moore-Gilbert, Bart (2009) *Postcolonial Life-Writing* (London: Routledge).

Life-writing – which includes biography, autobiography, and fictional works which fall somewhere within the boundaries of life-writing, such as Maxine Hong Kingston's *The Woman Warrior* – is a key new area of critical focus for postcolonial theory. Moore-Gilbert suggests that the centred subject or unified selfhood taken for granted by life-writing is problematic in the postcolonial context. This book considers different textual strategies and techniques employed by postcolonial writers to write the self.

Morris, Rosalind C. (ed) (2010) *Can the Subaltern Speak?: Reflections on the History of an Idea* (New York: Columbia University Press).

This collection includes both Gayatri Spivak's original and a later revised version of 'Can the Subaltern Speak?'. The other essays reflect on the issues raised by Spivak and apply them to separate contexts including slavery in the US and women's experiences of subalternity in Guatemala and Mexico. Spivak writes a response to conclude the collection, in which she considers the time at which she first delivered the original conference paper and the contexts in which her ideas are applied in 2010 and beyond.

Narayan, Uma and Harding, Sandra (eds) (2000), *Decentering the Center: Philosophy for a Multicultural, Postcolonial, and Feminist World* (Bloomington: Indiana University Press).

This edited collection of essays approaches questions of philosophy with a feminist commitment to inclusive and egalitarian thinking. The volume asks direct questions about specific living conditions and ways that philosophical thinking can be applied or adapted to the context of postcolonial global economies, communities and diaspora.

Bibliography

Achebe, Chinua (2003 [2001]) *Home and Exile* (Edinburgh: Canongate).

Achebe, Chinua (2006 [1958]) *Things Fall Apart* (London: Penguin).

Adiga, Aravind (2008) *The White Tiger* (London: Atlantic).

Allen, Paula Gunn (1980) 'A Stranger in My Own Life: Alienation in American Indian Prose and Poetry', *MELUS*, 7 (2): Between Margin and Mainstream, 3–19.

Anderson, Benedict (1991) *Imagined Communities* (London: Verso).

Ashcroft, Bill (2001) *On Post-Colonial Futures: Transformations of Colonial Culture* (New York: Continuum).

Ashcroft, Bill, Griffiths, Gareth and Tiffin, Helen (2000) *Post-Colonial Studies: The Key Concepts*, 2nd edn (London: Routledge).

Ashcroft, Bill, Griffiths, Gareth and Tiffin, Helen (2002 [1989]) *The Empire Writes Back: Theory and Practice in Post-Colonial Literatures* (London: Routledge).

Barry, Peter (2009) *Beginning Theory*, 3rd edn (Manchester: Manchester University Press).

Batten, Bronwyn (2009) 'The Myall Creek Memorial: History, Identity and Reconciliation' in William Logan and Keir Reeves (eds) *Places of Pain and Shame: Dealing with 'Difficult' Heritage* (Abingdon: Routledge), pp. 82–97.

Barber, Karin (1995) 'African-Language Literature and Postcolonial Criticism', *Research in African Literatures*, 26 (4), 3–30.

Barker, Clare and Murray, Stuart (eds) (2010) *Journal of Literary and Cultural Disability Studies*, 4 (2): Special Issue: Disabling Postcolonialism.

Bassnett, Susan and Trivedi, Harish (eds) (1999) *Post-Colonial Translation*. (London: Routledge).

Bayoumi, Moustafa and Rubin, Andrew (eds) (2000) *The Edward Saïd Reader* (New York: Vintage).

Bhabha, Homi K. (ed.) (1990) *Nation and Narration* (London: Routledge).

Bhabha, Homi K. (2004) *The Location of Culture* (London: Routledge Classics).

Bhabha, Homi, and Mitchell, W. J. T. (eds) (2005) *Edward Saïd: Continuing the Conversation* (Chicago & London: University of Chicago Press).

Bird, Charles S. (1999) 'The Production and Reproduction of Sunjata' in Ralph A. Austen (ed.) *In Search of Sunjata – The Mande Oral Epic as History, Literature and Performance* (Bloomington: Indiana University Press).

Boehmer, Elleke (1995) *Colonial & Postcolonial Literature* (Oxford: Oxford University Press).

Bolter, J. D. (2001) *Writing Space: Computers, Hypertext, and the Remediation of Print Culture*, 2nd edn (Mahwah, N. J.: Lawrence Erlbaum).

Bowers, Neal and Silet, Charles L. P. (1981) 'An Interview with Gerald Vizenor', *MELUS*, 8 (1): Tension and Form, 41–9.

Braude, Jonathan (1991) 'Reform for Hong Kong Sex Laws', *The Times*. 21 March.

Brontë, Charlotte (1994 [1847]) *Jane Eyre* (London: Penguin).

Buhle, Paul (1988) *C.L.R. James: The Artist as Revolutionary* (London: Verso).

Burns, James (2009) *Female Voices from a Ewe Dance-Drumming Community in Ghana: Our Music Has Become a Divine Spirit*. (Farnham: Ashgate).

Butalia, Urvashi (2000) *The Other Side of Silence: Voices from the Partition of India* (London: Hurst).

Carey, Peter (1997) *Jack Maggs* (London: Faber and Faber).

Césaire, Aimé (1972 [1955]) *Discourse on Colonialism*, Transl. Joan Pinkham (London: Monthly Review Press).

Césaire, Aimé (1969 [1956]) *Return to My Native Land*, Transl. John Berger and Anna Bostock (Harmondsworth: Penguin).

Césaire, Aimé (2002 [1969]) *A Tempest*, Transl. Richard Miller (New York: TCG Translations).

Childs, Peter, and Williams, Patrick (1997) *An Introduction to Post-Colonial Theory* (London: Harvester Wheatsheaf).

Chong, Kee Tan (2001) 'Transcending Sexual Nationalism and Colonialism: Cultural Hybridization as Process of Sexual Politics in '90s Taiwan' in John C. Hawley (ed.) *Postcolonial, Queer: Theoretical Intersections* (Albany, NY: State University of New York Press), pp. 123–37.

Chow, Rey (1993) *Writing Diaspora: Tactics of Intervention in Contemporary Cultural Studies* (Bloomington & Indianapolis: Indiana University Press).

Chow, Rey (1998) *Ethics after Idealism: Theory-Culture-Ethnicity-Reading* (Bloomington & Indianapolis: Indiana University Press).

Chow, Rey (2007) 'Translator, Traitor; Translator, Mourner (or, Dreaming of Intercultural Equivalence)', *New Literary History*, 37, 565–80.

Chrisman, Laura (2003) *Postcolonial Contraventions: Cultural Readings of Race, Imperialism, and Transnationalism* (Manchester: Manchester University Press).

Cocoa Board (2009) Official Ghanaian board, http://www.cocobod.gh (home page), date accessed 29 October 2009.

Conrad, Joseph (1994 [1902]) *Heart of Darkness* (London: Penguin Classics).

Conservative (pseudonym) (1935) '"Mother India" and Our MPs', *Saturday Review of Politics, Literature, Science and Art*, 159: 4138, 16 February, p. 212.

Craig, Maxine Leeds (2002) *Ain't I a Beauty Queen?: Black Women, Beauty, and the Politics of Race* (Oxford: Oxford University Press).

Dangarembga, Tsitsi (1988) *Nervous Conditions* (London: The Women's Press).

Dash, J. Michael (1995) *Édouard Glissant* (Cambridge: Cambridge University Press).

Deleuze, Gilles and Guattari, Felix (2004 [1987]) *A Thousand Plateaus*, Transl. Brian Massumi (London: Continuum).

Depestre, René (1972 [1955]) 'An Interview with Aimé Césaire' in Aimé Césaire, *Discourse on Colonialism*, Transl. Joan Pinkham (London: Monthly Review Press).

Desai, Kiran (1998) *Hullabaloo in the Guava Orchard* (London: Faber and Faber).

Desani, G.V. (1972) *All about H. Hatterr* (Harmondsworth: Penguin).

Dickens, Charles (1994 [1861]) *Great Expectations* (Oxford: Oxford University Press).

Diouf, Mamadou (2003) 'Engaging Postcolonial Cultures: African Youth and Public Space', *African Studies Review*, 46 (2), 1–12.

Djebar, Assia (1992 [1980]) *Women of Algiers in Their Apartment*, Transl. Marjolin de Jager (Charlottesville and London: University of Virginia Press).

Donnell, Alison (2003) 'Una Marson: Feminism, Anti-Colonialism and a Forgotten Fight for Freedom' in Bill Schwarz (ed.) *West Indian Intellectuals in Britain* (Manchester: Manchester University Press), pp. 114–31.

El Saadawi, Nawal (1985 [1974]) *God Dies by the Nile*, Transl. Sherif Hetata (London: Zed Books).

Fanon, Frantz (1967 [1961]) *The Wretched of the Earth*, Transl. Constance Farrington (Harmondsworth: Penguin).

Fanon, Frantz (1969) 'Algeria Unveiled' in Carl Oglesby (ed.) *The New Left Reader* (New York: Grove Press), pp. 161–85.

Fanon, Frantz (1986 [1952]) *Black Skin, White Masks* (London: Pluto).

Fast, Robin Riley (1995) 'Borderland Voices in Contemporary Native American Poetry', *Contemporary Literature*, 36 (3), 508–36.

Fischer, Gerhard (2000) 'Mis-Taken Identity: Mudrooroo and Gordon Matthews' in John Docker and Gerhard Fischer (eds) *Race, Colour and Identity in Australia and New Zealand* (Sydney: University of New South Wales Press), pp. 95–112.

Fransman, Laurie (1995) 'Foreword' in Werner Menski, *Coping with 1997: The Reaction of the Hong Kong People to the Transfer of Power* (London: Trentham Books).

Fraser, Bashabi (2008) *Bengal Partition Stories: An Unclosed Chapter* (London: Anthem).

Freud, Sigmund (2003 [1911]) *The Schreber Case*, Transl. Andrew Webber (London: Penguin).

Gandhi, Leela (1998) *Postcolonial Theory: A Critical Introduction* (New York: Columbia University Press).

Gandhi, Leela (2006) *Affective Communities: Anticolonial Thought, Fin-de-Siècle Radicalism and the Politics of Friendship* (Durham, NC: Duke University Press).

Garrard, Greg (2004) *Ecocriticism* (Abingdon: Routledge).

Ghana Tourism (2009) 'World Tourism Day' http://www.touringghana.com date accessed 29 October 2009.

Gibson, Nigel C. (ed.) (1999) *Rethinking Fanon: The Continuing Dialogue* (Amherst, NY: Prometheus Books).

Gikandi, Simon (1991) *Reading Chinua Achebe – Language & Ideology in Fiction* (Oxford: James Currey).

Gikandi, Simon (2000) 'Traveling Theory: Ngugi's Return to English', *Research in African Literatures*, 31 (2), 194–209.

Gilman, Sander L. (1998) 'Ethnicity-Ethnicities-Literature-Literatures', *PMLA*, 113 (1), 19–27.

Gilroy, Paul (1987) *There Ain't No Black in the Union Jack': The Cultural Politics of Race and Nation* (London: Routledge).

Gilroy, Paul (1993) *The Black Atlantic: Modernity and Double Consciousness* (London: Verso).

Gilroy, Paul (2004) *After Empire: Melancholia or Convivial Culture?* (London: Routledge).

Gilroy, Paul (2010) *Darker than Blue: On the Moral Economies of Black Atlantic Culture* (Cambridge, MA: Harvard University Press).

Glissant, Édouard (1997 [1990]) *Poetics of Relation*, Transl. Betsy Wing (Ann Arbor, MI: University of Michigan Press).

Gopal, Priyamvada (2009) *The Indian English Novel: Nation, History and Narration* (Oxford: Oxford University Press).

Gopalakrishnan, Shankar (2008) Letters, in response to 'Diary', Sanjay Subrahmanyam's review of *The White Tiger*, *London Review of Books*, 30 (23), http://www.lrb.co.uk/v30/n23/letters#letter3 date accessed 21 March 2010.

Grant, Colin (2009) Caribbean Voices – Part 1, BBC World Service. 22 July. http://www.bbc.co.uk/worldservice/documentaries/2009/07/090721_caribbean_voices_1.shtml date accessed 22 August 2009.

Gunner, Liz (1994) 'Mothers, Daughters and Madness in Works by Four Women Writers: Bessie Head, Jean Rhys, Tsitsi Dangarembga and Ama Ata Aidoo', *Alif: Journal of Comparative Poetics*, 14: Madness and Civilization, 136–51.

Haggard, H. Rider (1961 [1885]) *King Solomon's Mines* (London: Blackie).

Harper, Graeme (2002). *Comedy, Fantasy and Colonialism* (London: Continuum).

Harrison, Nicholas (2003) *Postcolonial Criticism* (Cambridge: Polity).

Hawley, John C. (ed.) (2001) *Postcolonial, Queer: Theoretical Intersections* (Albany, NY: State University of New York Press).

Holden, Philip (2008) *Autobiography and Decolonization: Modernity, Masculinity, and the Nation-State* (Madison: University of Wisconsin Press).

hooks, bell (1993) 'Postmodern Blackness' in Joseph P. Natoli and Linda Hutcheon (eds) *A Postmodern Reader* (Albany: State University of New York Press), pp. 510–18.

Hopkins, Lisa (2005) *Beginning Shakespeare* (Manchester: Manchester University Press).

Hopkinson, Nalo, and Mehan, Uppinder (eds) (2004) *So Long Been Dreaming* (Vancouver: Arsenal Pulp Press).

Huggan, Graham (1998) '(Post)Colonialism, Anthropology, and the Magic of Mimesis', *Cultural Critique*, 38 (Winter), 91–106.

Huggan, Graham (2001) *The Postcolonial Exotic: Marketing the Margins* (London: Routledge).

Huggan, Graham and Tiffin, Helen (2009) *Postcolonial Ecocriticism* (London: Routledge).

Indyk, Ivor (1993) 'Pastoral and Priority: The Aboriginal in Australian Pastoral', *New Literary History*, 24 (4), 837–55.

Islam, Syed Manzurul (1996) *The Ethics of Travel: From Marco Polo to Kafka* (Manchester: Manchester University Press).

James, C. L. R. (1938) *The Black Jacobins: Toussaint Louverture and the San Domingo Revolution* (London: Secker & Warburg).

James, C. L. R. (2000 [1963]) *Beyond a Boundary* (London: Serpent's Tail).

Jarrett-Macauley, Delia (1998) *The Life of Una Marson* (Manchester: Manchester University Press).

Jeyifo, Biodun (1993) 'Okonkwo and His Mother: *Things Fall Apart* and Issues of Gender in the Constitution of African Postcolonial Discourse', *Callaloo*, 16 (4): On Post-Colonial Discourse, 847–58.

Khan, Yasmin (2007) *The Great Partition: The Making of India and Pakistan* (New Haven and London: Yale University Press).

Kiberd, Declan (1995) *Inventing Ireland: The Literature of a Modern Nation* (London: Jonathan Cape).

Kincaid, Jamaica (1985) *Annie John* (London: Picador).

Kincaid, Jamaica (1988) *A Small Place* (New York: Farrar, Straus & Giroux).

Kincaid, Jamaica (1997) *My Brother* (New York: Farrar, Straus & Giroux).

Landry, Donna, and MacLean, Gerald (eds) (1996) *The Spivak Reader: Selected Works of Gayatri Chakravorty Spivak* (London: Routledge).

Lamming, George (1991 [1970]) *In the Castle of My Skin* (Ann Arbor: University of Michigan Press).

Lamming, George (1992 [1960]) *The Pleasures of Exile* (Ann Arbor: University of Michigan Press).

Macintyre, Stuart (2004) *A Concise History of Australia* (Cambridge: Cambridge University Press).

Manto, Saadat Hasan (1987) 'Toba Tek Singh' in *Kingdom's End and Other Stories*, Transl. Khalid Hasan (Harmondsworth: Penguin).

Marx, John (2004) 'Postcolonial literature and the Western Literary Canon' in Neil Lazarus (ed.) *The Cambridge Companion to Literary Studies* (Cambridge: Cambridge University Press), pp. 83–96.

Matzke, Christine, and Muehleisen, Susanne (eds) (2006) *Postcolonial Postmortems: Crime Fiction from a Transcultural Perspective* (Amsterdam: Rodopi).

Mayo, Katherine (2000 [1927]) *Mother India*, Mrinalini Sinha (ed.) (Ann Arbor: University of Michigan Press).

Memmi, Albert (2003 [1957 French]) *The Colonizer and the Colonized*, Transl. Howard Greenfield (London: Earthscan).

Memmi, Albert (2006) *Decolonization and the Decolonized* (Minneapolis: University of Minnesota Press).

Mercer, Kobena (1997) 'Bodies of Diaspora, Vessels of Desire: The Erotic and the Aesthetic' in M. Franklin Sirmans and Mora J. Beauchamp-Byrd (eds) *Transforming the Crown: African, Asian, and Caribbean Artists in Britain, 1966–1996* (New York: Caribbean Cultural Center), pp. 53–7.

Mernissi, Fatima (1987) *Beyond the Veil: Male-Female Dynamics in Modern Muslim Society*, 2nd edn (Bloomington & Indianapolis: Indiana University Press).

Mishra, Pankaj (2008) Letters, in response to 'Diary', Sanjay Subrahmanyam's review of *The White Tiger, London Review of Books*, 30 (22), http://www.lrb.co.uk/v30/n22/letters#letter1 date accessed 21 March 2010.

Moore-Gilbert, Bart (1997) *Postcolonial Theory: Contexts, Practices, Politics* (London: Verso).

Mudrooroo (1995 [1985]) 'White Forms, Aboriginal Content' in Bill Ashcroft, Gareth Griffiths and Helen Tiffin (eds) *The Post-Colonial Studies Reader* (London: Routledge), pp. 228–31.

Mukherjee, Ankhi (2009) '"Yes, Sir, I Was the One Who Got Away": Postcolonial Emergence and the Question of Global English', *Etudes anglaises*, 3 (62).

Munn, Christopher (1999) 'The Criminal Trial under Early Colonial Rule' in Tak-Wing Ngo (ed.) *Hong Kong's History: State and Society under Colonial Rule* (London: Routledge), pp. 46–73.

Nandy, Ashis (1995) 'History's Forgotten Doubles', *History and Theory*, 34 (2): World Historians and Their Critics, 44–66.

Narayan, R. K. (2001 [1978]) (ed.) *The Mahabharata* (London: Penguin Classics).

Nasrin, Taslima (1994) *Shame*, Transl. Tutul Gupta [Bengali (*Lajja*)] (New Delhi: Penguin Books India).

Nasta, Susheila (ed.) (1991) *Motherlands: Black Women's Writing from Africa, the Caribbean and South Asia* (London: The Women's Press).

Nayar, Pramod K. (2008) *Postcolonial Literature: An Introduction* (New Delhi: Dorling Kindersley (India)).

Ngo, Tak-Wing (1999) *Hong Kong's History: State and Society under Colonial Rule* (London: Routledge).

Ngugi wa Thiong'o (1973 [1972]) *Homecoming: Essays on African and Caribbean Literature, Culture and Politics* (New York: Lawrence Hill).

Ngugi wa Thiong'o (1981) *Decolonising the Mind: The Politics of Language in African Literature* (London: Heinemann Educational).

Ngugi wa Thiong'o (1993) *Moving the Centre: The Struggle for Cultural Freedoms* (London: James Currey).

Ngugi wa Thiong'o (2008) 'Freeing the Imagination', *Transition*, 100, 164–69, Available online: http://www.jstor.org/stable/20542547 date accessed 16 March 2010.

Niesen de Abruna, Laura (1991) 'Family Connections: Mother and Mother Country in the Fiction of Jean Rhys and Jamaica Kincaid' in Sushelia Nasta (ed.) *Motherlands: Black Women's Writing from Africa, the Caribbean and South Asia* (London: The Women's Press), pp. 257–89.

Nissan, Elizabeth and Stirratt, R. L. (1990) 'The Generation of Communal Identities' in Jonathan Spencer (ed.) *Sri Lanka: History and the Roots of Conflict* (London: Routledge), pp. 19–44.

Nixon, Rob (1987) 'Caribbean and African Appropriations of *The Tempest*', *Critical Inquiry*, 13 (3): Politics and Poetic Value, 557–78.

O'Brien, Paul (2007) 'Hibernian Evanescence: Globalisation, Identity and the Virtual Shamrock', *Postcolonial Text*, 3 (3), Available online: http://postcolonial. org/index.php/pct/article/view/713/483 date accessed 26 April 2010.

Ong, Walter J. (1982) *Orality and Literacy* (London: Methuen).

Owens, Louis (1988) '"Grampa Killed Indians, Pa Killed Snakes": Steinbeck and the American Indian', *MELUS*, 15 (2): Varieties of Ethnic Criticism, 85–92.

Polo, Marco (1958) *The Travels*, Transl. R. E. Latham (Harmondsworth: Penguin).

Prince-Hughes, Tara (1999) '"A Curious Double Insight": *The Well of Loneliness* and Native American Alternative Gender Traditions', *Rocky Mountain Review of Language and Literature*, 53 (2), 31–43.

Pulitano, Elvira (2005) 'Native Theory and Criticism: 2. United States' in *Johns Hopkins Guide to Literary Theory and Criticism*, 2nd edn, Available online: http://litguide.press.jhu.edu/cgi-bin/view.cgi?eid=190 date accessed 16 March 2010.

Quayson, Ato (1995) 'Orality – (Theory) – Textuality: Tutuola, Okri, and the Relationship of Literary Practice to Oral Traditions' in Stewart Brown (ed.) *The Pressures of the Text: Orality, Texts and the Telling of Tales* (Birmingham: Centre of West African Studies), pp. 96–117.

Race and Intelligence: Science's Last Taboo (2009) Channel 4, 26 October.

Rafferty, Kevin (1991) *City on the Rocks: Hong Kong's Uncertain Future*, 2nd edn (London: Penguin).

Reder, Michael (ed.) (2000) *Conversations with Salman Rushdie* (Jackson: University Press of Mississippi).

Renan, Ernest (1990) 'What Is a Nation?', Transl. Martin Thom, in Homi Bhabha (ed.) *Nation and Narration* (London: Routledge), pp. 8–22.

Rhys, Jean (1997 [1966]) *Wide Sargasso Sea* (London: Penguin).

Roy, Arundhati (1997) *The God of Small Things* (London: Flamingo).

Roy, Arundhati (1999) *The Cost of Living* (London: Flamingo).

Rushdie, Salman (1995 [1981]) *Midnight's Children* (London: Vintage).

Rushdie, Salman (1998) *The Satanic Verses* (London: Vintage).

Rushdie, Salman (2003) *Step across This Line* (London: Vintage).

Saïd, Edward W. (1980) *The Question of Palestine* (London: Routledge & Kegan Paul).

Saïd, Edward W. (1993) *Culture and Imperialism* (London: Chatto & Windus).

Saïd, Edward W. (1995 [1978]) *Orientalism: Western Conceptions of the Orient* (London: Penguin).

Saïd, Edward W. (2000 [1982]) 'Traveling Theory' in Moustafa Bayoumi and Andrew Rubin (eds) *The Edward Saïd Reader* (New York: Vintage), pp. 195–217.

Saïd, Edward W. (2001) *Reflections on Exile and Other Literary and Cultural Essays* (London: Granta).

Schwarz, Bill (2006) 'C.L.R. James's *American Civilization*' in Christopher Gair (ed.) *Beyond Boundaries: C.L.R. James and Postnational Studies* (London: Pluto Press), pp. 128–56.

Scott, Cleve (2007) 'Bussa's Rebellion (1816)' in Junius P. Rodriguez (ed.) *Encyclopedia of Slave Resistance and Rebellion*, volume 1 (Westport, CT: Greenwood).

Scott, Joan Wallach (2007) *The Politics of the Veil* (Princeton: Princeton University Press).

Sebastian, A. J. and Das, Nigamananda (2009) 'Drawbacks of Indian Democracy in Homen Borgohain's *Pita Putra* and Aravind Adiga's *The White Tiger* and *Between The Assassinations*: A Comparative Study', *Journal of Alternative Perspectives in the Social Sciences*, 1 (3), 635–44.

Selvadurai, Shyam (1994) *Funny Boy* (Toronto: McClelland & Stewart).

Sen, Aveek (2006) 'Voices of the Same Poverty', *Calcutta Telegraph*, 12 October, Available online: http://www.telegraphindia.com/1061012/asp/opinion/story_6857011.asp date accessed 28 October 2009.

Shakespeare, William (1980) *The Tempest* in *Shakespeare: Complete Works* (Oxford: Oxford University Press).

Sharma-Jensen, Geeta (2006) 'Close to her heart, if not her home', *Milwaukee Journal Sentinel*, 8 October, [online document ID: 114A4F20A24DA978].

Sharpley-Whiting, T. Denean (1998) *Frantz Fanon: Conflicts and Feminisms* (Oxford: Rowman & Littlefield).

Sherwood, Marika (1999) *Claudia Jones: A Life in Exile* (London: Lawrence & Wishart).

Shinn, Christopher A. (2008) 'On Machines and Mosquitoes: Neuroscience, Bodies, and Cyborgs in Amitav Ghosh's The Calcutta Chromosome', *MELUS*, 33 (4): Alien/Asian, 145–66.

Shoemaker, Adam (2003) 'Mudrooroo and the Curse of Authenticity' in Annalisa Oboe (ed.) *Mongrel Signatures: Reflections on the Work of Mudrooroo* (Amsterdam: Rodopi), pp. 1–23.

Singh, Jyotsna (1989) 'Different Shakespeares: The Bard in Colonial/Postcolonial India', *Theatre Journal*, 41 (4): Theatre and Hegemony, 445–58.

Slaughter, Charles (1901) 'The Aboriginal Natives of Northwest Western Australia and the Administration of Justice', *Westminster Review* 156 (4), 411–26.

Smertin, Yuri (1987) *Kwame Nkrumah* (New York: International Publishers).

Spencer, Jonathan (ed.) (1990) *Sri Lanka: History and the Roots of Conflict* (London: Routledge).

Spivak, Gayatri Chakravorty (1987) *In Other Worlds: Essays in Cultural Politics* (London: Methuen).

Spivak, Gayatri Chakravorty (1988a) 'Can the Subaltern Speak?' in Cary Nelson and Lawrence Grossberg (eds) *Marxism and the Interpretation of Culture* (Urbana, IL: University of Illinois Press), pp. 271–313.

Spivak, Gayatri Chakravorty (1988b) 'Subaltern Studies: Deconstructing Historiography' in Ranajit Guha and Gayatri Chakravorty Spivak (eds) *Selected Subaltern Studies* (Oxford: Oxford University Press), pp. 3–32.

Spivak, Gayatri Chakravorty (1999) *A Critique of Postcolonial Reason: Toward a History of the Vanishing Present* (London: Harvard University Press).

Suleri, Sara (1991) *Meatless Days: A Memoir* (London: Flamingo).

Suzack, Cheryl (2005) 'Native Theory and Criticism: 2. Canada' in *Johns Hopkins Guide to Literary Theory and Criticism*. 2nd edn, Available online: http://litguide. press.jhu.edu/cgi-bin/view.cgi?eid=191 date accessed 16 March 2010.

Tan, Tai Yong and Kudaisya, Gyanesh (2000) *The Aftermath of Partition in South Asia* (London: Routledge).

Thompson, Edward (1927) 'Three Books on India', *The Bookman* 72 (432), September, 322–23.

Trinh, T. Minh-ha (1989) *Woman, Native, Other – Writing Postcoloniality and Feminism* (Bloomington & Indianapolis: Indiana University Press).

Trinh, T. Minh-ha (1991) *When the Moon Waxes Red: Representation, Gender and Cultural Politics* (London: Routledge).

Trinh, T. Minh-ha (1992) *Framer Framed* (New York & London: Routledge).

Trinh, T. Minh-ha (1999) *Cinema Interval* (New York & London: Routledge).

Trinh, T. Minh-ha (2005) *The Digital Film Event* (New York & London: Routledge).

Valassopoulos, Anastasia (2004) 'Fictionalising Post-Colonial Theory: The Creative Native Informant?', *Critical Survey*, 16 (2), 28–44.

Vines, Stephen (1991) 'Hong Kong gay law reform paves way for Bill of Rights', *The Guardian*, 18 March.

Vizenor, Gerald (1992) 'Manifest Manners: The Long Gaze of Christopher Columbus', *Boundary 2*, 19 (3), 223–35.

Warraq, Ibn (2007) *Defending the West: A Critique of Edward Saïd's Orientalism* (Amherst, NY: Prometheus).

Watson, Karl (2009) 'Barbados and the Bicentenery of the Abolition of the Slave Trade', *Slavery and Abolition*, 30 (2), June, 179–95.

Welch, Pedro L.V. (2003) 'Barbados' in Alan West-Durán (ed.) *African Caribbeans: A Reference Guide* (Westport, CT: Greenwood).

Whitlock, Gillian (2000) *The Intimate Empire: Reading Women's Autobiography* (London: Cassell).

Wisker, Gina (2007) 'Crossing Liminal Spaces: Teaching the Postcolonial Gothic', *Pedagogy: Critical Approaches to Teaching Literature, Language, Composition and Culture*, 7 (3), 401–25.

Wolfreys, Julian (1998) *Writing London – The Trace of the Urban Text from Blake to Dickens* (London: Macmillan).

Wong, Day (2006) '(Post-)Identity Politics and Anti-Normalization: (Homo)Sexual Rights Movement' in Agnes S. Ku and Ngai Pun (eds) *Remaking Citizenship in Hong Kong: Community, Nation and the Global City* (Abingdon: Routledge), pp. 195–214.

Wong, Nicholas (2008) 'I for Illness' in Xu Xi (ed.) *Fifty-Fifty: New Hong Kong Writing* (Hong Kong: Haven Books), pp. 238–48.

Woodcock, Bruce (2003) *Peter Carey* (Manchester: Manchester University Press).

Worthen, W.B. (2007) 'Performing Shakespeare in Digital Culture' in Robert Shaughnessy (ed.) *The Cambridge Companion to Shakespeare and Popular Culture* (Cambridge: Cambridge University Press), pp. 227–47.

Young, Robert (1995) *Colonial Desire: Hybridity in Theory, Culture and Race* (London: Routledge).

Zack-Williams, Alfred Babatunde (2006) 'Kwame Nkrumah' in David Simon (ed.) *Fifty Key Thinkers on Development* (Abingdon: Routledge), pp. 187–92.

Zimra, Clarisse (1992 [1980]) 'Woman's Memory Spans Centuries – An Interview with Assia Djebar' in Assia Djebar, *Women of Algiers in Their Apartment*, Transl. Marjolin de Jager (Charlottesville and London: University of Virginia Press), pp. 167–87.

Index

Aboriginal Australia   40–2, 135–6
Aboriginal America   132
abortion   63, 178
Achebe, Chinua   32, 102, 130, 159, 160, 161, 166
   Things Fall Apart   163–5
Adiga, Aravind
   The White Tiger   150–3, 199, 203
Affective Communities (Gandhi)   42–5
Africa   2, 3, 7, 10, 21, 23, 28, 40, 42, 89, 91, 93–4, 99, 104, 106, 109, 115, 118, 119, 159, 200, 201, 205
   African literature   129, 137, 138, 159–68 *passim*
   African politics   3, 108, 130–1
   African university education   32–3, 127–30
   and neo-colonialism   11, 12
After Empire (Gilroy)   122–4
Ahmad, Aijaz   186
AIDS   187, 189
Alatas, Syed Hussein   139
'Algeria Unveiled'   30, 105
'The Algerian Family'   105
Algerian war of Independence 1954–1962   29
All About H Hatterr (Desani)   65–6
Ali, Monica   204, 209
Allen, Paula Gunn   132, 133
America   2, 3, 12, 13, 24, 25, 27, 40, 41, 44, 49, 83, 84, 85, 94, 117, 118, 119, 120, 131, 133, 145, 188, 201–2
   American War of Independence   176
American Sex Problems (Gadiali)   44
Anderson, Benedict   86–8
Anderson, Clare   207
Anderson, Michelle   27
Andrews, C.F. (Charlie)   43–4
'An Image of Africa: Racism in Conrad's *Heart of Darkness*' (Achebe)   130, 163
An Autobiography of My Mother (Kincaid)   187

Angelou, Maya   203
Annie John (Kincaid)   187
anthropology   79, 82, 98, 139, 140, 141, 142, 146
anti-capitalism   23, 124
Antigua   80, 81, 82, 158, 186, 187–8, 190
Antilles   37, 102, 103–4, 106–7, 109, 166, 167
Antonius, George   139
Anzaldua, Gloria   127, 201, 207
Arab, representations of   83, 85, 90
Arab scholars   29
Arab Awakening, The (Antonius)   139
Arabian Nights, The   85, 210
art   23, 79, 85, 109, 124, 128, 132, 143, 201, 210
Ashcroft, Bill   20, 43, 49, 50, 65, 128, 137, 193, 197–8, 206
Austen, Jane   18, 80, 81, 187
Australia   3, 40–2, 116, 127, 131, 135, 158, 169, 170, 176–8, 205, 209
authenticity   9, 96, 97, 99, 100, 115, 121, 133, 135, 136, 144, 152, 168, 186, 195, 208
authority   7, 17, 25, 33, 42, 71, 72, 73, 95, 111, 112–3, 114, 115, 141, 149, 164, 165, 168, 169, 174, 184, 199, 205
autobiography   24, 27, 135, 186, 187, 209, 210
Ayatollah Khomeini   186

Babri Masjid mosque   70
Bangladesh   46, 87, 102
Barbados   17, 18, 19–20, 34, 128
Barber, Karin   137
Bassnett, Susan   208
BBC   28, 123
beauty contests / pageants   27–8, 201
bestsellers   2, 135, 203–6
Beyond a Boundary (James)   24, 25
Bhabha, Homi   43, 86–7, 102, 105, 108, 112–5, 116–8, 120, 122, 133, 136, 141, 180, 184–5, 201, 202, 208
binary oppositions   39, 83, 92, 93, 112, 157, 162
biography   43, 135, 210

Black Atlantic, The (Gilroy)   119–21
Black Jacobins, The (James)   21, 25, 139
Black Skin, White Masks (Fanon)   37, 103,
       105, 108, 109, 111, 166, 167
Blake, William   126
Blood Relations (Malouf)   170
Boehmer, Elleke   82, 165
book publishing   203–6, 209
Booker Prize   9, 150, 152, 194, 203–4
Borderlands/La Frontera (Anzaldua)
       127, 207
borders   54, 59, 60, 61, 62, 63, 67, 68, 70, 73,
       112, 113, 115, 133, 160, 207
bourgeoisie   23, 108, 150
Brecht   95
Brick Lane (Ali)   204, 209
Britishness   88
Brown, Dee   132
Bury My Heart at Wounded Knee
       (Brown)   132
Bussa's rebellion (see slave uprising
       Barbados 1816)
Butalia, Urvashi   47, 60–3, 67–9, 70–5

Calcutta Chromosome, The (Ghosh)   199
Caliban   17–18, 32, 131, 143, 144, 170–2
'Caliban' (Brathwaite)   170
Canada   3, 88, 127, 158, 170, 179, 183, 188, 209
Canadian Native theory   131–2, 134, 135
cannibalism   6, 17, 32, 36, 110, 162, 177
capitalism   48, 52, 54, 55, 108, 123–6, 128,
       131, 151, 153, 198, 204, 206
   'liberal' capitalism   125
   print capitalism   87
Carey, Peter   158, 169, 175–8
Caribbean   1, 2, 17, 18, 19, 21, 24, 27, 28–9,
       33, 35, 37, 38, 42, 43, 80, 81, 103, 107,
       109, 113, 118, 119, 122, 123, 129, 157,
       158, 170, 172, 175, 187, 196, 201, 209
Caribbean Voices   28–9, 123
carnivals   26, 27, 42, 209
Carpenter, Edward   44–5
Cary, Joyce   32, 163
Cesaire, Aimé   21–3, 27, 31, 35, 37, 158,
       169–172, 208
Charter of Rights for Coloured Workers in
       Britain   26
Chicano/a   133, 207

Childs, Peter   45, 49, 51, 85
China   46, 48, 52–5, 56, 57, 150, 193, 202
chocolate   10–13
Chow, Rey   48, 75, 79, 82, 98, 100–1, 199
Chrisman, Laura   186
Coetzee, J.M.   203
Columbus, Christopher   132
The Cost of Living (Roy)   195
cinema   10, 96, 208
Cinema Interval (Trinh)   95
class   4, 12, 13, 20, 23, 26, 29, 48, 65, 81, 82,
       85, 91, 108, 114, 119, 123, 124, 145, 146,
       150, 151, 152, 180, 183, 205
Clow, Andrew   60
Cold War   84
Colonial and Postcolonial Literature
       (Boehmer)   82
colonization   2, 3, 4, 23, 31, 38, 40, 41, 42, 43,
       45, 49, 50, 54, 55, 69, 86, 109, 119, 132,
       157, 196, 197, 202, 209
Colonizer and the Colonized, The
       (Memmi)   38
Communist Party   23, 24, 26, 171
Congo   157, 159, 160
Constantine, Learie   25
contrapuntal music   80, 81, 120, 178–9
convicts   3, 40, 116, 176–8, 207
Covering Islam (Saïd)   89
Creole   42, 107, 109, 112–13, 202
cricket   24, 25
Critique of Postcolonial Reason, A
       (Spivak)   140, 141, 144, 145
Cuba Hasta Fidel (Retamar)   170
Culture and Imperialism (Saïd)   80, 82, 84,
       89, 176

Daily Worker   26
Dangarembga, Tsitsi   159, 166–8
Darker Than Blue (Gilroy)   120
Das Kapital (Marx)   126
decolonization   1, 13, 19, 38, 45, 46, 48, 49,
       86, 108, 128, 170, 196
Decolonization and the Decolonized
       (Memmi)   39
Decolonizing the Mind (Ngugi)   128
Deleuze, Gilles   35, 121, 146
Derrida, Jacques   116, 134, 146
Desani, G.V.   65–6

diaspora   2, 31, 39, 89, 90, 102, 114, 118–20,
    127, 129, 158, 167, 180–90, 193, 198, 201,
    207, 208, 209, 210
Dickens, Charles   18, 24, 158, 175–9, 185
digital publishing   199
digital technology   2, 120, 193, 199–201
disability studies   82, 205
Discourse on Colonialism (Cesaire)   23
Disgrace (Coetzee)   203
Dizzee Rascal   124–6
Djebar, Assia   30–1
documentary   28, 79, 82, 90, 94, 95, 96, 99
Donnell, Alison   28–9
double consciousness   118, 121
drama   25, 35, 98, 137, 209
Du Bois, W.E.B.   118, 121

Easter Rebellion, The (see slave uprising
    Barbados 1816)
East India Trading Company   79
ecocriticism   2, 193, 194–96
Ecocriticism (Garrard)   194
education   2, 11, 18, 24, 25, 28, 29, 39, 42, 43,
    58, 82, 83, 104, 106, 109, 128, 143, 151,
    157, 159, 166–8, 170, 181, 187, 209
Egypt   84, 87, 145, 148
El Guindi, Fadwa   29
El Saadawi, Nawal   148–50, 152–3
Emecheta, Buchi   209
Empire Writes Back, The (Ashcroft, Griffiths
    and Tiffin)   65, 137
Empress Orchid (Min)   203
Englishness   24, 88, 186
Enlightenment, The   116, 196
ethnography (see also anthropology)   39,
    98, 115, 139, 140, 141, 142, 146
eurocentrism   49, 59, 116, 117, 163, 207
Evaristo, Bernadine   209
exile   18, 27, 35, 63, 87, 89, 119, 130
exotic   4–13, 98, 201, 204, 209

fair trade   10, 11
Famished Road, The (Okri)   138
Fanon, Frantz   30, 31, 37, 38, 46, 69, 102,
    103–11, 116, 166–7, 208
fatwa   186
feminism   27–9, 30, 31, 50, 68, 95, 101, 105,
    117, 144, 169, 172, 173, 174, 208, 210

film   79, 90, 91, 93–4, 95–9, 200, 208
First World War   3, 139
food   9–10, 10–13, 54, 64, 149, 168, 184
Foucault, Michel   83, 146
France   3, 22–3, 35, 37, 49, 103–4, 107, 108
Francophone postcolonial studies   208
Frankenstein (Shelley)   143–4
French Revolution   22
Freud, Sigmund   84, 116, 146
Funny Boy (Selvadurai)   180–3, 188

Gandhi, Indira   47, 64, 70, 71
Gandhi, Leela   26, 42–5, 50, 116, 134, 208
Gandhi, Mahatma   38, 44, 60, 63
Garrard, Greg   194–5
gay activism   56, 57, 75, 169, 201–2
gender   28, 29, 30, 81, 82, 91, 99, 105, 108,
    119, 134, 138, 147, 149, 201, 205
Genette, Gerard   97
Ghosh, Amitav   199
Gikandi, Simon   130, 160
Gikuyu   129, 130
Gilbert, Helen   209
Gilroy, Paul   102, 115, 116, 118–24, 125
Gitā   141–3
Glissant, Édouard   31, 34–5
globalization   2, 4, 12, 13, 84, 90, 98, 116,
    118, 120, 150, 152, 153, 193, 198, 200,
    204, 205, 207, 209
God Dies by the Nile (El Saadawi)   148–50,
    152–3
God of Small Things, The (Roy)   194–5, 203
Google   200
Gordimer, Nadine   113, 203
Gramsci, Antonio   12, 146
Great Expectations (Dickens)   169, 175–9
Griffiths, Gareth   49, 65, 128, 137
Guattari, Felix   35, 121
Guha, Ranajit   139, 146, 150, 208

Haiti   22
Half of a Yellow Sun (Adichie)   203
harem   29, 90, 94, 209
Harrison, Nicholas   49–50, 51, 134
Hatem, Mervat   105
Heart of Darkness (Conrad)   130, 157,
    159–63, 168, 196
Heat and Dust (Jhabvala)   204

Hegel   142–3
hegemony   12–13, 50, 91, 92, 146, 197
Highlife for Caliban, The (Johnson)   170
Hiroshima   144
history   2, 3–4, 5, 25, 39, 41, 47, 49, 50, 58,
   70, 72, 73, 122, 124, 125, 126, 144, 150,
   181–2, 197
   ahistoricism   143, 196–7
   alternative histories   4, 47, 51, 59, 60, 61,
   70, 71, 72, 118, 185, 198
Hollywood   90
Homecoming (Ngugi)   128, 129, 130
homosexuality laws   45, 55–7, 201
Hong Kong   45, 46–9, 51–5, 55–8, 75, 200,
   201, 202, 208
hooks, bell   105, 117
Huggan, Graham   9, 136, 193, 195, 196,
   203–4, 209
Hullabaloo in the Guava Orchard
   (Desai)   9–10
hybridity   43, 86, 87, 101, 102, 112–15, 116,
   117, 120, 121, 122, 140, 180, 184–5, 186,
   201–3
hypercorrection   107
hyphenated identity   89, 91
hysteria   36

Ibo   33, 157, 159, 163–4, 165
Imagined Communities (Anderson)   86
imperialism   6, 7, 9, 12–13, 32, 37, 45, 50,
   51, 80, 81, 82, 84, 89, 100, 113, 116, 140,
   142, 144, 158, 160, 162, 169, 172, 174,
   176, 187, 196, 198, 207
India   5, 8, 9–10, 13, 30, 38, 43–4, 47, 48, 51,
   58–60, 63, 64, 65–6, 68, 69, 74, 82, 87,
   109, 113, 144, 147, 150–2, 158, 169–70,
   177, 183, 186, 193, 195, 197, 198, 205,
   208, 209
   independence   46, 59
indigo   21
Industrial Revolution in Britain   21
Inheritance of Loss, The (Desai)   9, 203
In Other Worlds (Spivak)   142
interdisciplinarity   2, 117, 193
internet   50, 120, 193, 199, 200, 205
interpellation   43
Interpreter of Maladies, The (Lahiri)   203
In The Castle of my Skin (Lamming)   28, 33

IQ tests   82
Ireland   21, 200, 201, 209
Islam   83, 85, 100, 186

Jack Maggs (Carey)   158, 169, 175–9
Jamaica   28–9, 172
James, C.L.R.   21, 24–6, 43, 81, 139
Jameson, Fredric   116
Jane Eyre (Bronte)   169, 172–5
Jewish diaspora   119
Jews   38, 119
Jeyifo, Biodun   165
Jia (Family) (Ba Jin)   98, 100
Jones, Claudia   26–8
Jones, William   84, 109
Justice   44

Kashmir   46, 66, 75
Kawakubo, Rei   144–5
Khan, Yasmin   59, 60, 62, 66, 68, 69, 70, 73, 74
Kiberd, Declan   209
Kikuyu (see Gikuyu)
Kincaid, Jamaica   113, 180, 186, 187–90
King Solomon's Mines (Haggard)   6–8
Kipling, Rudyard   18, 125

Lacan, Jacques   82, 116
labour   2, 10, 13, 17, 19, 21, 33, 81, 123, 124,
   131, 146, 148, 166, 187
Lamming, George   17–18, 28, 31, 33–4,
   127–8, 170
language   11, 17, 18, 22–3, 33, 35, 38, 39, 65,
   87–8, 100–1, 102–3, 103–7, 108, 109–10,
   112, 113, 115, 121, 122, 127–8, 129–30,
   134–5, 137, 145, 163–4, 167, 171–2, 181,
   193–4, 200
   Englishes   202
Latin America   49, 131, 207
Lessing, Doris   203
Leung, William   56, 57
life-writing   132, 210
liminality   114, 115, 133
literary canon   2, 9, 18, 31, 65, 80, 126, 157,
   168, 174, 194
literary prizes   2, 9, 41, 150, 152, 194, 203–6
Location of Culture, The (Bhabha)   108,
   113, 117
logocentrism   116

London   26, 28, 65, 66, 102, 114, 160, 162,
    176, 177, 178, 183, 184, 185, 186, 209
Loomba, Ania   193

Macaulay's Minute of 1835   109
Madagascar   23
madness   36, 62, 159, 168, 185
Malaysia   139
Man Booker Prize *see* Booker Prize
Manifest Destiny   40, 132
Mansfield Park (Austen)   80, 81, 187
Manto, Saadat Hasan   61, 72
Map of Love, The (Soueif)   145
margins   34, 48, 58, 72, 73, 87, 90, 91, 93, 96,
    115, 117, 123, 137, 140, 142, 146, 163,
    165, 172, 173, 175, 176, 181, 183, 198,
    199, 209
Mariners, Renegades and Castaways   25
marketing of literature   203, 209
Marquez, Gabriel Garcia   203
Marson, Una   28–9, 43, 123
Martinique   22–3, 34–5, 37, 107, 110
Marx, Karl   26, 126, 146, 151
Marxism   23, 25, 26, 27, 50, 85, 108, 116,
    117, 151, 196, 207, 208
Master of the Ghost Dreaming
    (Mudrooroo)   136
Masters and Servants Act 1840   20
Maverick Club   25
Mayo, Katherine   43–4
McDonaldization   13
McLeod, John   209
media   11, 13, 87, 104, 120, 122, 124, 125,
    181, 193, 200, 205, 210
Memmi, Albert   37–9
Mercer, Kobena   201
Mernissi, Fatima   29, 30, 209
Mexico   133, 207, 210
Midnight's Children (Rushdie)   64–5
migration   43, 47, 48, 51, 67, 68, 70, 71,
    73, 74, 86, 102, 103, 107, 108, 110, 112,
    115–16, 119, 127, 152, 157, 158, 170, 180,
    182–3, 185, 193, 202
Milton, John   24, 189
Mishra, Pankaj   151–2
Miss America   27
missionaries   11, 32, 80, 84, 105, 136, 157, 159,
    163–4, 165, 166, 167, 168, 174, 177, 208

Mister Johnson (Cary)   32, 163
Mistry, Rohinton   203
Moby Dick (Melville)   25
Modern Language Association (MLA)   131
monolith   89
Montagu, Mary Wortley   94
Moore-Gilbert, Bart   50, 134, 186, 210
Morrison, Toni   203
Mother India   63, 66, 74
Mother India (Mayo)   43–4
Much Ado About Nothing (Shakespeare)   66
Mudrooroo   41–2, 135–6
music   10–13, 23, 81, 89, 98, 120, 122, 123,
    124–6, 200
Muslim League   63, 68
Mūtiiri   130
Myall Creek massacre   41
My Brother (Kincaid)   113, 180, 186, 187–90
Myth of the Lazy Native, The (Alatas)   139

Naipaul, V.S.   203
Naked Spaces: Living is Round (Trinh)   93,
    94, 97–8, 99
Nandy, Ashis   196–7, 198
Narmada valley   195
Nasrin, Taslima   71
nation   86–9, 110, 112, 115–16, 119, 131,
    185, 187, 200
nationalism   24, 87, 119, 121, 125, 139, 150,
    181, 207
Nation and Narration (Bhabha)   86
Native American   40, 131, 132, 133, 136, 167
    Culture   134
    Literature   132, 134–5
Native Canadian   131, 132, 134–5
native informant   100, 127, 138, 139–45
nativism   128, 131, 133, 139, 140, 145, 147
negritude   23, 27, 36
neocolonialism   2, 4, 11, 12, 13, 49, 84, 100,
    116, 117, 139, 140, 193, 195, 200, 203,
    204, 205, 209
*Neo-Colonialism: The Last Stage of
    Imperialism* (Nkrumah)   12
Nervous Conditions (Dangarembga)   157,
    159, 166–8
Ngugi wa Thiong'o   127–31, 145, 206
Nigeria   26, 32, 138, 159
Nkrumah, Kwame   12, 13

Nobel Prize for Literature   203
Notting Hill Carnival   26, 27

Obama, Barack   13, 188
objectivity   5, 47, 72, 75, 79, 86, 94, 95, 96,
   97, 122, 146, 165
O'Brien, Paul   200-1
Okri, Ben   138, 203
Ong, Walter   136-7
'On the Abolition of the English
   Department' (Ngugi)   129
opium   53
Opium Wars   46, 53
Oprah's Book Club   203
oral literature   129, 131, 137
Orality and Literacy (Ong)   136-7
Orientalism (Saïd)   79, 83, 89
Orientalists   79, 83-6, 89, 90, 109, 204
Othello   169
other   5, 6, 48, 75, 79, 80, 81, 82, 86, 89-90,
   90-2, 94, 95, 99, 100, 101, 113, 115, 116,
   132, 133, 172, 173, 174, 185, 201, 203-4
othering   5, 75, 81, 82-5, 91, 114
Other Side of Silence, The (Butalia)   60, 73
Owens, Louis   132-3

Pakistan   46, 47, 58, 59, 60, 61, 62, 66, 67, 68,
   70, 74, 87
Paradise Lost (Milton)   143
Parry, Benita   141
Partition   45, 46-8, 58-66, 68-75
Pemulwuy   40
penal colonies   40, 176
performance   8, 12, 42, 98, 132, 136, 138,
   172, 185, 209
phallocentrism   116
philosophy   116, 130, 134, 140, 141, 142,
   143, 145, 208, 210
Pioneer Press   29
The Pirate's Daughter (Cezair-Thompson)   203
plantations   1, 2, 17, 18, 19-21, 80-81, 109,
   180, 187, 194, 195
Pleasures of Exile, The (Lamming)   17, 170
Polo, Marco   4-6, 7
postcolonial, the (definitions)   2, 3, 4, 45, 49-51
Postcolonial Ecocriticism (Huggan and
   Tiffin)   196
'Postmodern Blackness' (hooks)   117

postmodernism   51, 117, 132, 186, 208
poststructuralism   51, 132, 208
pre-colonial society   23, 32, 128, 168
pregnant women   63
print capitalism   87
prison, prisoners   3, 26-7, 40, 44, 53, 56, 70,
   73, 125, 148, 176, 207
Prospero   17, 18, 32, 131, 170, 171-2
prostitution   25, 43, 45, 74, 151
pseudo-science   82, 104, 177
psychopathology   104, 109-10
Pulitzer Prize   203

Quayson, Ato   137-8
queer   50, 55, 58, 75, 118, 182, 201-2
Question of Palestine, The (Saïd)   89

race   20, 23, 26, 29, 74, 80, 82, 88, 104, 107,
   108, 109, 111, 114, 120, 122, 123, 157,
   167, 170, 182, 207
racial reclassification   91
racism   23, 26, 29, 36, 104, 106, 112, 114,
   117, 122, 130, 160, 163
Radcliffe, Cyril   59, 60, 63
Rafferty, Kevin   52, 53, 54, 55
rape and violence against women   63, 67,
   72, 73, 74, 75, 105, 149
Reassemblage (Trinh)   97
Registry Bill   20
religion   11, 20, 31, 41, 42, 48, 59, 62, 63,
   66-8, 69, 70, 71, 72, 74, 75, 88, 96, 119,
   148-9, 164
representation   3, 5, 6, 7, 9, 24, 29, 34, 35, 37,
   40, 42, 51, 71, 72, 79, 80, 81, 83, 86, 88,
   90, 91, 92, 97, 98, 100-1, 107, 117, 119,
   120, 122, 132, 136, 137, 139, 144, 145,
   146, 147, 151, 152, 157, 160, 163, 165,
   171, 172, 174, 175, 176, 177, 181, 182,
   186, 193, 201, 207, 210
reservations   133
Return to My Native Land (Cesaire)   35, 171
rhizome   35, 121
Rhys, Jean   169, 172-5
The Richard & Judy Book Club   203
Riley, Joan   209
Robinson Crusoe (Defoe)   196
Rousseau   82
Roy, Arundhati   194, 195, 203

Rushdie, Salman   9, 64, 65, 66, 102, 130, 183, 185, 186, 203

Saïd, Edward   13, 75, 79–90, 91, 92, 93, 94, 95, 96, 99, 100, 116, 120, 139, 140, 160, 162, 163, 176, 177, 179, 187
San Domingo revolt 1791   21–2
Sanskrit   113
Sapir, Edward   102–3
Sapir-Whorf Hypothesis   102–3
Sardar Sarovar megadam   195
Satanic Verses, The (Rushdie)   102, 114, 180, 183–6
sati (Hindu widow burning)   8, 30, 129, 144, 147, 149
Scheherazade   209
Schwarz, Bill   25
Second World War   3, 28, 69, 84, 125
Selassie, Haile   28
Selvadurai, Shyam   180–3
Selvon, Sam   209
sexuality   2, 45, 55, 56–8, 82, 91, 105, 106, 111, 180, 182, 183, 193, 201–3, 205, 207
Shakespeare   8, 17, 18, 24, 31, 65–6, 95, 126, 127, 128, 154, 157, 158, 169, 170–2
Shame (*Lajja*) (Nasrin)   71
Shelley, Mary   143
Shohat, Ella   208
Siege of Krishnapur, The (Ballard)   204
silence   35, 72–3, 95, 96, 146, 147, 148, 149, 150, 157, 158, 160, 166, 172, 194
Silent Spring (Carson)   194
Singh, Jyotsna   8, 169
Sister India (anonymous)   44
slave uprising Barbados 1816   19–20
slavery   1, 2, 13, 17, 19, 20, 21, 22, 23, 36, 37, 109, 110, 111, 119, 171, 187, 210
Small Place, A (Kincaid)   187
Smith, Zadie   209
Social Darwinism   82, 104
Soueif, Ahdaf   145
Souls of Black Folk, The (Du Bois)   121
South Africa   91, 111, 113–14, 200, 207
Soviet Union   84
Spencer, Jonathan   181
Spivak, Gayatri Chakravorty   139–47, 148, 149, 150, 172, 173, 174, 178, 179, 210
Sri Lanka   158, 180–83, 202

Staying On (Scott)   204
sterilization   64
Stonewall riots   202
subaltern   139, 144, 145, 146, 147, 148, 149, 150, 151, 152, 153, 185, 207, 208, 210
Subaltern Studies Group   139, 146, 150, 208
sugar   18, 19, 20, 21, 80, 187, 204
Surname Viet Given Name Nam (Trinh)   94, 95, 97, 99
swastika   125

Tagore, Rabindranath   44
Tale of Love, A (Trinh)   95
Tamil Tigers   180, 181
Tamil United Liberation Front   181
tattooing   74, 204
tea   29, 53, 178, 195
Tempest, A (Cesaire)   31, 169, 170, 171
Tempest, The (Shakespeare)   17, 18, 31, 143, 157, 169, 170
terra nullius   40
theatre   8, 95, 170, 171, 172, 209
Thackeray, William Makepeace   24
Thatcher, Margaret   125
This Island's Mine (Osment)   169
Things Fall Apart (Achebe)   163–5
A Thousand Plateaus (Deleuze and Guattari)   121
A Thousand Splendid Suns (Hosseini)   203
Tian'anmen Square massacre   48, 52
Tiffin, Helen   49, 65, 128, 137
'Toba Tek Singh' (Manto)   61–2, 72
Tompkins, Joanne   209
torture   21
tourism   13
Toussaint L'Ouverture   21–2
translation   8, 9, 31, 39, 41, 79, 84, 85, 100–1, 105, 109, 112, 113, 115, 130, 134, 141, 142, 145, 153, 163–4, 168, 170, 184, 200, 205, 208
travellers   4–5, 79, 82, 94, 118, 193, 195, 205
Travels (Marco Polo)   4–6, 7
'Travelling Theory' (Saïd)   85, 92
Treaty of Nanking   53
Treaty of the Bogue   53
Trinh, T. Minh-ha   79, 88–100, 139, 141, 146
Trinidad   24, 25, 26, 42
Trivedi, Harish   208

True India, The (Andrews)   43, 44
Tunisia   38, 108
Tutuola, Amos   137, 138

*Uncle Sham: Being the Strange Tale of
    a Civilisation Run Amock* (Gauba)   44
United States (see also America)   28, 35,
    49, 111, 158, 180

Valassopoulos, Anastasia   145
veil, veiling   7, 29–31, 94, 105, 210
vernacular   33, 34
Vietnam   23, 90, 94, 95–6, 98, 99
*Vintage Book of Indian Writing, 1947–1997,
    The* (Rushdie and West)   9
Vizenor, Gerald   132, 134

Walcott, Derek   203
West Indian Gazette   27
When the Moon Waxes Red (Trinh)   91, 93
Whorf, Benjamin   102–3
white *engages*   21

white slaves   21
White Teeth (Smith)   209
White Tiger, The (Adiga)   150–3, 199, 203
Wide Sargasso Sea (Rhys)   158, 172–5, 178
widows' hostels   64
Williams, Patrick   45, 49, 51, 85
Wisker, Gina   204
Woman, Native, Other (Trinh)   93, 95
Woman Warrior, The (Kingston)   204, 210
Women of Algiers in their Apartment
    (Djebar)   30, 31
Wong, Day   57
Wong, Nicholas   58
Wretched of the Earth, The (Fanon)   37, 38,
    46, 108, 166
Writing Diaspora (Chow)   82

Yorùbá   138

Zimbabwe   159, 166
Zingolo   10–13
Zionism   119

Printed in Great Britain
by Amazon

61435497R00142